G000060704

Spell

Old English Heroic Legends

Kathleen Herbert

Anglo-Saxon Books

BY THE SAME AUTHOR

Queen of Lightning
Ghost in the Sunlight
Bride of the Spear

Illustrations by Nicole Ryan © 1993

Copyright Kathleen Herbert 1993

First Published 1993
Reprinted 1993

Published by
Anglo-Saxon Books
25 Malpas Drive
Pinner
Middlesex
England

All rights reserved. No part of this publication may be reproduced without prior permission in writing from the publisher, except for the quotation of brief passages in connection with a review written for inclusion in a magazine or newspaper.

ISBN 0–9516209–9–1

Printed by
Antony Rowe Ltd.
Chippenham
Wiltshire
England

CONTENTS

Acknowledgements

Particular reference is due to the following:

A stanza from *The Battle of the Goths and the Huns* from *The Saga of King Heidrek the Wise,* ed. Christopher Tolkien, Nelson's Icelandic Texts 1960.

Riddle 73 in *The Earliest English Poems* p. 101, Michael Alexander, Penguin Classics 2nd ed. 1977.

Extracts from *Ragnarsdrapa* from *Edda*, p. 123, Snorri Sturlson trans. Anthony Faulkes, Everyman's Library, J M Dent & Sons, Copyright David Campbell Publishers Ltd. 1987.

Land of the Tollund Man p.90 para 3, Palle Lauring, trans. Reginald Spink, Lutterworth Press 1957.

Two short passages from *Germanic Legend in Old English Literature,* Roberta Frank in The Cambridge Companion to O.E. Literature ed. M Godden & M Lapidge, CUP 1991.

The comparative translations of *Deor* lines 14-16:

  (a) *The Earliest English Poems* p. 36, Michael Alexander, Penguin Classics 2nd ed. 1977.

  (b) *Anglo-Saxon Poetry* p. 364, S A J Bradley, J M Dent & Sons Ltd. 1982.

  (c) *A Choice of Anglo-Saxon Verse* p. 91, Richard Hamer, Faber & Faber Ltd. 1970.

The Oxford Book of Medieval English Verse ed. C & K Sisam Oxford, Clarendon Press 1970.

Foreword

"Germanic legend holds our interest because it is extraordinary, a strange and enchanting offspring of the real and the dreamworld . . ."

Roberta Frank: *Germanic Legend in Old English Literature.*

One Old English poem about Germanic legend begins with the words: 'Widsið (Far-Journey) spoke out, he unlocked his word-hoard . . .'

Widsið was speaking as a *scop*, a king's poet and singer. Such men were living memories of the English, Saxon and Jutish tribes and their dynasties. In their songs, the great kings, queens and heroes of the past still lived on, long after their funeral fires had died to ashes, or their bodies and treasure had been laid under mounds.

What Widsið unlocked from his word-hoard included seventy-one names from the Heroic Age of the Germanic peoples and their Finnish, Greek and Hunnic neighbours. The unspoken promise of the poem is that there is a story to every name and that the *scop* can tell them all.

The Angelcynn brought these stories with them when they came to Britain. Their poets could mention a name – Ingeld, Mæðhild, Heremod – sure that their listeners would know it and enter at once into the story-world that was being created.

Nowadays, readers can find the skeletons of these stories in the notes to *Beowulf* and other Old English poems. The bare summaries at least show that they were tales of adventure, passion, bloodshed and magic, set in a wild northern world where a grave mound might house a dragon guarding its treasures, a beautiful ice-hearted princess could order death for any man who dared to look at her, a raven might speak to a king out hunting and tell him the number of days he had left to live.

The treasures found in the graves help us to see this world with the mind's eye: the queens glittering with golden ornaments, the champions in their boar-crested helmets, armed with jewel-studded pattern-welded swords, the great drinking vessels made of aurochs' horns, the lyres, the gaming pieces. There are even the shadows of a royal ship and a great palace marked out in the soil.

As Roberta Frank says, the world of these stories is 'strange and enchanting' yet real at the same time. Theodoric Amaling, the Ostrogothic prince, was educated in Constantinople, consul in the year 484, and 'Lord of Italy, king of the Goths, governor of the Romans' from 493 to 526. In the stories the English knew about him, he made a foray into the land of the giants and was trapped. He was set free by his comrade Vidigoia (Widia), son of Weland the Smith by the princess he had raped as an act of revenge on her father.

In spite of their power and strangeness, very little creative work has been done recently with these stories, though their tone and atmosphere can be sensed throughout *The Lord of the Rings*.

A story in a foot-note is just a skeleton. Stories only live while they are being told and enjoyed. True telling means re-making the story every time it is told, even when the teller is reciting words that have been learned by heart. No two performances of *Hamlet* are the same, even when given by the same cast in the afternoon and evening of the same day . Also, the tale varies with the teller. The account of Hamlet that Shakespeare unlocked from his word-hoard is not like the one that Saxo wrote about him in Latin four hundred years earlier. Any poem chanted some six hundred years before that, just after Amleth had killed his uncle and avenged his father, would have been different from both.

Can these stories come to life at the end of the 20th century? The only way to find out is to try. When I began, as a practising novelist, to work with this material, I did not know what the results would be like – or even if there would be any results. I had no need to invent plot-lines: the legends offered events, arranged in order and leading to endings. They also supplied the names of the leading characters and stated their motives. As every writer knows, this is not enough. Sometimes material is impossible to work with. The story will not move, the people will not live, you can find no reason or emotion behind the action, no creative satisfaction in following it through to the end.

I was startled to find how quickly these legends came alive for me. The stories told themselves in my imagination. Their world took shape in my mind's eye. Whenever I asked a question, the old material itself gave me the answer. I found that the summaries in the annotated texts are not dry bones; they are dry seeds with life inside them.

That is why this book is in two parts. First come the stories – a mere handful, there are many more of them – as they told themselves to me. After that, there is a selection of the source material, with information about where it can be found and some discussion about how it can be used. Mainly I hope, for pleasure, for the excitement of exploring a world that is both reality and dream. Partly, to add to the pleasure of those who are studying Old English literature.

But also, I hope, for creation. There are fine stories here to be told by word of mouth, novels and plays to be written, operas to be composed, paintings and designs to be made. The material is very old, it comes from deep in our past, yet because it has not been hackneyed and worked to death, it is still 'strange and enchanting'.

'. . . ic hwile wæs Heodeninga scop,
dryhtne dyre. Me wæs Deor noma.
Ahte ic fela wintra folgað tilne,
holdne hlaford, oþþæt Heorrenda nu,
leoðcræftig monn, londryht geþah
þæt me eorla hleo ær gesealde.'

(For a while I was the poet of Heoden's court, dear to the
prince. Deor was my name. For many years I held a high
position, had a generous lord - until now Heorrenda, a man
skilled in song-making, has received the estate that the
nobles' protector formerly gave to me.)

I The Everlasting Battle

When he first took sword, Heoroweard son of Heaðoric made a boast in front of all the warriors on the ale-benches. He swore that he would only bed or wed women of outstanding beauty.

His father was king of the Wulfings, who live in the rich Amber Lands around the mouth of the Oder. In due course, Heoroweard succeeded him. He was a big, fine-looking man, a savage fighter with a powerful war-band to back him. What he was not given, he took. He had no trouble living up to his boast.

His first queen, Ælfhild, was so lovely that men said she must be kin to the light-elves. She bore a son, Heoden, who had his father's strength and stubborn will, with a good share of his mother's beauty. He was a young man when he became king in his turn. As he was free-handed and cheerful as well as brave, a troop of young nobles flocked to his service, proud to be known as his hearth-companions and to fight in his war-band.

One afternoon Heoden was riding alone through the forest, on his way back to the royal hall from one of the near-by farms. The goodwife there was his old nurse; he was fond of her. She was abed now with a broken leg, wretched because she could not tend her house or oversee her maids. Heoden had been to visit her, taking a flask of his small, costly store of southern wine as a gift to help cheer her.

It was Blotmonað. The weather was still fine and sunny, though the days were short. The harvest, a good one, had long been gathered in; ships were beached safely in the havens; the cattle had been slaughtered and salted. War was over for the year, so the young king could give most of his mind to his second-best love, hunting.

Round a bend in the forest track, a woman came in sight, riding towards him on a small shaggy pony. Her kirtle was bright green with scarlet borders. The westering sunlight flamed against her jewelled headband, her necklace and brooches, the gold threads of her embroidery. She seemed to be on fire.

Heoden wondered why a woman of such wealth should be mounted on a wretched little nag; also, how she dared to travel alone with the worth of a nobleman's blood-price flaunted on her body. He stopped wondering when she drew near enough for him to see that she was riding an enormous wolf. Her bridle reins were live snakes. Her face could have stopped a war-host in full charge.

Grey elf-locks straggled under her veil. Her body was shaped like a barrel but the skin of her face was drawn so tightly over the bones that it looked like a skull. Her eyes were bloodshot and red-rimmed; her nose had flaring black nostrils like a deer's; black hairs bristled on her chin. She had a wide, surprisingly fleshy mouth; her lips were moist and red as if she had just been chewing raw meat.

Heoden drew his horse aside from the path to let her pass and raised his hand in greeting. Courtesy costs nothing.

'A good day to you, lady.'

'It'll prove a good day to both of us, I hope. There's still some time left before nightfall and the grass is warm from the sun. We could have a happy hour together behind those bushes. If the evening air gets chilly, your cloak's wide enough to wrap us both.'

Heoden had a hunter's steady nerves. He did not shudder.

'I'm too young and untaught to be fit company for you, lady. I wouldn't know how best to entertain you.'

'Then it's high time you had a lesson, dear lad. You'll do better all the rest of your life for what I can teach you.'

She looked worse when she smiled; it showed her fangs. Heoden smiled back.

'You'd be wasting your time, lady, you'd find me un-teachable. I'm my father's son. It takes a woman of matchless beauty to rouse my – interest.'

The troll-woman's face turned grey and still like a piece of weathered stone. The wolf snarled; the snakes hissed from her fingers. Heoden watched her, making no move but ready to draw his sword in an instant if she flew at him.

Then she nodded. Her eyes shone as red as her garnets.

'May you have what you want – *always!*' It sounded like a curse.

She tightened her fingers on the snakes. The wolf turned aside; he and his rider vanished among the trees. Heoden was glad to be rid of her so easily.

Feasting in the royal hall an hour later, Heoden washed away her memory with ale and mead. His mind was full of next day's hunt. He ordered the companions to be ready to set out at the first glimmer of dawn, to make the most of the shortening daylight.

They were ready, with their weapons and horses, their foot-servants and their hounds. They waited till sun-up, yet there was no sign or sound from the king.

Deor was Heoden's scop, his kinsman (their mothers were sisters), one of the bravest fighters in his war-band and his best friend since childhood. He had the right to go into the king's bedroom and rout him out of bed.

Heoden had not left last night's feast any drunker than usual, but now he was lying like the dead. It was some time before Deor's shaking and calling brought any sign of life. At last his lips began to move and mutter:' . . . beautiful . . . eyes . . . sparkling blue like ice-crystals . . . long hair . . . bright and pale as the first sunbeams of spring . . . breasts . . . white as untrodden snow . . . beautiful . . . '

His eyes opened. He stared blankly at Deor. It was clear that he did not know where he was or who Deor was. Then he remembered. He scowled.

'Why in Hel's name did you wake me *now?*'

'You said you wanted to make an early start. We've been waiting for you since first light.'

Heoden half-grunted, half-snarled. He got up, though, and was soon leading the hunting-party out of the stronghold. In spite of the late start, they had a very successful day. Heoden played his usual reckless but skilful leading part in the sport but he did not show his usual joy.

That night he left the feast early. The next day he told Deor that he must have wrenched a muscle during the hunt. Now, he could hardly stand. The companions could go hunting or amuse themselves as they chose, he would keep to his bed that day while his body set itself to rights. He refused Deor's offer to stay with him and help pass the time with stories and songs.

Next day Heoden did not wake at all.

The leech and cunning-women worked on his body while he slept. They found no sign of injury or sickness; the king had not been elf-shot. The household priest sacrificed to the gods; there was no answer. The companions nearly took the king's hall apart, hunting for hidden sleep-runes. They found nothing. Then the old herb-wife came and told them that the last day the king hunted, he had asked her to brew him a strong sleeping-potion.

Then they knew that Heoden had put his body to sleep so that his spirit could get out of it. They were horrified.

Masters of sorcery can go on spirit-journeys but only after years of hard training. Even then, it is deadly dangerous. Other folk can be lured or harried out of their bodies against their wills. But not even the oldest and wisest counsellor in Heoden's witan had ever heard of anyone, not a sorcerer, who had deliberately sent himself on a spirit-journey. Where had their king gone? Would he – could he – ever get back? And was it possible to break a spell that a man had put on himself?

A wind came shrieking out of the north, bringing the first snow of winter. Heoden slept on. When the wind dropped, Deor called a council.

'We must act now, winter or no. If we wait till spring, the king will be lost for ever. His body will weaken; it could be dead and rotting by the time he comes back to it – if he ever does.'

'What can we do that we haven't done already?' said one of the elders.

'We want someone cunning enough to find where he's gone and strong enough to bring him back,' said Deor. 'That needs more magic than we've got among our folk, so it seems. But I know there are such powerful sorcerers in Middle Earth, because all the tales speak about them.'

He stood up.

'Now, listen to me, Heodenings, I am making a vow: I will not rest for storm, snow and the Dark Days of midwinter, till I meet a wizard who can bring back our king. Whatever sacrifice is needed, I will make it. Whatever price is asked, I will pay it.'

As Deor said this, a shadow fell over him. They all looked round. Someone was standing close by, watching them.

He was short and squat, dressed from head to boots in catskins striped grey and black, with snow-shoes bound to his feet, a pouch at his belt and a skin bag over his shoulder. Under his hood straggled locks of coarse black hair. His skin was sallow; his nose was broad and flattish; his eyes were set slanting in his head. They were bright and hard as jet beads; other folk could not see into their depths and track his thoughts.

By his looks, he was one of the Scridefinnas from the farthest north. Because they live on the outer rim of Middle-earth, they know more than most about what lies beyond the edge. They are uncanny folk, skilled in sorcery. The companions were startled to see him so close. They had not heard him coming, no guard had challenged him, no servant had announced him.

'Who are you? What's your business? Why have you come here?'

'I am Heorrenda. I'm a – gleeman. I've come here because one of you called me' – the slanting black gaze moved from face to face and rested on Deor – 'though the one who needs my help isn't among you'.

Whatever he called himself, he was clearly a shaman, so they told him about their king's plight. Heorrenda listened attentively but Deor sensed that he was hearing nothing he did not know already.

They took him to see the sleeping king, crowding round the inner doorway, watching his every move. He did very little. He lifted Heoden's eyelids and stared for a second into his blank eyes. He clamped his hands round Heoden's head, pressing his thumbs to the centre of the brow. He pulled back the bed-covers and laid his ear against Heoden's chest as if listening. Then he replaced the coverlets and stood up.

'Well, have you found him?'

Heorrenda shook his head, unconcerned.

'First, I must know what he's looking for. He hasn't found it yet but it's drawing him. Depends how far he's managed to go without a guide.'

He laughed.

'He hasn't the slightest knowledge or skill in these matters but he has enormous courage and desire. That could take him far into the spirit world. I might fly on ahead and wait for him, or call him back to me. We shall see.'

He marked out a circle of protection round the king's bed. Then he took his drum and began to dance inside the circle, stepping to the drumbeats and to the sounds that came out of his mouth. It could hardly be called singing. The words – if there were any words – must have been Finnish. Sometimes there were gruntings rising from his belly, or purring that made his body tremble; sometimes croaks and high-pitched screams like bird-calls. As he circled faster and faster, closing in on the king's bed, Deor seemed to glimpse the shadow of wings – not one but a pair of falcons gliding and wheeling round each other on a homeward flight.

The drumming stopped. Heoden sat up, glaring furiously at the shaman.

'How dare you break my dreams!'

'I have a message for you, lord'.

'I don't want to hear it.'

Heoden's voice blurred; he turned on his side and pulled the coverlets up round his ears.

'Not even about – eyes sparkling blue like ice-crystals? Long hair, bright and pale as the first sunbeams of spring? Breasts –'

Heoden jumped up and gripped the shaman's shoulders.

'Who is she? Where is she?'

He glared round, yelling for the servants to bring his clothes, then turned back to Heorrenda while they helped him to dress.

'How can I get to her?'

'She is Hild, King Hagena's daughter, of the Holmrygas.'

The companions looked at each other.

The Holmrygas were their nearest neighbours to the east – but not very near. They lived round the mouth of the Vistula; there were two hundred miles of desolation between the tribes' strongholds, with little worth raiding in all those miles. So the Wulfings and the Holmrygas were enemies, as neighbours must be, but not deadly foes because they did not meet often enough to keep blood-feuds going. The Wulfings traded and fought with the tribes to their west and south, the Danes, the Angelcynn, the Frisians. The Holmrygas dealt mostly with the folk of the north-east. There was a lot of Wendish blood in them, even in their royal house. The Wulfings looked on the Holmrygas as outlanders, ill to meddle with and dangerous to trust.

'One other thing,' added Heorrenda casually. 'The princess is a wælcyrie, one of Woden's women.'

Heoden looked taken aback for an instant, then stubborn.

'But wælcyrian do mate with kings and heroes. There are stories about them.'

He glanced eagerly at Deor, to back him up on this.

'A few. I never heard of one that ended happily.'

'The princess has certain skills that King Hagena isn't eager to let go out of his tribe. Her father's wishes wouldn't count, of course, if the girl wanted to have a man, but she doesn't. She's made a vow that no one will ever have her maidenhead with her consent, except Woden. So any man, churl or thane or prince, who comes to the Holmrygas' stronghold and only looks his lust at her – is killed.'

There was a pause.

'I can get her for you,' said Heorrenda softly. 'I'm the only one you're ever likely to meet who can do it.'

He stroked his fur – cats' fur. Cats are the goddess Freo's creatures.

'Only Freo's man has a hope of taking one of Woden's women. I'm willing to promise never to leave your service before Hild is in your power.'

Heoden was radiant.

'Wyrd was smiling at me when she brought you here. When do we start? How long must I wait till I have her?'

The shaman said very gently, 'It will be costly.'

Suddenly, Deor knew what was coming. He felt the sick horror of watching a man step into a quicksand, with no time to shout a warning.

'You can have whatever you ask, even to half my kingdom.'

'Oh, I've no wish for even half a kingdom. I wouldn't know what to do with it. A man should stick to his own craft; it's taken me half a life-time to learn mine. I've been wandering far and wide in Middle-Earth seeking for knowledge. It's time I settled down. I want a noble's place in your household, with landright.'

'It's yours.'

'I want to be your scop.'

Heoden hesitated, glancing furtively at Deor.

'I've already got one.'

'That's no hindrance. I heard him making a vow this very day, in front of all these elders and warriors, that he alone would be the one to pay my price.'

Heoden laughed with relief.

'That's settled then.'

So it was that Heorrenda, the outland shaman, became the royal scop in place of Deor, the king's kinsman and shield-friend.

Later, the king spoke to Deor alone.

'I'll make it up to you.'

Deor knew he meant golden ornaments, jewelled weapons, a high-born wife. No outward honour could make up for the public insult to his scop's craft as maker and master-wordsmith, his very selfhood. He looked at Heoden and said nothing.

15

'Besides, it won't last very long. That breed never stay long anywhere. I'll make a wager with you – any odds you like – I won't have had Hild in my bed half a year before he's away to the northlands again.'

He clapped Deor on the shoulder.

'Soon everything will be back just as it was.'

Nothing would ever again be just as it was. Deor said nothing. Heoden stopped smiling.

'I've always looked on you as my most faithful friend, utterly true to me. I know I can trust you, come what may.'

Deor sighed. 'Yes, you know you can trust me, come what may.'

At least Heoden was right about that.

Yule came and went; days lengthened; ice melted, earth grew green, ships could put out to sea again. The king was eager to set off and win Princess Hild. Heorrenda told him not to try war, or an embassy to her father. They would go as merchants. Once inside the Holmrygan stronghold, the shaman would use his arts to enchant the king and his companions, then lure the girl to come away with him and give herself to Heoden of her own accord.

The companions thought this was an excellent joke. The king had, of course, picked the thirty strongest, bravest, wildest of his war-band to crew his ship. All Deor's best friends were going – Helmstan, Wulfhere, Oslaf, young Eadric – and Deor himself.

It seemed to Deor during those last days that there was a laughing madness on all the rest of them. They roared when they saw the 'merchandise' loaded into the ship: rotting sacks, frayed lengths of rope, fleeces from sheep that had died of the scab, rusted iron pins.

Heorrenda sang over the rubbish and it took the form of Greek brocades, golden girdles, splendid furs and jewelled brooches. He sang over the royal warship and she took the shape of a broad-beamed Frisian trading cog. He sang over the picked warriors and they took the shapes of plainly-dressed, leather-skinned, salt-caked seamen.

Only Deor, a scop with his own craft of weaving word-spells, was not quite tricked by the illusion. From time to time, he could see through the webs of magic that had been spun round them. Whenever that happened he felt giddy, almost scared. He told nobody, but he was aware that Heorrenda knew and was amused.

The ship was pushed off from the beach. The crew braced themselves for the long dreary pull to the mouth of the Vistula. But as the ship came out of haven, a mighty current took her and sent her rushing forward the way she should go. The sea-bed churned up; the air was full of the smell of seaweed; behind their stern the wake was gleaming silver for miles with shoal after shoal of fish; thousands of seagulls came down around them in screaming clouds.

'What is it? What's happening?'

Everyone looked at Heorrenda.

'Wada has come – the giant who keeps the sea-bed, the master of currents, the fish-herd. You can ship your oars, he's got the hull in his grasp. I've put a binding-spell on him to take us quickly to the Holmrygas and bring us away even quicker.'

So they stretched their legs and lounged on the thwarts while the ship raced eastwards with its thousands of finned and winged followers. No one on sea and shore seemed to notice them. But when they got near to the great lake at Vistula mouth, Heorrenda told them to take to the oars. They came into the haven like any other merchant ship.

The Holmrygas were wary and unwelcoming to westerners. The port-reeve set guards to watch the ship, forbade all but a small party to carry goods up to the royal stronghold, would not let anyone bear arms ashore.

Heorrenda, as ship-master, was meek and obliging. The whole crew would stay aboard till he himself brought them leave from the king. (He looked warningly at the companions to show he really meant this.) The port-reeve's own men could carry the goods up from the haven. Just he and his mate (pointing at Deor) would come up with them to pay their respects to the king. They would take nothing with them but their harps. They both had some skill as gleemen; they would be glad to offer their services to the king to amuse him and his household.

The piles of rubbish were unloaded; the port-reeve's men carried them carefully up to the stronghold. Deor watched with mingled horror and choked-back laughter as the Holmrygan nobles, their wives and daughters draped themselves delightedly in the sacks and mangy fleeces. He wondered how long the shaman had made the spell to last.

The feast began. Heorrenda and Deor took their places humbly by the door, on the lowest bench. Deor looked anxiously towards the high seat.

King Hagena was a powerfully-built man, almost a giant, who looked as if his temper was as ugly as his face. But the girl beside him was the loveliest creature the scop had ever seen or imagined – long hair flowing under her diadem, bright and pale as the first sunbeams of spring, eyes sparkling blue like ice-crystals, skin as white as untrodden snow. In spite of his jealousy and anger, Deor understood Heoden's desire for her and his readiness to sacrifice anything, or anybody, to have her.

As the shaman got up, harp in hand, to entertain the hall-guests, he muttered to Deor, 'Wait till I've started, then slip out to relieve yourself and stay outside the door till I come. *Don't* cross the threshold again.'

He stepped out into the middle of the hall and began to recite *The Queen of Romeburh*. This was a ribald lay telling the exploits of a widowed Empress of Constantinople, as she tried out one young man after another for the position of her next consort. They all failed to stand up to her gruelling tests.

The Holmrygas were soon helpless with laughter, eyes streaming, fists pounding the tables, gasping for breath, exhausted. No one noticed Deor go out. When he came back to the door, though, they were all still as stones.

Heorrenda was singing of love, so sweetly that Deor felt the fingers on the harp-strings plucking the heart out of his breast. He saw women of unearthly beauty taking shape among the shadows, offering themselves to him – swan-maids with breasts as soft as down, amber-eyed elf-women, their hair swirling round them like autumn leaves, a young wælcyrie with a body as lithe and slim as a boy's and wild-fire in her blood –

Deor's feet began to walk him into the hall towards the singing; his will had a struggle to pull him back. The shaman's voice and harping grew more and more drowsy. The folk in the hall sank to sleep. He moved towards the door, playing a delicate, beckoning little tune. The girl on the dais got up and followed him. As they came out, the shaman nodded to Deor to take her hand. Following the music, they went past the sleeping guards and servants, back to Heoden's ship. The companions were lining the side, staring at the shore-folk, sleeping where they had fallen.

Deor helped Hild climb aboard; her eyes were open but her face was blank. Her spirit seemed asleep – or fled elsewhere. The shaman told the companions to cast off and get the ship out of haven fast.

18

Heoden saw nothing but Hild; he clasped her tightly in his arms.

She clasped him tightly in her arms.

'I've been dreaming of this moment,' he whispered.

'I've been dreaming of this moment,' she whispered.

'Now you're mine for ever!'

'Now you're mine for ever,' she agreed.

They kissed, open mouth to open mouth.

The companions were grinning, congratulation spiced with envy. The girl seemed as love-possessed as Heoden. Perhaps she, too, had seen him in dreams and had been longing for him.

Deor felt a cold touch of fear. Hild was not talking to Heoden or kissing him. Her spirit had been sent flying somewhere else at Heorrenda's command. Heoden was enjoying nothing but his own desire; his lust was moving and speaking in her empty body as well as in his own.

By now, the ship was out of haven. Wada took the hull in his mighty grasp and thrust it out to sea. The companions shipped their oars. They wedged two spears at either end of the stern thwart and slung cloaks like bed-hangings between the shafts. They piled more cloaks in the stern to make a couch for the lovers. Heoden and Hild turned as one body and went behind the curtain. Heorrenda played his harp till the others fell asleep. The ship hurtled through the night like a flying spear.

When Deor woke, it was daylight. He saw they were heading due north, still at the same unearthly speed, followed by tribes of sea-birds and fishes. He was not surprised at their course. Heorrenda had told them that Wada would set off northwards, make a great sweep beyond Bornholm and bring them home to the Oder from the west, as from a friendly visit to the Jutes or the Angelcynn.

Deor glanced back along their wake. To the south a great bank of cloud was slowly rising from the horizon. Just for a moment, against the brightness between the cloud and the sea, he glimpsed other ships, coming after them. He called Heorrenda.

'Look!'

Heorrenda smiled.

'King Hagena and his men have heads like pigs of iron. No spell could bind them for long.'

'But how did they get on to our track?'

19

'They're *in* our track. Wada's striding at such a rate, his current'll be running for miles. Hagena's fleet must have got swept into the far end of it. And if they're using their oars as well, they're probably catching up a little. Don't worry. No mortal eye can see you now. And you'll never see King Hagena's ships coming into Oder mouth, I can promise you that.'

Deor never felt easy when Heorrenda smiled.

The companions were waking up, yawning and stretching. Heoden came from behind the curtain to join them. They caught a glimpse of Hild, dishevelled, drowsing among the cloaks. Heoden must have slept for some part of the night; he looked alert and full of zest, in the best of tempers.

They had brought barrels of ale and mead. Heoden proposed to beach the ship at a suitable place, land a hunting-party and hold his wedding-feast ashore over their kill. The shaman nodded, went to the prow and began chanting. The ship turned at once, like a horse obeying the bridle rein, and took them east into a long narrow inlet, winding away out of sight among wooded cliffs. Heoden picked Deor and five others to come with him, leaving the rest to guard the ship and the sleeping girl. The shaman chose to come with the hunters.

When they had killed their first deer, Heoden glanced round at the wild highland country.

'What is this place?'

'Norway.'

'*Norway!*' They stared at him in horror.

'I told you we were coming north first.'

'But in Hel's name, why as far as Norway?'

'It's the best place for me to get back to my own country.'

He sniffed the air. 'The ice is melting up there, the reindeer are moving north. It's time I was on my way.'

He turned up a steep path among the trees.

'You can't leave us now – you promised –'

'I promised never to leave your service before Hild was in your power. She is in your power. What happens now is your concern. If a man can't keep his own woman, nobody else can keep her for him. I've got you off to a good start.'

'Traitor! You call it keeping a promise – misleading us miles from home, then deserting us on the coast of Norway?'

'Wada is taking you home. I've put a binding spell on him. He's making a circle, as I told you, to mislead your enemies. West from here, along the north coast of Britain, south among the islands, east between Britain and Gaul, north past Frisia, round the land of the Jutes – and there you are!'

He smiled.

'Fare you well on your journey home. I'm off to mine.'

He moved away among the trees.

'You're staying here!'

Heoden snatched a bow and shot at him. He meant to bring the shaman down and cripple him, but he did not give himself time to aim carefully. The arrow went over Heorrenda's head and stuck in a tree. He whirled round to face them. For a second they stared at a huge wildcat, fur bristling, ears flat against its head, lip raised in a snarl, paw lifted to strike. The creature spat at them, then streaked up the bole of the nearest tree and vanished.

They turned back gloomily to the shore with their kill. Each man knew that Wyrd was not friendly to them.

Matters were not friendly on board the ship, either. She had changed back to her real shape. So had the companions. They were crowded near the stern, clutching their weapons, except for young Eadric. He was slumped on a thwart, clutching his half-severed arm. The makeshift screen of cloaks had been thrown down.

Hild was facing them, her back to the stern-post. Her neck and breast were dripping red with ruby pendants on a collar of wrought gold. More rubies gleamed in bracelets on her wrists. These were Heorden's greatest treasures, looted ages ago from the Greek lands in the south. He had brought them with him as his bride's morning-gift; he had clasped them on her during a bout of love-making. Hild had a spear in her left hand; her right gripped Eadric's sword. That was also dripping red, with Eadric's blood.

The warriors made a move towards her. Heoden rushed forward, followed by the hunting party.

'Stop that!'

He leaped aboard.

'I'll kill any man who strikes at her!'

Hild saw that they took orders from him. She turned to stare at him. Her spirit was back now, glaring furiously out of her eyes.

'Who are you? How did I get here?'

'I am Heoden, king of the Wulfings. You came here with me, your husband.'

'Husband? You mean you stole me, crept up on my people unawares, you coward! Did you cut their throats while they slept? Did you stun me in my bed and rape me while I was helpless? Or did you hire a traitor in our household to drug our mead at the feast, you maggots!'

She glanced at the side as if she meant to throw herself overboard. Only then did Deor realise that the ship was racing out to sea again. Heoden took a step towards her. She readied her weapons.

'I swear to you – I'll take any oath you like to put on me – that we came to your people in peace. My men took no weapons ashore. No drop of your people's blood was shed. There was no need. You came down to the ship, hand in hand with my kinsman. You embraced me in the sight of all these warriors. You gave yourself to me last night – the only bloodshed was then – and you were laughing for joy. You're wearing my morning-gift round your neck.'

She dropped her spear and put her hand to her neck, fingering the pendants.

'I remember nothing of this.'

'You were in a trance of love. We both were.' Heoden smiled at the memory. 'Freo is a mighty goddess. No mortal can stand against her.'

She was staring at her wrists.

'You lost no time putting your slave-collar and manacles on me.'

'Don't belie me, woman! Those are a queen's treasures, worn by my queen.'

She gazed round desperately as if seeking a way of escape. She looked at the clouds of gulls diving and soaring above her. She saw the wake, silver with shoals of fish all the way back to the horizon. She noticed that the ship was rushing through the water with no one at the oars. Then she went to the stern and leaned over, staring down into the depths.

Heoden raised his voice impatiently to her back.

'I have every right to claim you and keep you as my wife and queen. You vowed yourself to me last night.'

She turned to face him, smiling now, her eyes sparkling blue as ice-crystals.

'And you may be quite sure that every vow I make, I keep.'

She laid aside her weapons, sat down on the cloaks in the stern and began to braid her hair. Heoden was thankful that she had calmed down and accepted her fate. He decided to let well alone for a while. He came forward and joined the others in a game of dice.

Deor glanced at Hild from time to time. She was watching the gulls wheeling round her, flying off into the distance then swooping back to her again. She lifted her arms to them; to his amazement they perched on her hands and shoulders, tame as doves. Her lips moved as if she was talking to them; then she bent her head to their beaks as if they were talking to her. She seemed quite content.

By and by she began to sing softly in Wendish. Her voice was very sweet. For a while Deor was happy to listen – then wondered with a start how he could possibly be hearing her through the screaming of the gulls.

But the gulls were not screaming any more. The sky was empty of them, except for one or two hovering specks away towards the horizon.

He cried out, 'The gulls have left us!'

They all stared. Hild had her back to them, gazing out over the stern. She spoke over her shoulder.

'The gulls went after the fish. The fish went after Wada.'

The ship was no longer racing over the waves. She had lost way and was starting to wallow. Heoden cried out in fury and despair.

'Wada has deserted us!'

She shook her head. 'I undid the binding-spell and sent him away. Don't worry, I thanked him politely before he left, for both of us. And I gave him a parting gift, from both of us.'

She turned to face them, holding out her arms. Her wrists were bare. The ruby bracelets had gone overboard.

The ship lurched as a wave slammed her amidships. Hild laughed.

'You'd better get the oars out.'

Deor signed to the others to do as she said, remembering how Heorrenda had forewarned them that she had certain skills. He thought of the ships he had glimpsed far to the south in the dawn light. He guessed the gulls had told her that Hagena was on her track and that she had sent him word by them.

Heoden went up to her. She did not flinch.

'Why have you done this?'

'I don't recall that I said farewell to my father before I left. I wouldn't like to think of him complaining about my manners.

Also – husband – I haven't yet had the pleasure of seeing how well you fight.'

She glanced ahead, where a scatter of islands was rising into view.

'Oh, look – Orkney! I've often flown here with my battle-sisters.'

Some of the islands were mere rocks, walled with sheer cliffs, but there were broader, lower lands beyond. Hild pointed to one of these.

'Better make for Hoy. You'll have plenty of room there to meet my people.'

Heoden felt her anger and ill-will striking at him like lightning. Still, he made his moves as coolly as if he had planned the coming battle before he set out to gain his bride. He told the companions to row past the obvious landing, a wide sheltered bay, where Hagena would certainly beach his ships. They went a good way further north, hid their ship in a little cove and climbed inland to a steep ridge with a deep, fast-flowing burn at its foot. Hagena would have a rough march to come in sight of them, then the burn to ford before he could get at them.

Hild gazed south.

'Father's in a hurry, to have come so close behind us. He can't wait to meet the man who raped his daughter and took her as a slave.'

'You know that's not true!'

'Do I? Anyway, father doesn't know it. Shall I go to meet him and show him my morning-gift? I'd rather he thought of me as your wife than your whore.'

Heoden stared at her, trying to read her mind. For the first time since he had become besotted with desire for Hild, he thought about his own folk. They had been left without their king and the best part of his war-band, easy prey now that the raiding season had started.

Was there any need that he and Hagena should fight to the death for Hagena's daughter? He was a king and he had made Hild his queen. What harm had he done? He had not shed one drop of Holmrygan blood in warfare. He could lay the blame for the trickery on Heorrenda. He had merely sent his scop and his kinsman to ask for the girl's hand in wedlock – how could he have foretold the use of sorcery? He himself had been a victim of it.

If Hild would play the woman's part, as peace-weaver, the two tribes could be allies, each stronger for the other's friendship. Could he trust her to go to her father and not stay with him? Then the men he picked to escort her would go to their deaths; he would be left to face Hagena with fewer warriors. Perhaps that was what she wanted.

He could not reach her mind. She read his.

'I'll come back, whatever father says. I promise I'll never leave you now, after what has passed between us. You can send as many men as you like to follow me but I doubt if they can keep pace.'

She set off down the ridge. It was steep, jagged with boulders and loose stones, thick with clumps of heather, ready to break a bone at each careless step. Hild went down it like a waterfall, cleared the burn with a flying leap and ran across the moorland. She moved so quickly that it was hard to see her clearly. Heoden fancied she was running over the tops of the heather clumps rather than following the sheep-tracks through them. There was no hope of catching her now.

Hagena was overseeing the beaching of his ships and the landing of his war-gear when his daughter walked up to him.

'Well?'

'Heoden sent you this.'

She unclasped the Byzantine collar from her neck and held it out to him. Hagena looked at the shoulder-wide bands of wrought gold, set with medallions and huge cabochon rubies, the pendants edged with filigree, tipped with rock crystals. Hild looked at her father's face. She saw amazement, admiration, greed.

'So he has some real treasures, as well as that rubbish he unloaded on us.'

He took the collar into his hands and fingered it lovingly. He was summing up its worth, what it told him about the worth of Heoden as a son-in-law, whether it was worth his while to trade Hild and peace to get it. She watched her father working out the sum.

'Oh yes, he's rich. He inherited King Heoroweard's gold-hoard as well as his habits. Any woman he wants he takes, but he can afford to pay for his pleasure. He's ready to fight you if you dare try taking me away from him, but he's willing to pay you this for my hire.'

Hagena's fingers tightened on the collar. The muscles in his arms bulged; he crushed the delicate gold-work. Then he laid it on a flat-topped rock, took his battle-axe and hammered it till both gold and jewels were in fragments.

'Go and tell him that you watched me smash his paltry trinket and soon you'll be watching me smash him.'

In spite of Hild's vow, Heoden had not been sure he could trust her to keep it. When he saw her coming back, he felt as much guilt as joy. He hurried to take her in his arms.

'You father kept the necklace!'

He could not quite keep the relief out of his voice.

'My father smashed the necklace with his battle-axe. He told me to say he'll do the same to you.'

She smiled at him.

'He has five shiploads with him, so the odds are only five to one against you. Never mind, that's not your fault, husband.'

She sat on an outcrop of rock to watch.

It was quite late in the afternoon when Hagena's men were seen plodding up from the south. Heoden went down to face his father-in-law across the burn. Hagena wasted no time on formal preliminaries.

'You thieving bastard, got by a troll on a Hunnish whore! Can you scrape up enough courage to come within reach of my sword?'

'If you can scrape up enough courage to step across this stream, you'll find out.'

Heoden had decided to hold his side of the burn; he had the ridge behind him to fall back on at need. By nightfall, Hagena's men had not won their way across the water, but ten of Heoden's thirty lay dead on the nearest bank when the fighting broke off.

Neither Heoden nor Deor slept during the first watch of the night. Heoden was keeping guard. Deor was waking for his friends Helmstan and Wulfhere, who had not come back to camp. Something moved among the corpses down by the water's edge. There was a shimmer of pale gold hair in the moonlight. Hild had gone down to the dead; she was singing to them. Deor thought she was chanting the death-song over the men who had fought for her and her husband. Then he blinked; he thought the moonlight had cheated his eyes; perhaps they were already blurred with tears. The dead had seemed to stir.

They were stirring, stretching their limbs, standing up, gathering their weapons, coming back uphill to camp.

Hild the wælcyrie, Woden's priestess and lover, had certain skills. One of them was the art of singing the dead quick again. No wonder her father did not want to lose her.

Deor felt a surge of joy as Helmstan and Wulfhere came over the crest of the ridge between the watch-fires. He called their names, stretched out his arms to greet them and clasp their hands. Then he drew back in cold despair as they passed him without a glance, dead eyes in blank faces. Whatever was moving in their bodies, he knew he would never meet his friends again.

He heard Heoden chuckling.

'Good lass! I knew she'd stand by me. She doesn't want to lose me now, after only one night.'

'Heoden – they're still dead.'

'I don't care what they are, so long as they can still use weapons and fight on my side.'

But then he began to curse. Hild had lifted her hands towards the further bank. She sang to the Holmrygan dead; there were many more of them. They too stirred, rose and made their way back to Hagena's camp. Hild strolled carelessly back up the slope. Heoden blocked her way.

'What have you done to harm me now?'

'Harm? I've just sent warriors to strengthen your thinning ranks, husband. I'm a dutiful wife.'

'Then why did you raise Hagena's men as well?'

'I'm a dutiful daughter. Besides, I knew you'd hate to take an unfair advantage over anyone by using magic.'

Heoden was too proud to amuse her by trying to argue.

Next day, the fight raged from dawn to sunset. Hild watched from her rock. Hagena's men got across the burn but were thrown back from the ridge. That night, though, they camped at its foot. By then, only Heoden and four of his men were truly alive. The sleepless dead stared all around them, their eyes gleaming in the light of the watch-fires. The newly-slain lay on the rocky slope beneath. Deor saw the pale shape with golden hair move singing among the corpses till they stirred and rose and climbed the hill.

Heoden put a hand on his shoulder.

'I want you to go – now. Tide's in, the ship'll be floating at anchor. You can easily push her off with the steering oar. Mainland's close by; the Picts there will respect you as a scop.'

'I'm not a scop any more – remember? Do you want to destroy my honour as a warrior too? Have me live to be pointed out as the one who broke faith with his lord, left him to die on the battlefield?'

'Your lord broke faith with you. I'm sorry about that, Deor; I was witched out of my senses. Anyway, a warrior is only bound to die for his lord if his lord calls on him to do so. Tomorrow, I mean to die for my warriors and set them free from this horror. But I'd like you to tell my story. I'm asking this as a favour from a friend.'

Deor clasped his hand and went away, down the far side of the ridge.

On the third day of the battle, Heoden fought with the fury of Woden. His last three men died behind him, the dead fought all around him but because he no longer cared to live, no power could bring him down. He cut his way towards Hagena.

Hagena did care to live; he was desperate not to die till he had killed the man who had carried off his daughter and was using her as his whore. Giant though he was, he could not match Heoden in the force and speed of his blows.

So in the end Heoden nearly thwarted his own purpose. His sword smashed down on Hagena's helmet, slicing away part of his skull and cutting into his brain. Hagena tottered a moment before he fell, still gripping his sword. There was just time for Heoden to impale himself on its point, driving his body along the blade; time to feel a moment of joy that he had ended Hild's feud with him and her hideous revenge.

His death would pay Hild for the love-death she had died in his arms three nights ago. She would not forgive him – 'forgive' was a word no wælcyrie would ever speak, let alone act on – but she would have done with him.

But she hadn't. It is said that she has not done with him yet, nor will have done till the world's end.

Deor had only half obeyed his kinsman's last request. He had waited hidden among the rocks, to see where Heoden fell. In spite of the risk, he meant to pile a cairn over his body and to chant a death-song for his friends.

Then he saw the pale shape with golden hair gliding towards Heoden's corpse, heard her singing, saw Heoden stir and get to his feet. His scop's vision looked through the ages to come, saw the bodies hidden as outcrops of rock by day, raised to fight the endless battle through all the hours of dark, unable to rot, unable to rest, unable to win free.

His nerve broke. He fled to the ship, slashed the anchor rope and pushed off. He did not care whether he drowned or the Picts cut his throat.

A wind came shrieking after him out of the north and drove him away from the islands into the open sea. It was not the time of year for such a wind; its sudden rising was uncanny. Perhaps Hild had called the wind, to destroy the last of Heoden's men and make sure his story was never told. Or perhaps, since scops and sorcerers are both workers of magic, Heorrenda had sent it from the northlands to help a fellow-craftsman.

The ship was smashed up at last among the Lindisfaran islands, but the Lindisfaran islanders got Deor safely to land. Their chief, Ida, had just set himself up as king of Bernicia; he was delighted to take a royal scop into his household.

'Ides sceal dyrne cræfte,
fæmne hire freond gesecean, gif heo nelle on folce geþeon
þæt hi man beagum gebicge.'

Old English Maxim

(A high-born lady, a maiden, must meet her lover with
cunning stealth if she does *not* want to do well and
achieve a formal offer of marriage.)

II Board Games and Gaming Pieces

The First Game

King Dene of Scedenig was a great king. He had a
powerful war-band, overthrew many tribes, cast down
their kings, burned their royal halls and made their
nobles pay him tribute. He was the first of the Scyldings to
grasp lands overseas. He took Sillende and the near-by islands.
He meant to take the land of the Jutes but before he could
bring that about, he died.

He had two sons, both tall and handsome. In battle, they
had both shown themselves fearless, skilled with their
weapons, daring leaders. The younger, Hloðhere, really was so.
Hunlaf, the heir, with his father's power to make him dreadful,
his father's war-band at his back and Hloðhere at his side,
played his part with swagger and bluster. Even the warriors
and scops believed in him, at first.

It is not easy to cheat a brother's eyes, especially a brother
who comes hunting and stands shoulder to shoulder in the
battle line. Hloðhere knew his brother was a hollow man. Their
little sister Hereswið guessed as much but she was too young
to put her feelings into words. She worshipped Hloðhere; she
shrank away from Hunlaf when she was in the same room with
him. As he had no time for her, he did not see this.

Before King Dene's mound was ready to receive him and his
treasures, Lord Beornwald came looking for Hloðhere.
Beornwald was one of Dene's most powerful nobles and had
once led his war-band. He found Hloðhere in the women's
bower, comforting Hereswið. Their mother was some years
dead; the child was lonely and frightened.

Beornwald told Hloðhere that he must go at once as Hunlaf
wanted to be rid of him.

Hereswið clutched her brother; he looked bitterly amused
but not surprised.

'He's sending me into exile – so soon?'

31

'He's going to have you killed. He's bribed some of the hostages to do it after the king-making feast, when everybody's drunk. He's promised them they can leave his court and won't have to pay any more tribute. And that's true – because he and his men are going to kill them for murdering you. If you defend yourself so well that you're still alive when the avengers turn up, you'll be killed in the following skirmish.'

There was a pause. Then Hloðhere said slowly, 'I always knew he was worthless. I hadn't thought my father's son would sink to treachery.'

'You must slip away quietly and come to my stronghold. Don't try to bring any of your gear with you; someone would tell Hunlaf. I'll supply you with everything you need – weapons, armour, servants. My men will see you safe out of the kingdom.'

Hloðhere sneered.

'I'm sure they will. I'm sure if I go alone and in secret to your stronghold, I'll never be seen again. And I'm sure Hunlaf will pay you well – how much does he think my death is worth?'

'My lord, you've no right to say –'

'I have every right. If my own brother can betray me to death, so can you. So can everybody.'

Hereswið burst out crying.

'I can't! I won't! I'll always, always keep faith with you – to the last drop of blood in my body. Say you trust me! Say it, say it!'

Hloðhere's face softened. He hugged his sister.

'Yes, I trust you. I know you love me with all your heart.'

He held out his hand to Beornwald.

'Forgive me and forget what I said. It was my bitterness speaking, not myself.'

'My son Beornfrið is ready to go with you as your companion in exile.'

Hereswið said eagerly 'So am I! And your best friend Osmund – he'll go too! Shall I tell him in secret?'

'If the young men come with me, Hunlaf will brand all their kin as traitors – and I know now what he's ready to do to anyone he fears. Anyway, I can go quicker and quieter by myself. As for you, darling, you're the only kin left to me. Keep a place warm for me here, in your heart. I'll send you word of me when I can – listen for the seagulls and you'll hear from me.'

Next day, he gave a friendly challenge to some of Hunlaf's closest cronies. These were the ones, he was sure, who would come to his rescue when the bought killers struck – to make sure that he was dead. He bet that his horse could out-go any of theirs for speed and staying-power. They were braggarts; it was easy enough to goad them into fixing a course through wild overgrown country.

He put his byrnie under his leather hunting tunic, his helmet along with some bread and cheese in his saddle-bag, armed himself with his sword and seax, took his best horse – and soon lost his company.

Hunlaf would have been glad to believe that Hloðhere and his horse were lying with broken bones somewhere out on the fells, feeding the crows. He sent out searchers but the bodies were never found. He could not be sure that his brother had not made a bolt into exile. Yet there was no word of him among the Geats, the Swedes or the Jutes; no word that he had taken ship to Sillende or Angeln and fled south into the German lands. He was surely dead.

Hunlaf settled down to enjoy his kingship. At first, the dread of his father's name and his father's war-band kept the tribute flowing in. But soon, his cronies had the chief places in his household. Beornfrið was passed over as leader of the hearth-troop. He went to his father's lands on the Geatish border. His kinsfolk were too mighty to be attacked; they kept themselves to themselves from then on, neither friends to the king nor open enemies. A number of the older nobles, Osmund's father among them, did likewise.

The new king was in no hurry to take a wife of his own, though he took the wives and sisters of his cronies whenever he wanted. The men he called his friends were glad enough to trade their womenfolk for his gold. He picked the best-looking of the pack, a lively, light-hearted young woman, to take charge of Hereswið. He settled them in the dead queen's bower.

He gave his chief mistress a free hand with the gold-hoard, so traders, jewelsmiths and entertainers came flocking to the bower. The girl was not mean or spiteful; she let the little princess spend money as recklessly as herself and left her free to deal with anyone she chose.

There was a merchant who owned a ship called Mæw; Hereswið bought his goods whenever he came and listened eagerly to his news.

A visiting scop made a song about a seafarer who had suffered dreadful hardships when he was caught by the winter storms. Yet every spring he would feel his heart flying out of his breast like a sea-mew, crying to be away overseas again. The song caught Hereswið's fancy; she asked the scop to come and sing it again just for her. They talked together for a long time; she rewarded him lavishly for his entertainment.

Once a Geatish wanderer came asking for a night's shelter; he was making his way home from the south. He paid for his bed and food with stories of the strange lands he had passed through. Hereswið was pleased to listen and asked that the man should be seen safely on his way to the Geatish border.

The stranger thanked her for her kindness. He was not a beggar, he made her a present of a little silver bowl from Romeburh, wrought with a story in pictures all round the outside. It showed a hero parting from his young bride; he was lost at sea but his ghost came back to her, drawn by his undying love. The bride's heart broke and she died but the gods took pity and turned the lovers into sea-birds, so that they could live together again, careless and free.

Hereswið loved the story and the bowl; she gave the wanderer a jewelled arm-ring in exchange. It was one of the royal treasures but Hunlaf did not mind. Gold flowed though his hands like water through a sieve. Dene's folk saw nothing wrong in that, for the first years of his reign. Kings should be free-handed.

So, by obeying Hloðhere's parting words, to '*listen for the seagulls*', Hereswið heard from her brother at times and nobody else at Hunlaf's court was any the wiser. When, some five or six years later, some of the Danish folk wanted to find him, she was able to tell them where to go looking for him.

Hloðhere had gone east, then south down the Vistula, into the drifting wreckage of tribes and dynasties that had been left after the Huns smashed Eormanric's empire. In those days, a man who was reckless and ruthless, free of any ties to lord or kin, could shape his life as he chose, while it lasted. He could win a kingdom. Even better, he could make a name that would live for ever in song and story.

At first, Hloðhere had kept his name and family to himself, in case his brother had sent hunters on his track, or put a price on his head. By the time he had become a famous champion and no one would have dared to attack him under his old name, he had already earned himself a new one that fitted his mood and his way of life. He was Heremod.

He won his name fighting with the Goths against the Huns, then fighting with the Huns against the Eastern Empire. He went into Rome with Alaric and took a vast amount of looted treasure. When Alaric died, he joined Athaulf's war-band, helped them cut their way into southern Gaul and carve out a kingdom. That is where the Danish envoys found him.

During his exile, he had sent messages to Hereswið whenever he could, using the seagull password. But there was one time, the first year of his wanderings, when he had not been able to send messages. Later, when he was alone with his sister, he told her something about that time and she wished she had not heard it. After he was gone, his bodyservant claimed that he had talked in his sleep and made a fearsome tale of his nightmares. By then, folk were willing to believe anything that was said about him.

He had known that his brother would have eyes watching for him in the creeks and harbours of Sillende and Jutland, would have ears open for news of him at the Geatish and Swedish courts. So he went north along the wild marches, through the forests and lakelands, up into the mountains. Before he turned south again, he had passed through the lands of the Finnas and the Cwenas. He had also passed through a northern winter.

He fought bears; sometimes, in the dusk that fell sooner every day, he fought huge fur-clad shapes that loomed over him and struck at him with the force of giants or trolls. He was attacked by wolves, drawn by the smell of blood or roasting flesh from the game he killed. His horse was so badly savaged, he had to put his sword into the poor creature.

He endured the battering of storm-winds, the cruel grip of frosts, the closing in of darkness. He struggled against the dread of loneliness, the fear that haunts the wastelands. He began shouting, to hear a human voice and rouse an echo to answer him:

'I am Hloðhere the Scylding! Hloðhere the Scylding!'

The scops say that whenever a lonely wayfarer calls out in the wasteland, someone always comes.

Troll-women need not look hideous. They can make themselves fair enough for a while, if they choose. The alder-wives who beckon to passers-by on the edge of swamps in the gloaming are lovely and elf-sheen in the moonlight, though their backs are hollow rotting tree-stumps. Then there are the glimmering girls who dance light-footed on the marsh pools, the mist-wraiths, the wandering night-shadows, cold creatures who enjoy the warmth of a man and want his seed.

It is said that once they take hold of a man and lie with him, no woman of flesh and blood can ever rouse his desire.

Sometimes Hloðhere crawled into a cave for a night's shelter, or pushed his way to the middle of a clump of stunted trees, then found he had come into a great hall, blazing with torches and hearth fires. Lordly warriors greeted him, fair queens glittering with jewels gave him a smiling welcome. They seemed to have been waiting for him. He filled himself with rich food from silver platters; he drank southern wine in golden goblets; he was bedded in furs with a naked queen in his arms. He always woke on the cold hillside, aching and starved, as if his guts had been eaten away by worms.

The last gleam of daylight died; the two months' night began. He would have died in the wasteland among the shadow-folk and the trolls, if he had not staggered into a Finnish *sita*. He was crazed and sick; the shaman took him into his own hut and cared for him.

Hloðhere lay by the hearth during the dark time, drinking potions that burned like liquid fire inside him and talking to the shadows that came to him out of the hearth-smoke. Yet for much of the time, his spirit was hurrying somewhere else. He was climbing in desperate haste up a huge tree that grew so high its branches had broken through the sky-roof. Something was clambering much faster behind him – soon it would be close enough to clutch his feet – then he was a crane, flying from the branches in stupid panic, though a huge hawk was circling overhead ready to take him –

Death was very near.

The shaman healed his body and called his spirit back into it. When spring came, the Finnas set him on his way to the south. He reached the Gothic lands at last and put his sword to hire. In body, he was as strong and well-fleshed as he had been in the days when he lived as a king's son, and much harder. He was on the way to becoming Heremod the champion. But he had been into the Old Darkness on the edge of Middle Earth – and the Darkness had come into him.

Meanwhile, Hunlaf was merrily scattering his father's gold-hoard but doing nothing to win any gold of his own. He bedded a well-born girl who had been promised elsewhere. Her bridegroom and his kin did not think so well of their king that they were willing to take his leavings. The bride's family were not over-joyed to be left with a bastard to keep, who might turn out like his father.

Some of the subject tribes stopped paying tribute. Hunlaf blustered and threatened but did nothing to punish the rebels. Word of this went all round the borders of Scedenig and the islands. The Jutes promptly took Sillende and killed every one of the Danish folk who had settled there.

Now Hunlaf would have to act. The Danish nobles waited for him to summon them with their house-troops. But the king was in no hurry to take the field. He let the rest of the year's fighting season go by in big talk about the mighty war-host he would have gathered by next spring. He ordered the forging of weapons and armour that he could not pay for. Worst of all, he had shown that he was a craven who had no mind to risk his life fighting for his lands and his folk.

His sister was now husband-high. He betrothed her to his closest boon-companion, a man as drunken and lustful as himself but cruel as well. He named this man to lead his host for him in the coming war with the Jutes.

Hereswið turned to Osmund for help. In the old days he had been her brother Hloðhere's dearest friend; as boys, they had shared their weapon-training and hunting trips. Yet he had taken a place in Hunlaf's household and stayed on at his court after most of the young warriors who cared about their good name had left to follow other lords. She knew that loyalty to Hloðhere had kept him there, so that she would have one man near her whom she could trust.

Osmund went to Lord Beornwald's stronghold. The old war-leader and his son Beornfrið had already made up their minds that it was time to be rid of Hunlaf. They knew other powerful kindreds who thought the same. Hereswið had told Osmund where her younger brother had gone. After Haligmonað, when fighting was over for the year but before the winter storms had closed the sea-roads, Osmund took a boatload of Danish warriors south, to look for Hloðhere and offer him the kingship.

They found him at last in southern Gaul. He was rich, powerful and famous by the name of Heremod the champion. Scedenig was drab and chill in his memory. Its kingship was a poor bribe to a man who had looted Rome and was lord of a great estate in Aquitania. Yet when he heard that his sister was crying for his help, he gave up his land-right, took his leave of King Athaulf, packed his Roman treasure and turned his back on the south.

Heremod came to Scedenig early in Hreðmonað. The Danish folk welcomed him like the young Bealdor, coming back from Hel's kingdom with the springtime to make the earth green again. Hunlaf's companions left him; they fled and only fought when cornered. Hunlaf did not fight at all. Heremod dragged him from under his bed and put his sword through him without a word. Folk said that death by the sword was only too good for a worthless craven. For a long time, the Danes were ready to say that everything Heremod did was right.

He took Sillende again and killed every Jute there. That was fair enough, as the Jutes had killed all the Danish incomers. He gave some of the best-looking young captives as an offering to the gods. That was also right and wise – but he made the offering in a way that was new to the Danes and kept some of them from quiet sleep for a night or two after. He hanged the men, of course; but he had it done by hooks driven into their bodies between their thighs, so that instead of dancing for Woden, they wriggled like spiders dangling from the trees. The girls were stretched out over ruts in the road, with their arms and legs tied to stakes. Then loaded carts were driven over them, to smash their bones like the captured Jutish weapons, before they were all thrown into the holy lake.

Heremod's men settled their doubts by telling each other that this must be a southern rite he had learned in the Gothic wars. Truly, the gods must have been pleased by it; Heremod never lost a battle during his kingship. All the chiefs that King Dene had beaten in the old days hurried to swear good faith to their new lord. They gave him their sons as hostages. Tribute came pouring in again.

Heremod did not sit back to enjoy his wealth and get slack. He kept on the move, visiting all the subject tribes to take their oaths, be feasted by them and scare them into keeping quiet when his back was turned. Then he made war further afield, into Jutland and along the southern coasts of Norway. His nobles and fighting-men were proud of their victories and pleased with their loot.

The new king also kept a sharp eye on his nobles, going the rounds of their estates, checking their taxes and sitting-in on their law-suits. He was merciless to law-breakers, however small their wrong-doing, and never gave the benefit of a doubt.

Decent folk agreed that this was right and proper; a king should keep good order in his land.

Unlike his brother, he did not lust after women. His witan smiled and nodded their heads over that; a king should keep a court, not a whore-house. Until he chose to make a royal marriage-alliance, his sister would preside over his household, carry the first mead-cup to him at his feasts, welcome his guests and see to the comfort of the house-troop.

In those first months of his rule, Hereswið was radiant with joy and pride in her brother. At fifteen, she was a very lovely woman, with the golden beauty of the Scylding House and gracious manners. Now that the Danish fortunes were on the mend, there were some splendid offers for her, from powerful neighbours in Angeln and Geatland. Heremod refused them all. He seemed to take the proposals as insults; his answers certainly were.

The witan still nodded and smiled. The counsellors agreed that Heremod was wise not to jump at the first offers. He showed that he was not afraid to defy great kings. He was telling the world he put a high price on Danish friendship. One crafty old lord hinted that it would be foolish to send Hereswið out of the kingdom yet. Till the king had a queen and sons of his own, he could do without a brother-in-law on his borders and a foreign nephew as his only heir.

In the royal hall soon after, the mead was flowing and the young warriors were out-doing each other in boasting what they would do to show their loyalty to their king. Osmund took the harp and began to chant Heremod's praises.

He sang of the king's feats in distant lands, his victories all round the Danish borders, the terror of his name, the glory of his court, the might of his war-band, the treasure he had won.

The young warriors shouted their approval and hammered on the tables.

Then Osmund sang of the greatest treasure in the Danish court, the jewel of the Scyldings, the Lady Hereswið. He praised Heremod for refusing to let any foreign king carry off this jewel from the Danes and wear it on his breast. Might every noble warrior in the war-band fight like the heroes of old to be worthy of her!

The hall shook with the noise of cheering and stamping. Heremod did not join in the applause at his own praises. He sat like the carved image of a god, unsmiling. He never lounged in the high seat, like Hunlaf, shouting banter at his drinking companions and roaring with laughter at jokes against himself.

A few days later the king was in the armoury, checking the weapon-store. He picked up a battle-axe and brought it down on Osmund's skull, felling him like a horse-sacrifice.

The other men were not ready for Osmund's death. He was the king's childhood friend; he had served the king well. No crime had been charged against him; no angry words had passed. Everyone stared at Heremod.

He told them calmly that Osmund was a traitor, one of the vermin of Hunlaf's court. He had been playing a clever game: using his false friendship to seduce his king's sister while she was a child. He had been planning to seize her, kill his king and take the kingdom. He had been justly struck down before he could carry out his plot.

Heremod did not sound mad or drunk, though he was clearly in a cold fury. He was not playing a part, as kings sometimes do when they want a pretext for destroying a powerful lord. He believed every word he said.

The warriors and counsellors, talking among themselves, told each other that Heremod could be right. His sister was a beautiful woman. She had trusted Osmund as her brother's friend, she had met him secretly to ask for his help against Hunlaf. Perhaps she had let Osmund take some harmless freedoms with her and then – young men will be young men. Still, a brother must guard his sister's honour. Even the war-leader, Beornfrið Beornwald's son, who had liked young Osmund, agreed that no one could say a word against such a killing.

Hereswið had more than a word to say. She set out from the queen's bower to confront her brother. She met him coming to meet her; she began to protest against the wrong he had done Osmund and the slur on her name. He gripped her arm, drew her back into the bower, told all her servants to get out and closed the door.

'Why did you butcher Osmund – your best friend?'

'Best friends make the worst traitors.'

'Osmund was no traitor – and how dare you think I would play the whore with him?'

'How could I think anything else? He as good as boasted about you in the hall – he thought I was fool enough not to catch his meaning. You were brought up among whores and whoremongers. You stayed on with them, year after year, you never came to me!'

'You told me to stay here! And how could I have made my way to you?'

'You knew where to find me. You sent Osmund to fetch me fast enough, when you wanted me to rid you of a man you loathed and clear the way for the man you wanted, so he could kill me and lie with you. That's a very cunning game the two of you were playing – and cheating at it, too!'

'That's a lie! Osmund was as innocent as I am!'

'If you were innocent, how would you know guilt when you met it? How could a girl brought up by Hunlaf's bitches be innocent?'

'So what must I do to clear myself? Carry a red-hot spit in my hands for fifty paces without getting burned? But you'd say I'd whored with all the judges beforehand to make them give me cold iron! Send to The Lady's temple, then! Ask the priestesses to come and test my body – No! Take me to the temple. If they find I'm a true maiden, I vow I'll offer them my body as a sacrifice to Freo. I'll tell them to cut my heart out and give it to you. I dare you to eat it. If you swallow one tainted spot of flesh, may it poison you. But if it's all clean wholesome meat, then I order you to stand up in the assembly and swear you believe I've been true to you!'

He caught her in his arms and kissed her again and again.

'I do believe it! My poor little sister, I should never have left you here unguarded. I'll take better care of you from now on. I'll make sure no speck of dirt ever comes near you and no foul word is ever spoken about you.'

The royal township was very large. The old queen's bower and storehouses had been built well back beyond the royal hall, so that she might not be disturbed by the comings and goings of the warriors, the din and stench from the cooking-hunts, forges, brew-houses and byres. Some apple-trees grew behind the bower, sheltered by the earthwork and stockade that girded the township. There was also a bed of herbs.

Heremod had the bower newly hung with embroidered cloths and furnished with the richest of his Roman treasures. He set a troop of churls to work laying out the little orchard and herb plot till they became a faint ghost of the gardens he had seen in the south.

He ordered the woodwrights to make a strong fence all round, so tall that even if men stood on the earthwork they

could not see over. He tested this himself. Then he sent men
into the wasteland to uproot hawthorns and brambles. These
were set to grow inside the fence, so that the garden and the
bower were ringed by a hedge of thorns.

When all was complete, he told Hereswið that he had made
her the fairest dwelling in all Scedenig. Since there was no good
reason to leave the best for the worse, he expected her to stay
in it.

He gave her costly dresses and precious jewels. He bought
southern wine for her from every visiting merchant, and rare
spices to make her food tasty. He sent her musicians, jugglers,
dancers to pass the time for her. But he was her only visitor of
noble rank. And all those who served her or entertained her
were women.

At first, Hereswið was glad to get away from the talk about
Osmund and the watching eyes in the royal hall. She was proud
to show her brother that he had been wrong about her. As the
years went past, she grew restless in her costly cage. She began
to complain to her favourite maid that it was very hard her
brother should think she would play the whore unless he kept
her locked up. The day came when she said grimly that since
he believed she was a whore, she might as well act like one and
have the pleasure of it as well as the punishment.

Among the king's hostages was a young Norwegian, a
chief's son from Tovdals. It was only a little lordship – a haven,
some coastland and farms scattered up the river valleys. It
hardly seemed worth Heremod's notice. But he had just taken
Vendsyssel; he wanted to warn the Norwegians from raiding
across the Skagerrak, so he struck hard all along their southern
coast, then made them pay for peace.

A hostage can enjoy a very good life. At the court of a
powerful and generous king, he can learn courtly manners, get
the best weapon-training, meet the famous champions and
collect rich presents. A wise king will do his best to turn his
hostages into devoted friends. Hostages have gladly fought to
death for their lords.

Heremod was not a convivial man. He was free-handed to
his Danish warriors; he needed to be, to keep them loyal to
him and eager to fight. His gifts were usually fine armour and
jewelled weapons, not trinkets or goblets. He would not give a
sword to an enemy's son, or teach him how to use it.

Eirik was well-fed and lodged; he ate in the king's hall,
sitting on the lowest bench, ignored by the king and the nobles

of his hearth-troop. He lounged away his time among the grooms and huntsmen. They were good-natured enough; they let him follow the hunt with them. He never rode among the king's friends. He stood about with the armourer and serving-lads, watching the young nobles of the hearth-troop at their weapon-play. He was never given a chance to show how well he could do.

All the while, his rage was growing. He was very proud and as wild as a gull. He was longing to be out at sea instead of cooped-up and useless, living like a stablehand or a turnspit.

Eirik made up his mind to break free. He would rather live as a wolf's head in the forest, or be hunted to death there by Heremod's men, than stay under Heremod's roof. But before he went, he was going to hit back at Heremod, make him pay for his insults.

He knew that Heremod's men would cut him down before he got within striking distance of the king. He decided to take Heremod's greatest treasure, not steal it but smash it – or kill it, if what he loved was a hawk, a horse or a hound; he could see that the king loved neither man nor woman – then leave the wreckage for all to see and for Heremod to remember.

He listened more carefully to the servants' talk. He began to ask idle questions, to fish with hints, to learn what the king prized most. He had to take his time to find the answer; folk were scared to talk about the king's sister. When he first came to the court he had guessed she must be deformed or mad, hidden away for shame and decency. When he learned that she was lovely and that the king treasured her so dearly he would not let any other man look at her, he knew what his revenge would be.

He would get at Hereswið, rape her and, if luck held, leave her with his seed growing inside her.

Heremod had meant to make sure that no man could come near his sister, or even catch a glimpse of her in the distance. Getting into the secret garden would be the first test of Eirik's skill. He felt he was playing a game of wits against the king, it gave some spice to the dullness of his daily life.

There was a narrow stretch of waste ground between the garden and the earthwork. Kept dark by the high wall and the stockade, it was overgrown with rank weeds and brambles. Eirik had strolled round the top of the earthwork once or twice with the guards for something to do and had looked down on it. He had heard about the bristling shield-wall of thorns inside the garden fence. There was no way in except by the gate from the courtyard.

Erik played with the idea of seducing one of the maids and coaxing her to smuggle him into the bower dressed and veiled as a woman. He would need time to get a girl besotted enough to take such a risk for him. Could he trust any of Heremod's folk not to betray him? Would a girl who had risked her life for love of him stand by while he bedded another woman? How could he get the princess alone and keep her quiet amid a houseful of maidservants?

While he was thinking out the next moves in his game, he lounged idly in the courtyard, watching who came and went in and out of the bower. He counted the number of women and made sure he knew them all by sight.

At last, one evening when dusk was falling, he risked going round to the back of the bower, along the stretch of waste ground between the garden fence and the earthwork.

Seen from above, it looked completely overgrown but when he pushed in among the tall nettles, he found a faint path. The earth had not been trodden bare but the plants made a little way for him as if something solid had already passed between them, winding in and out so as not to mark a straight line.

Then suddenly, the path ran against the fence and stopped, just where the undergrowth was darkest and thickest. He looked closely at the fence, feeling up it as high as he could reach, then down to the ground. The planks had been planed straight and smooth, fitting tightly together. He found no crack, no hinge, no keyhole. Yet he knew that a living creature had come to this part of the fence before now and had somehow passed through it. What others could do, so could he. Stealthily, giving no outward sign of what he was doing, he kept a daily watch on the waste ground.

It was about this time that Hereswið, sitting in the garden with her favourite maid, said angrily:

'I won't be treated like a whore for nothing! I'm taking the punishment – too bad I've never had the pleasure as well!'

Her maid looked at her with pity. This girl, Wynn, was as lively and pleasant as her name. She was a seaman's daughter; her father had been killed boarding a Jutish ship. She did her work heartily; the rest of her time she pleased herself.

'It's a wicked shame to keep you cooped up here. More so as it's Midsummer. He ought to let you out for the Sun Dance and the games. He should be leading the dance himself, like our other kings did. Even poor Hunlaf never failed at that! It's your duty – you're the Barley King's children, come from the Sheaf. King Heremod and his nobles only look up to Woden – they leave The Lady and the Barley King to us churls nowadays. Where would the warriors be, I'd like to know, if The Lady didn't bring men and women together? Or if the Barley King didn't give us his body to eat and his spirit to warm us up? You ought to dance, for luck of our folk, if the king won't. Tell him, lady!'

'Whatever I tell him, he'll never let me go. When I make up my mind to leave, I'll have to let myself out – with a knife or a noose.'

'Don't say that, my lady! You mustn't even think it – you'd bring death on us all. The king would have our blood!'

'I'm sorry, Wynn. I wish no harm to you or the other girls. But I can't bear this half-life much longer and there's no other way out for me.'

'There is another way, if you'll swear to be secret. It's almost time for the meal. Complain about the heat and the smell of food. Tell me to come out and walk with you in the cool of the evening.'

Later, when they came back into the garden, they strolled to the far end of the orchard, close by the thorn hedge. A thick ivy-tod was growing on an old trunk. Wynn moved it aside and showed Hereswið a gap between two of the thorn bushes. Beyond, there seemed to be an unbroken tangle of spiky branches and bramble trails. In fact, a crooked path had been opened between them by removing shoots here and there and keeping them cut back.

They edged their way along till they came to the fence. Wynn pressed her hands against the edge of one of the planks. The other edge moved inwards, then as she went on pushing, it slid back along an inner groove that had been made in the top and bottom sills. The gap was just big enough for a slender body to squeeze through; it gave on to the patch of waste ground. Wynn let Hereswið look for a second, then pushed the plank back into place.

'Who did that? Who would dare –'

'The woodwrights, of course. When the king had the fence made, the word went round that we were all to be walled up inside. The gate would only be unlocked once a day to send in our food. You know how folk talk. Well, the king can do what he likes in his own family and anyone can do what they like with their slaves. But craftsmen are freemen, like seamen and farmers. They weren't going to have their daughters and sisters and sweethearts locked up in prison for no wrong they'd done. So the woodwrights made this way out. The slave-girls don't know about it, we don't trust them that far. As it happens, we don't need to use it much, only for our secret meetings.'

'But you're defying the king's wishes. He's killed folk as traitors for less.'

Hereswið was bitter, thinking of Osmund.

'Nobles vow themselves to their king. Slaves have to obey their owners. But we're free churls, we do our work and pay our taxes. For the rest, we do as we choose. I'm trusting you to keep our secret.'

'You can trust me.'

'Forget about killing yourself then, and come to the Midsummer dance. The Lady will be pleased with you. She'll send you some good luck.'

Heremod never joined in the Midsummer revels, so neither did his hearth-troop, his household officials or anyone whose service was needed for the royal hall. Everyone else made off as soon as possible. Eirik watched Hereswið's maids and slave-girls hurrying out of the bower in two's and three's until he had accounted for all of them save one – the lively girl with curly brown hair who had a joke for every man she met.

So Hereswið, kindly mistress, had let her womenfolk go to the Sun Dance, all but one maid. He would never have a better chance to get at her. Somehow he must break into the bower today.

He went to the back and lay in the long grass in the shadow of the earthwork, thinking of the moves that would take him over the fence and past the thorn-hedge. He saw, without being seen, the two serving-women coming along the hidden path, then heading for the township gate. One was the lively brown-haired girl. Her friend was taller and shyer, she kept her veil folded round her head. He had never seen this woman before.

Watching these pieces moving out across the board, he was sure that his game was nearly won. He let the women get well ahead, then followed them. Many others were going the same way; if the women saw him at all, they would think no harm.

Beyond the township, with its ploughland and pasture, were the woods, then the open moors. Just beyond the woodland was a low hill with a flattish top and rounded sides, tufted with scattered birch trees and hawthorns. Here folk lit the Midsummer fire and sent the blazing sun-wheels hurtling down the hillside. In the middle was the Troiaburh.

The road to Troiaburh was marked out by a double row of stones that circled the hilltop, coiling and doubling back upon its track in loop after loop, leading inwards then turning away to the outer rim. Folk who trod the maze, two steps forward one step back, had a long way to go to reach the centre but their journey was well worthwhile. As they went along, the amber walls of Troiaburh rose up around them. At the centre, they saw the gods in all their brightness.

At Midsummer, the Sun Dance went on all day, and all night too by the light of fires and torches. As folk arrived from the farms and villages all around, they joined the chain of dancers winding through the maze. The last man in the line, already stepping to the beat, grinned at Wynn, holding out his hand. She let go of Hereswið's arm and linked herself to the chain.

Hereswið, shy and uneasy in Wynn's clothes, hesitated. She was tired from the long walk over rough ground, after three years inside her garden wall. She was sure that everyone who saw her would guess who she was. Above all, she was frightened of losing Wynn in the crowd and did not want to let go of her – but in the Sun Dance, a woman takes a man's hand, a man takes a woman's.

In the moment that she stood alone and bewildered, a man came up from behind, linked his hand to Wynn's, then turned smiling and beckoning her to join him. She was glad to be near Wynn; as she took the man's hand, someone linked on to her other side and she was in the dance.

At first, she kept her head bent. She watched the feet of the man in front, fitting her steps to his – two steps forward, one step back with a sway and a stamp, two steps forward – over and over again. The dancers were singing, their steps beat time to the tune.

The men sang:
> *'Who dances between the stones*
> *out there in the green grove?'*

The women answered:
> *'Maidens are dancing between the stones,*
> *lightly they dance in the green grove.'*

Then they asked:
> *'Who dances between the stones . . .?'*

and the men chanted:
> '*Spearmen are dancing between the stones . . .*'

The man who had beckoned Hereswið into the dance was very tall. He had thrown his hood back on to his shoulders, his hair shone like ripe barley. His steps were longer and livelier than hers but as the dance went on and on, his heat and strength flowed into her through their linked hands. They were dancing as one body with eight limbs.

Now the dancers were singing:
> '*Who dances between the stones*
> *out there in the green grove?*
> *Freo is dancing between the stones . . .*
> *Beow is dancing between the stones . . .*
> *lightly they dance in the green grove.*'

By this time, it seemed to every link in the living chain that there were only two dancers on the sacred way. The Barley King was dancing the Sun Dance with The Lady. The gods were dancing in the dancers' bodies; they were all filled with godhead. Slowly, the shining walls of Troiaburh rose up around them. They entered the Golden Hall.

As each dancer reached the heart of the maze, where the chain swung round to unwind, he or she turned to kiss the one who followed. Then the dance circled slowly back to Middle Earth. The walls of Troiaburh vanished; there were just stones laid out in a pattern on the hilltop.

Hereswið had been circling and stepping so long, singing the same words over and over again under the noonday sun, that the dance was still going on inside her when she came out of the maze. The world was spinning round her. She staggered; the tall stranger put his arm round her and held her up. He took a small leather flask from the pouch at his belt and put it to her lips. She was parched and swallowed eagerly. She drank Beow's Blood – it was the first time she had tasted barley spirit; it lit a Midsummer fire in her blood.

The world spun even faster but now she was turning with it, dancing lightly in the green grove. The stranger steered her downhill towards a clump of birch trees. She was laughing as she danced beside him. The Midsummer song was singing itself inside her head. He laid her down, pulled up her skirt and came inside her. One body with eight limbs, they went on dancing the love-dance on the warm turf.

She was very beautiful, of royal blood, King Heremod's jealously guarded treasure – and Erik had her on the ground under him, drunk and silly, as if she were a farmer's slave-girl. He enjoyed his revenge.

When Wynn found her, she was fast asleep under the trees, with the stranger sprawling lazily beside her, looking up into the leafy branches. It was long after noon, though the sky would be light for hours yet. Wynn shook her.

'We'd better be off home now, sister – we daren't stay for the fire-wheels and the rest of the games, our brother wouldn't like it!'

Hereswið did not move but the man turned his head. Wynn saw he was the king's Norwegian hostage and went cold with terror. He laughed at her.

'No matter. We've already finished our games.'

He picked up the sleeping Hereswið and strode off through the woods towards the royal township. Wynn followed. Neither spoke again till they were within sight of the earthwork. Then she said,

'In The Lady's name – for your own sake as well as ours – keep quiet about this.'

'You'll find I'm very quiet and easy to deal with, if no one crosses my will or puts me out of temper.'

He pulled his hood well down on his brows, wrapped Hereswið's veil tightly round her head, then slung her over his shoulder with her face against his back. He tramped though the gateway, a stable-hand lugging his drunken sweetheart home from the dance, while Wynn kept the gate-guards busy capping her jokes.

There were few folk about. Wynn led the way behind the barns and work-sheds to the waste ground and slid the plank. Eirik saw which one it was and how she handled it. He carried Hereswið into the deserted bower and laid her on her bed. As he turned to go, Wynn told him to put the plank carefully back into place.

'Trust me. And I'll open it carefully again, every time I come for her.' He looked down at Hereswið. 'Once I've been inside a place, I can always find my way back again.'

He whistled a few notes of the Sun Dance, making it sound like a thrush calling.

'When she wakes up, tell her whenever she hears that whistle in the orchard, she'll know I'm waiting.'

Eirik had enjoyed his revenge – but he had also enjoyed the pleasure of his body, his youth and strength, the woman's beauty, the sunlight, the dancing, the Midsummer magic. It was a heady brew, stronger and sweeter than mead. He wanted to enjoy it again before he made his break for freedom – and again – and again –

Wynn thought it would more dangerous to refuse him than to risk being caught. Hereswið had no thought of refusing him; she did anything he wanted.

Eirik had meant to trap her into playing his game, by her woman's feelings, her body's needs and the threat that he would talk about her. But folk who start playing games with Freo's powers are apt to find suddenly that they are not planning their moves any longer – that they are pieces on the board, moving wherever *She* decides to put them.

Eirik had trapped himself as well as Hereswið. When he thought about making his escape, he knew that he could not live without her. Hate and lust had turned to love. When he left Heremod's court, he would have to take her with him.

Lying with her in the long grass near the orchard fence, while Wynn sat on watch, spinning and singing ballads as if to pass the time for her lady, he whispered his plans.

'We'll wait a month or two, till the nights grow longer. I'll steal a rope – we'll go over the stockade at dark of the moon. You won't be frightened, sweetheart? Till then, guard your tongue. Don't give away a word of this, even to Wynn.'

In the end, which was not long in coming, Eirik gave himself away. He was very careful. No one saw or guessed his visits to the bower. He never let himself get drunk enough to set him boasting or dropping hints that he would soon be even with Heremod. He was betrayed by his joy. To Heremod's suspicious eyes, he looked as bright as the Midsummer sun. His mind seemed to be filled with some secret thought that was giving him intense pleasure.

To Heremod, secret thoughts were plots, plotters were traitors and the right way with traitors was to strike them down first. Also, the darkness in his spirit shrank from the light of Eirik's joy. It would have to be quenched.

He became more friendly to Eirik, as if he had been too busy with war and statecraft to notice his young guest till now and wanted to make up for his neglect. Eirik seemed pleased and grateful to be noticed, chuckling to himself at the cunning game he was playing with Heremod, hiding his own feelings while cheating him.

After harvest, the king went hunting. This time, Eirik was mounted on one of the king's best horses and rode at his side.

The hunters brought a boar to bay in a thicket. Before the hounds were loosed to drive him out, Heremod stepped back and graciously waved Eirik to take pride of place in the ring.

Eirik was proud to show the Danes his skill and courage. He knelt and readied his spear. At the moment the boar charged, Heremod drove his own spear-head into Eirik's back and held him pinned at the end of the shaft while the boar savaged him with its tusks. By the time the hounds had dragged the boar down, Eirik was ripped to bloody pulp. When he had stopped twitching and moaning, Heremod pulled his spear from the corpse. He was calm and smiling.

'I've made the Haligmonað sacrifice for us to the Lord of the Boar. May his favour shine on our helmet-crests when we go to war next spring.'

His companions were taken aback but told themselves that the dead lad was only a Norwegian hostage; his life had always been in the king's hands.

Hereswið was sickly in the fall of the year. Heremod did not visit her for some time. After harvest, he always rode the borders to make sure all was well before winter set in. When he next came to the bower, his sister was not waiting in her hall to greet him.

Wynn met him instead. Her belly was swelling; several of the other women were in the same way since Midsummer. They were carrying 'barley-children' and were pleased about it; churls thought such babies were lucky.

Wynn told the king that between the hot noons and the cold nights, his sister had been attacked by mist-wraiths and could not shake them off. She would never be well so long as the mist-wraiths could come up to the bower from the water-meadows and forest pools to get at her. He ought to send her to the coast, where the sea winds would drive the mist-wraiths away and where Wynn's grandmother, a famous cunning-woman, would surely heal her.

Heremod gave no answer. He walked into the room behind the hall. Hereswið was lying on her bed, almost buried under a pile of rugs and furs. Her face was wasted almost to a skull, her eyes seemed to be sunken in her head, her hair was dank and tangled into elf-locks. She was streaming with sweat.

'Why have you piled all this bedding on top of her?'

'I told you. She's got a fever. One moment she's burning, the next she's shivering and icy cold.'

Heremod was watching his sister's face. He saw death's shadow there and had a foretaste of happiness. Once she was dead, shut away in her death-house with her mound piled over it, no man could rob him of her or turn her against him. He could love her in peace.

Hereswið muttered something; he could not catch the words.

'What did she say?'

Wynn looked puzzled.

'She said she had to listen for the seagulls.'

Heremod's eyes filled with tears; he turned his head away so that the maid should not see he was weeping.

'Very well, let her go to the sea. Take her to your grandmother. Let her have everything she wants.'

He hurried away and did not see her again. When they were alone, Wynn pulled back the pile of coverlets that had hidden her lady's growing belly, dried the sweat and dressed her in a clean shift.

Next day, Hereswið's bed was put into a covered wagon. She was taken down to the haven, followed by a train of pack-horses laden with her gear. Wynn was the only maid who went with her; she said there would be plenty of women to look after her lady at her grandmother's homestead.

The grandmother, Wulfwaru, was a famous and highly-respected witch, who lived well on the gifts she got for cures, friendly seas and good catches. She took Hereswið into her own bed and tended her carefully. Wynn had a little sister who lived with her grandmother and served as her maid. Also, her mother and her youngest aunt were widows for the time being, so they were free to help nurse Hereswið. Wynn stayed beside her too, as long as she could; though by the time spring came she had enough to do for herself. When she was seen outside again, strolling down to the shore to joke with the men, she was carrying a boy in the crook of each arm.

In spite of Wulfwaru's skill and care, Hereswið died in the spring because she did not want to live any longer. Only Wulfwaru and her kinswomen knew that she had borne a son. Wynn swore to rear him as her own.

'Call him *Healfdene*,' whispered Hereswið. 'It's the truth – and it's not a name that will catch my brother's notice. My clothes and jewels are for you and your family. You've been kinder to me than my own kin. My brother will never ask you for them. Likely he'll burn everything else that was mine. Use the goods as you think best, but look -'

Her fingers scrabbled in her jewel-casket.

' - this brooch, this bracelet and this ring. Never part with these. They were my father's. I hid them when Hunlaf was wasting our gold-hoard. They're Scylding treasures, for the king's wearing. You'd be in danger if anyone saw them. I leave it to your good sense whether you ever let Healfdene know who he really is. If you do, give him these jewels - tell him I loved his father - and was proud to bear his child.'

She rested her head on Wynn's shoulder, sighed and was dead.

Heremod did not send for his sister's body. He had a mound raised for her on the headland that guarded the haven. There were always gulls flying and crying round it; perhaps she listened to them as she lay alone, walled inside her house.

'ᛈ : Peorð byþ symble plega and hlehter
wlancum on middum ðar wigan sittaþ
on beorsele bliþe ætsomne.'

The Rune Poem

(A gaming-piece always means a sporting combat
and laughter among high-spirited folk, where
warriors are sitting together in merry mood in the
feasting-hall.)

The Second Game

Barley-children, got at Midsummer when the sun is at full strength, are born to thrive. Wynn's two boys were big and strong. Healfdene was tall and golden-haired. Saewulf, the younger twin, was shorter and stocky, with his mother's thick brown curls. The twins were always good-tempered with each other. When they began to run around outside their hut, they backed each other up in every game and fight they had with their neighbours' children.

Some time after they were weaned, Wynn took up with a shipwright who was kind to his two stepsons. He was glad to have a couple of handy lads growing up to help him in his craft. Meanwhile, they spent their early years along the shore, playing, fighting, fishing, swimming and giving a hand with the boats as soon as they were old enough. They were as much at home on the water as on land; they would put to sea on anything that floated. Healfdene always took the lead. He was the one who thought of new games and set the most reckless dares. Saewulf cheerfully followed him into every scrape. By the time they were ten years old, the brothers ruled as chiefs over all the boys in the haven and along the near-by coast.

It was already clear that the twins were going to be seamen, not shipwrights, when they came to manhood. Helped by their stepfather's craftsmanship, their grandmother's power and the wealth that Wynn's grateful mistress had left her, they were soon shipmasters. From fishing they went on to trading, venturing further and further along the whale-roads. Whenever they saw the chance, they added raiding to trading.

They usually headed south-west, working along the coasts of Britain and Gaul. Here they found the best merchandise, the readiest customers, the richest spoil. And here, listening to gossip and travellers' tales at ale-booths, they first heard of Queen Irminburg.

There was a chaos of tribes swarming over the wreckage of the old Roman frontier between Frisia and Gaul. A group of Saxons, led by a Woden-born chief and his war-band, had pushed west on their own. They were now cut off from the rest of their folk. They had reached the eastern side of the Rhinemouth. Beyond were the Franks, who did not give a kindly welcome to strangers crossing their borders.

The Saxons meant to ship to Britain, where there was more and better land for the taking. Meanwhile, they settled down to pass the winter along the last seaward stretch of the old frontier road, from the city of Traiect to Lug's Dun and the fort at the harbour mouth. The city's walls and some of its buildings were still standing. They took it for their stronghold and set about gathering food-rent from the fishermen and farmers.

Then they took a terrible blow that nearly destroyed them as a free folk. They had to fight hard to hold their new-won land against other rovers, desperate for somewhere to settle. In one fierce battle, as they broke their enemies' shield-wall and put them to flight, their chief, Garðrist, was brought down – run through the guts and his hip-bone smashed. He was still alive when they carried him into Traiect but it seemed impossible that he could live much longer. If he did, he would never fight, or even stand, again. He had no brothers, no near kinsman to hold the tribe together. The war-band would likely have cut itself to pieces, fighting for the leadership. Then the folk would have been lost, wiped out by the next tribe to attack them, or dragged down to serfdom by the Franks. They were saved by Freo and the chief's kinswoman, Ælfrun.

She was a priestess of Freo, a rune-mistress and a very wise woman. The Lady loved her and often came to talk to her. She had a younger sister, Irminburg a shield-maiden who had vowed herself to Woden. Irminburg fought alongside the men but had no use for them except as comrades in arms.

Ælfrun had Garðrist carried into the Roman bath-house she had taken as Freo's temple and hallowed precinct. She could tell by the remains of pictures on the walls and floors, as well as the carved images, that the place had always been used for The Lady's rites. She told Irminburg to keep guard at the chief's bedside, but would not let any man near him. Three days later, she came out to the warriors who were keeping vigil at her gate and gave them a message from Freo.

The Lady had taken Garðrist under her protection. She would keep him lodged in her house, far from all sights and sounds of war, till his wounds no longer troubled him. She had ordered him to take Woden's daughter Irminburg as his wife. Irminburg must rule them as queen until their king was ready to take his place among them.

The men were in awe of Ælfrun and believed every word she said as if they had heard it from Freo's own mouth. They had fought alongside Irminburg and knew she was the kind of warrior who wins battles. As soon as the priestess stopped speaking, the most powerful warrior in the war-band, Hrefn, the king's dearest shield-friend, called out that he was for Queen Irminburg and was ready to kill anyone who was against her. No one was.

Between them, the two sisters and Hrefn kept the Saxons firmly in hand. They could not take ship for Britain while the king was lying in Freo's house, so they set about enlarging their kingdom at the Rhinemouth. By the end of another year, most of them were calling it "home". Freo must have been pleased with them; they had good crops and won all their battles.

Healfdene picked up stories about Irminburg in the harbours of Gaul and among the Saxon settlements in Britain. He made up his mind to see her on his way home. Winter was coming on; he had made a good haul and did not need any more loot. This visit was to be friendly and peaceful, unless she gave trouble. If he liked her, he meant to do her a favour in return for her hospitality. As he said to Saewulf, a man ready and able to give her a good ride in bed would come to her as a pleasant change from a husband who was bed-ridden.

The queen was at one of her farmsteads near Lug's Dun when the Danish ships rowed into harbour. Harvest had been gathered in; her lords had gone to their own lands for the winter season to oversee the payment of their food-rents. War and trading were over for the year. So Irminburg had only a small bodyguard with her when Healfdene and forty crewmen marched in to pay their respects.

She gave no sign that she was taken aback. She set herself and her household to keep the Danes in a good mood, till she could gather her troops to see them off. She looked delighted to welcome them; she said she liked nothing better than listening to merchants telling of the strange lands they had seen. When the company sat down to feast in her hall, she had Healfdene placed by her side and he was able to take a good look at her.

Irminburg was a big woman, as tall as he was, and somewhat older, likely a year or so past twenty. She was broad-shouldered and strong-boned, as she needed to be, to carry a helmet and byrnie in battle as lightly as other women wore their gowns and veils in the bower. Yet she was neither bulky nor wiry. Her long arms were well-rounded, so were the full breasts curving out under her embroidered gown; her golden girdle clasped a waist as firm and supple as a boy's. Her hair, braided under a jewelled headband, was bright red; her eyes seemed to be grey but when the torchlight shone in them, they glinted like emeralds.

She was the most splendid woman Healfdene had ever seen, a worthy bedfellow.

When the food was cleared from the tables, the queen asked him pleasantly if he and his men wanted beds for the night – or would they rather go back to their ships? The port-reeve would see that the ships were safe, of course, but perhaps he would sleep easier if he lay next to his cargoes?

'My goods are safe enough, I left some of my lads to watch them. We're staying here – but you needn't trouble to make up a bed for me, I'm coming into yours.'

He grinned at her. 'One good turn deserves another.'

The queen smiled back at him.

'I'll drink to that,' she said.

Healfdene drank to it as well; he gulped his wine-cup empty. Seemingly, the queen drained hers; she tilted her head and swallowed, then held her goblet back over her shoulder for a servant to fill it again. Healfdene drank to her health and strength; then they drank turn and turn about to each other's bodily parts, trying to out-do each other in bawdy flattery and laughing at each other's jokes. Irminburg's servants followed their lady's lead, getting the Danes drunk but keeping them good-humoured.

When Healfdene got up and headed for the room behind the hall, he would hardly have got through the doorway without the queen's strong arm round his shoulders. She was quite steady on her feet. She told her waiting maids to get out, saying, 'We can see to our own needs.'

Healfdene laughed at that till the tears ran down his cheeks.

He pulled off his clothes in a great hurry to get at her. His hands fumbled with the buckles of his boot-straps; when he bent down to his feet, the room pitched under him like a ship in a storm. He gave up and fell sprawling across the bed with his boots still on and his breeches round his ankles.

The queen was a tidy woman; not even lust could make her careless with her goods. Her headband and jewelled hair-pins were carefully taken off and set aside; each bracelet and finger-ring was put back in its own place in her jewel casket. She placed her shoes side by side next to her clothes chest, untied her garters, rolled down her hose and laid them on the lid of the chest. Then she began to unpin the brooches that held up her gown.

Every time she took off a piece of her clothing, she looked at Healfdene on the bed and smiled very sweetly at the thought of joys soon to come. He saw her lift her hands to her head to take down her plaits. The torch flame was dazzling his eyes, so he closed them.

Irminburg waited a while, listening to his breathing. Then she lit a taper from the torch and held it near enough his chest to singe the hairs and scorch the skin. When she was sure he would not wake, she put her clothes on again much faster than she had taken them off, then called her servants. They all had work to do that night; some had to ride fast and far inland. There was clattering in the stables and much movement in the hall but Healfdene and his men, lying like the dead, knew nothing of what was being done.

When the Danes woke up, they were thick-headed and bleary-eyed. The servants brought them buckets of water to dowse their heads and mugs of ale to wash away the fumes. The hall-thane came out of the queen's room with a message from their captain. He wanted them to go back to their ships at once and see to the stowing of the gifts that the queen had sent down to the harbour for them. He would follow shortly, when he had talked over some last few matters with the queen.

Saewulf and his mates leered at each other and set off. They had a dim sense that there were more folk about this morning – more spearmen – than they had seen overnight. Perhaps they were still seeing double.

Their ships were safe. The night-watchmen said that the port-reeve had been friendly; he had sent them food and ale from his own table. The queen's parting gifts had already been stowed aboard: there were two large heavy chests and a great bundle wrapped up in what looked like a straw mattress. The port-reeve had told them to take care how they handled it; they guessed it was precious glass table-ware from Frankland.

They waited for Healfdene; he was taking his time saying farewell to the queen. There was a crowd of spearmen on the beach. They took no notice of the Danish ships but their numbers made Saewulf uneasy. Time went by and still Healfdene did not come.

The Saxons were engaged in weapon-play; they had formed into two bands; one group was attacking the harbour as sea-raiders, the others were trying to drive them back. They all looked to be ugly fighters. The Danes hung over the sides of their ships to watch. Saewulf was still uneasy. He kept gazing landward for Healfdene. His glance fell on the padded bundle; the ship was lying quiet at her moorings but the bundle was heaving up and down. It was also growling.

Saewulf pounced on it and cut the ropes that tied it. Healfdene, naked and gagged, rolled out. He was trussed like a chicken ready for roasting; his golden hair had been shaved off; his bare scalp had been coated with tar and stuck all over with chicken feathers. He was red with fury and from struggling.

Saewulf cut his bonds, thanking the gods when he saw that no other harm had been done except to his brother's pride. He pulled his own leather cap over Healfdene's scalp and put his cloak round him before he called the crew.

Luckily Healfdene had kept hold of his wits and could still keep hold of his men.

'That Hel's witch put a spell on me – stuck me with a sleep-thorn, so I shouldn't have her.'

He looked grimly at the Saxon warriors milling on the beach.

'Get the ships out to sea at once – and don't give them a sign or a word of what's happened to me. We can't fight them and I won't give them a chance of laughing at us.'

When they were well away, Healfdene opened the two chests that the queen had sent with him. They were full of acorns – pig-food.

He had the ships beached on one of the deserted islands south of the Rhinemouth, while he cleaned his scalp and brooded on his wrongs. He had no fear that his men would think any the less of him for the mishap; he was too strong a leader. No strength is proof against sorcery: one witch can get the better of a whole war-band.

Saewulf said, 'She must have liked you, really. She could have had us all gelded while we were helpless, then sold us as slaves.'

Healfdene was aware that Irminburg had not used witchcraft, she had just made game of him with the oldest and simplest trick in the world. He knew he would never be easy till he had paid her back, trick for trick, and shut her mouth from telling the story against him. While he was getting the chicken feathers off his scalp, he worked out his moves to trap her.

After dark, the ships rowed quietly back to a winding creek north of the Saxon harbour; they tied up in the woodlands, well hidden.

Healfdene went ashore alone. He was dressed in the filthiest rags he had collected among the crew. His face and body were grimed with dirt. Saewulf's leather cap was pulled down over his brows and he had a patch over one eye. He was carrying a wooden box, full of the poorest and shabbiest trinkets that had been carelessly gathered up with their loot. A couple of good pieces had been laid on top of the rubbish. He scratched a Thurs on the box-lid – a play on his name as ▶ is half a Day-rune.

'If I'm not back in three days, don't come looking for me. Be off home. Saewulf, you're to have my ship and my share of the cargo.'

In the early dawn he set off through the woods towards Irminburg's farmstead. Where the trees grew thickest, he buried the box among the roots of an oak in an overgrown hollow. Then he sat down to wait for the evening.

Towards dusk, the queen's cowherd was shutting the cattle into the byre when he saw a one-eyed hunchback come skulking into the yard.

'Spare a crust for a poor old man?'

'Be off! I've enough to do to feed my own.'

'Life's very hard. I've got a kingdom's treasure all to myself yet I'm starving to death!'

'King Guðhere of the Burgundians, wandering in exile, are you?'

'Don't mock me. I was hunting for puff-balls in the wood. I've found a chest of Roman treasure hidden among the roots of an oak. Enough to live like a lord – only I'd be killed if anyone saw a glint of gold on me. The queen would pay me well if I told her – but I'd never be let come near her. Would you speak for me? You'd get a good reward.'

The cow-herd hesitated, wary and doubtful.

'I'm telling the truth. Come and see for yourself.'

The cowherd followed him through the woods and down into the hollow. The beggar scrabbled among the roots, pulled up the box and took out a jewelled brooch and a golden goblet.

'Give her these and tell her there's a box full of other treasures if she cares to come and take it. I'll stay here to guard it. Now, remember to tell her I'm afraid for my life. I know these woods like the palm of my hand. I'll be watching

61

and listening. If she brings anyone else with her besides yourself – if she leaves any spearmen lying in wait – I'll be off and she can whistle to the wind for the treasures.'

He sat down against the oak; the cowherd hurried away. The beggar waited for a few minutes, then shadowed him to the wood's edge, where he stayed on watch amongst the bushes.

Irminburg had been told that her troublesome guests had put out to sea. She ordered her troops to stay on guard at the harbour in case they came back again when they had unpacked their captain.

She was not in the mood for another night's feasting. After a quiet meal with her household, she had gone to her room to brood over the dangers that threatened her kingdom. Garðrist was failing; Ælfrun had said that for all her prayers and sacrifices, The Lady would not promise to keep him alive for another year.

Irminburg was not in her first youth; what would happen when she could no longer fight at the head of her warriors? She had vowed her maidenhead to Woden; she could not take a man if she wanted one – and she did not want any man. Yet once Garðrist, the last man of their Woden-born stock, was dead, her nobles would start fighting for the kingship. One or another would try to take her by force to strengthen his claim. The visit of the Danish sea-rovers had shown how easily that might happen.

When Ælfrun had given her warning, at the beginning of harvest, the sisters had talked over the coming danger with Hrefn. There was still one great rite that they had not yet performed, one last sacrifice that they could make to win the favour of Freo and Woden, so that the two great gods would join their powers to give them a new king.

Garðrist had given his glad consent to the offering; his three friends had taken oath to him and to each other that they would keep faith and play their parts in the ritual.

But mankind is frail and the gods are fickle. They will wipe out whole tribes for a quarrel amongst themselves, or for a whim, or to settle a bet. Freo had promised that Irminburg would rule over the Saxons until they had a king ready to take her place but Irminburg had no way of knowing how The Lady would do so – or whether it would be a lucky day for the Saxons when it happened.

She was still dwelling gloomily on her doubts when a maid told her that the cowherd had come with a message for her.

The queen's mood brightened at the news of the treasure. A fine war-band expects fine gifts; she needed all the gold she could get her hands on. She smiled grimly to hear that the beggar was frightened of spearmen and would meet no one but the queen. She buckled on her sword, flung her cloak round her and went out quietly with the cowherd.

Down in the hollow, she saw a hunched figure crouching among the oak roots. The cowherd hurried forward to help lift the box. As he bent down, the beggar sprang up, towering over the churl, and hit him on the back of his skull with a lump of rock. He fell, stunned. The beggar stepped over his body and came towards her, smiling. She saw he was the Danish sea-captain. Under his rags he was wearing a sword. She gripped the hilt of her own.

'Well met again, my lady. You won't need your sword, I don't mean to kill you. I've just come to play out the game we started the night before last. I hate leaving a match unfinished. We can lie down over here. There aren't any nettles or thistles, I've already looked.'

'Oh no.'

'It's just as you choose, my lady. I always play fair with those who act fairly by me. We can have our bout, just the two of us, and then go our own ways. I've got two ships' crews waiting for me, lusty lads and sharp-set after being at sea. If you don't want me, you can have them, all of them, one after the other. I leave it to you.'

For a second, they stared at each other. Then she said calmly, 'Very well, I'll have you'.

'Throw your sword belt over among the oak roots. I'll put mine beside it. Now get down.'

It should have been the sweetest pleasure of his life. Besides the joy of having tricked her and forcing her to obey him against her will, he had never wanted a woman so much as he wanted her. Now he had her – yet he had not. He could not win the slightest sign of feeling from her.

Healfdene was young. He had never met with any trouble from girls, even the ones he carried off on his raids. Secretly, he had hoped that when he showed Irminburg what kind of man he was, she would give way and enjoy herself, in spite of her pride. Failing that, her shame, anger, fear, even disgust, would all have been gratifying. He got nothing.

She played fair. She did not struggle, tense herself or close her legs. She let him do what he wanted. All the time, she watched him without making a sound. Apart from those coldly watchful eyes, he might have been inside a newly-slain corpse before it had begun to stiffen.

After his first lust was spent, he worked away as long as he could but without zest – she made sure of that. When he came out of her, he swaggered so that she should not see how disappointed he was.

'Well, you tricked me, I've tricked you, so we're quits. No hard feelings.'

Silence.

'And remember, if you tell stories about me, I've got a good one to tell about you.'

Silence.

'You can have what's in the box. I brought it to pay for my lodging.'

Silence.

He buckled on his sword and left her. When he got back to his ships, he told his men that he'd taught the bitch not to make game of Danish seamen. They set off for home.

Irminburg got to her feet, smoothed her dress and buckled on her sword belt. She put her sword through the cowherd's body and left him for the woodland creatures to pick his bones. No one had seen her coming into the woods with him. She looked at the box and saw that it was full of cheap trumpery. Still, she took it back to her hall and put it carefully away in one of her chests.

'Ful oft wit beotedan
þæt unc ne gedælde nemne deað ana,
owiht elles; eft is þæt onhworfen,
is nu fornumen swa hit no wære
freondscipe uncer.'

The Wife's Lament

(Often and often we vowed that nothing would separate us
two except death alone, nothing else; that has changed,
since. Our loving partnership is annulled now as if it had
never been.)

The Third Game Wins The Match

Healfdene and Saewulf had good weather for their voyage home. When they brought their ships into haven, they found they had landed in trouble. Their king had gone away into the world of Darkness and there was a terrible storm brewing.

Between harvest and the onset of winter, Heremod always rode the borders and visited his great lords to see that all was well. Since Hereswið died, his spirit grew ever gloomier and more suspicious. He sent no word ahead to warn his hosts of his coming so that he could catch any treason, or slackness, unawares.

When he rode up to the homestead of Beornhelm, Beornfrið's son, the young lord and most of his hearth-troop were away. They had gone hunting a pack of wolves' heads who lived in the wastes between Scedenig and Geatland, raiding both south and north.

So Beornhelm's lady would have to welcome the king when he rode into her courtyard and then entertain him at a feast, without her husband's support. Lady Osðryð was frightened. She was Osmund's niece, though she was too young to have known her murdered uncle. Most of the lords had fought shy of her family ever since his killing, knowing that the king hated the sound of his name. She was grateful to Beornhelm for choosing her; now she was in dread lest she should harm him. If the king found fault with his welcome, he might blame her husband as well as herself. His anger was terrible.

She was heavy with child and near her time, so she was breathless and flustered as she hurried out with the wine-cup to greet him. She asked him to dismount and come into her hall. She wanted to show him that she was happy to see him, that she felt no ill-will for her uncle's death and the slur on his name.

She was very young; she played her part clumsily. She was too eager; she smiled too much; she chattered too long about how glad she was that he had come, how she would do everything for his pleasure, how she hoped his night's lodging would refresh him –

Heremod's face grew darker and more grim. Suddenly he hurled the wine-cup to the ground, splashing her gown with red drops, and screamed at her.

'Whore! So you think you can use me for your pastime? How often have you cheated your lord since he wed you? Whose bastard are you carrying?'

Before the horrified girl could speak, he drew his sword and drove the blade into her womb, then hacked at her in a fury as she stumbled and fell in a bloody heap.

The king's hearth-companions were used to watching him commit murder. They sat blank-faced, staring over their horses' heads. Osðryð's household seemed turned to stone.

Next moment, Heremod's frenzy had left him. He looked around calmly at the silent watchers. His voice was steady and reasonable.

'This quean was bringing shame on her husband, a king's thane. I've given her king's justice. You all saw how she tried to rouse my lust.'

Osðryð's household had seen nothing of the kind. They saw a good wife butchered by her guest as she welcomed him.

A stable-lad kicked up a loose cobble and threw it at the king. It struck him over the brow, tearing the flesh so that blood streamed into his left eye. The sight of his blood set the churls free from their horror. They all began to prise up the cobbles and stone him. Heremod lunged at them with his sword but they kept out of reach. Someone ran to let the hounds loose.

Heremod yelled at his men.

'To me! To me! Cut them down!'

None of them moved to help him.

Worse than the pain of the blows was the pain of betrayal. His own folk had turned on him, they wanted to kill him, just as his brother had done. They would not even give him a sword-death, so that he could go proudly to Woden, fighting against odds. They were stoning him down to be torn by their dogs, as if he were a wolf or a fox cornered in a farmyard. He howled with agony and rage.

Many of the cobbles struck his horse. The hounds had scented Osðryð's blood on his sword; they were leaping and worrying at the horse's legs. It kicked out and reared, then bolted with its rider out of the courtyard. The hounds went after them for a while. No man gave chase.

Heremod vanished into the wasteland, as he had done once before. This time there was no hope of returning – no sister to listen for word of him, no friend to go in search of him. His body was never found. Maybe the creatures of Darkness who had been waiting for him so long took him back into their dwellings.

Heremod was the last of the Scyldings. With all his faults he had been a strong king. By force and terror he had kept Scedenig orderly and safe from its enemies. When word went round that he was gone, his lords mustered their spearmen to fight each other for the kingship. The neighbouring kings counted up the number of Scylding marriages their forebears had made, that would give them a claim to the Scyldings' lands. They also began to gather their troops.

This was the story that the sea-rovers heard from everyone they met after they had beached their ships. Healfdene had more to hear from Wynn as soon as she could talk to him alone. She showed him the Scylding jewels and told him the truth about his mother.

Healfdene made up his mind to take the kingdom. He was in the mood for one more daring raid to end the season and lift his spirits after his hollow victory over Irminburg. He had as much right to the royal hall and the gold-hoard as anyone in Scedenig, he was sister's son to the last king. He put this point to his foster-brother and his crewmen. Zestfully, they agreed to back him.

Now that her tongue was free, Wynn made the most of her tale. She said that Hereswið had seen, almost from the moment her brother came back from exile, that he had brought the powers of Darkness with him. She had prayed to her forefather, the Barley god, to save the Danish folk. She had offered him her maidenhead and her life as a sacrifice for them. Beow had heard her prayer. He came to her in the Midsummer dance; he gave her a son and took her life in return. She had begged Wynn to foster her child and keep his birth a secret till the time of need. He was a man now, the boldest sea-king on the whales' road.

It was a good story and she told it well. It went from mouth to mouth up and down the coast and spread inland. When Healfdene marched on the royal stronghold, he had a army of tough seamen behind him, also a great host of country folk.

He could not have come at a better time. The older and wiser lords knew that they could not withstand the attacks that would come across their borders next spring – if the Swedes and Geats, the Jutes and English would even wait that long. They needed to join their war-bands under a king but none of them would give way to another. There was already bad blood between many of the great kindreds.

Healfdene claimed to be a Scylding and looked like one. He had no blood feuds in Scedenig. He had an army that could fight as well at sea as on land. The witan decided to believe his story. The scops changed the king list, putting him in as a son of the Barley god. Heremod's name was taken out; it would never again be recited in hall or at folk-moot as one of the Scyldings. He was not forgotten, though; he came as a dark shadow into many a winter's tale.

The new king showed from the start that a man who can hold a steering oar in a heavy sea and keep a ship's crew under his command can hold a kingdom. He spent the winter getting ready for all-out war in the spring.

Irminburg's Saxons had also been waiting anxiously for what the next year would bring. During the winter, the queen grew listless and out of spirits. She no longer went hunting; she did not once put on her armour and challenge her champions to try their swordsmanship against her. More and more often, she went to Freo's house in Traiect, to take part in The Lady's rites and help tend the king. By year's end she was spending all her time in the temple precinct.

Mothers' Night had passed. The days were getting longer; the roads were fit to travel. The queen sent riders to her lords, who had been wintering in their own strongholds, with a message from Freo.

Woden had long wanted Garðrist in his own war-band of dead heroes; he had meant to take him in his last battle. Now, he would wait no longer. Freo had told him she had promised the Saxons they would never be left without a king. Out of his great love for The Lady, at her own wish, Woden had come to her priestess Ælfrun and had given her a child. The two gods had said that he would be a great king, ruling a mighty kingdom.

Folk who came to The Lady's House could see for themselves that Ælfrun was indeed with child. She was glowing with joy, full of the power of the goddess. She had carried out the will of the gods; she had given herself to Woden with all the due rites; Freo often came to her and told her over and over again that the promises would come true. She never spoke of her *'child'*; she always said, *'My son Ælle'* as if he were already in his cradle.

Woden the shape-shifter had taken Hrefn's shape to bring this great gift to the Saxons. For all the treasures that Hrefn and Irminburg had offered to the god, the runes they had cut, the charms they had repeated, the blood they had poured out in his honour, neither of them could feel so sure as Ælfrun that Woden would keep faith. The last months of waiting were harder for both of them to live through than all their battles. Irminburg was very ill for once in her life; she had to take to her bed for a time.

A fortnight before Midsummer, in the presence of the priestesses and the wives of the great lords, Ælfrun bore her son Ælle, big and healthy. He was nursed in Freo's House, under the eyes of the goddess. His aunt, Queen Irminburg, would foster him at her court to teach him war and statecraft. His champion, Hrefn, would lead the war-band till he was old enough. Ælle had a good start.

When the cunning-women were sure he was alive and sound, one of the priestesses ran and knocked at the king's door. Irminburg opened it a crack, heard the news, praised The Lady, then shut herself in again with the king. She was wearing her helmet and byrnie.

Garðrist was out of bed, propped in a chair. He too was wearing his armour, though he could hardly bear its weight and the mail-shirt hung loose on his wasted body. He had overheard the news of Ælle's birth; he dragged himself to his feet, his left hand gripping the chair-back. Irminburg took a spear that had stood propped against the wall by the king's bed all the time of his sickness. They smiled at each other; Garðrist nodded. He drew his sword and aimed a feeble blow at her. She drove the spear into him with all her force, crying joyfully, 'Woden has you!'

The king died on his feet, sword in hand, giving his life for his folk. He had earned his place in Woden's feast-hall.

Healfdene spent the year driving invaders across his borders and teaching them to stay away. He was a good king and well-liked. His time at sea had taught him how to make men obey him without hating him, willing to follow him to death. He saw to it that folk were afraid to attack him or break his laws. Away from the battle-field and the judgement seat, he was cheerful and open-handed.

He made Saewulf, his foster-brother, lord of the great island of Sillende. He also built a hall there for himself. He had strongholds in all his lands, going from one to the other to hear law-suits and use up his food rents but he made his home on Sillende. It was not haunted by memories of his father's cruel death, his mother's grief, his uncle's tormented spirit.

He married Sigerun, the sister of Sigehere, one of the island kings. She was a good wife, wise and kindly. She gave him three sons and a daughter, who was later betrothed to Saewulf.

As he grew up, Heorogar, the first boy, showed signs of a dark brooding temper that worried his parents. Their counsellor, Beornhelm, asked himself, shuddering at his memories, whether Heremod's unlaid ghost had taken lodging in the lad. Perhaps it was as well that Heorogar died from wound-fever while still a young man.

The second boy, Hroðgar, was the son that any father – most of all a king – prays for. He was brave but prudent, even-tempered and utterly trustworthy.

The youngest, Halga, was his father's boyhood self, born with the sea in his blood, growing up to be a sea-king, as hardy and skilful as he was reckless. The king loved and valued Hroðgar, his heir, but Halga warmed his heart. Whenever Halga came home from sea, rushing into the hall like a sea-wind, laughing as he told the tale of his latest exploits and shared out his spoils, Healfdene felt that he was living his own youth again.

South of Lug's Dun, on a ridge overlooking the islands, there was a small village; folk had lived there time out of mind. It was a poor place: a cluster of huts inside a stockade, some fields cleared from woodland and scrub, cattle grazing on the saltings. Its only treasure was a holy spring. The water was good for fever and gripe in the guts; it also healed bad eyes. Like all good gifts that come from the earth, the spring belonged to the Mother. She lived on the southernmost island and ruled the waters and coasts all around; she cared for seamen and traders as well as farmers. The islanders and shorefolk had always called her Nehalennia.

The Mother wanted her spring to be kept by maidens, so the girl who gathered flowers for its garlanding, took the humble offerings that were brought to the goddess and kept the grass clear of cattle-droppings was always very young. Whenever a keeper gave away her maidenhead, she went to live in her man's hut and a younger sister or cousin took her place.

Lifetimes ago, a Roman officer with an inflamed wound had been healed after bathing in the spring and drinking its waters. He had built a little stone house beside it for the goddess and her nymphs; he had also enclosed the well-head by a stone wall with steps going down into the water so that folk could bathe more easily.

Later, but still long ago, a wandering holy man had come to the village. He said he had good news for everyone, so the villagers gathered round him to listen.

He told them that the Lord, the Son of the Sky-God and the Virgin Mother had come to earth and been put to death but had risen to life again. They knew that already. The Bealdor died every year and the whole earth joined with the Mother in weeping and mourning for him but he always came back again in Eostremonað.

He also told them new names for calling on the Lord and the Mother: Jesus Christ and Maria. That was useful to know; gods listen best when they are called by their favourite or secret names.

The good news was that when he came back from Hel's kingdom, the young Lord had asked a boon from the All-Father. From now on, all who called on him by his name and took him as their only Lord would be welcomed into All-Father's royal hall and given a place at the everlasting feast. That was wonderful. They had always thought that the hall and the feast were only for kings and heroes.

The priest said no; the Lord's death had opened heaven to everyone, rich and poor, men and women, even slaves – so long as they honoured him, served him and shared in his sacrifice. The villagers were touched as well as pleased. They asked eagerly what sacrifice the Lord wanted – cattle, children, men?

This made the priest angry. The Lord's death was enough to pay for all, it seemed. All he asked in return was that they should be faithful to his name, obey his orders and be willing to lay down their lives for their friends. Puzzled but relieved, they promised that they would. So he dipped them in the holy well in the Lord's name, showed them how to keep off evil spirits with a cross-sign and taught them a prayer to All-Father.

Before he left, he told them that the girls who looked after the shrine, the handmaids of the Lord, must keep their maidenheads unbroken as long as they lived. The villagers thought that a cruel burden. What use was an old maiden? This must be the sacrifice the Lord wanted: the girls were laying down their lives for their friends.

From time to time, other priests of Christ came to see that the folk were still faithful and to tell them more stories about the Lord. Then the wild tribes from the east broke in across the Roman border, killing, looting and stealing the best farmlands. No raiders came to the village by the holy well. Perhaps the Mother of the Lord was watching over it. The land was poor and out of the way; there was nothing much to steal.

Life was hard and dangerous. No more priests came but the villagers stayed faithful, dipping their sons and daughters in the holy well, making the sign of the cross and saying the Lord's prayer. They worshipped the Mother too, of course, as they always had done time out of mind; they held all her festivals at the proper seasons.

Then the Saxons came and stayed. They made the farmers give them cattle and crops but they held other raiders at bay. When Irminburg took stock of her kingdom, she gave the village with the Mother's well to her sister, the priestess of Freo.

Ælfrun had larger and richer lands to visit; she sent one of her reeves to the village to collect her dues. Then one year she came herself, to speak to the village headman, Farro, and his wife Bobilla. A maid came with her, carrying a girl-child in a basket. Ælfrun had brought her to Bobilla to foster.

'Her name is Ursa. She was born to a woman in Freo's House, who can't rear her. I'll forgive you your rent to pay for her keep. You can set her to work for you as soon as she's old enough. Beat her if she needs it, otherwise see she's kept whole and untouched. When she's man-high, I'll dispose of her. If I find she's lost her maidenhead, you'll be sorry.'

Ursa was a big girl, with red-gold hair. Her temper was sunny, so she did not get beaten much, only for her own good to keep her from running into danger. Nothing seemed to frighten her. When she was old enough to help on the farm, she more than paid for her keep even without the saving of the rent, as she was hard-working and sensible. Farro trusted her with the herding and milking. He and Bobilla loved her dearly. They brought her up as a Christian like themselves. Ursa liked their stories about the Bealdor Jesus; she learned them by heart and would tell them over again to herself to pass the time while she was out herding.

When Ursa was twelve, the lady Ælfrun came and gave orders about her. She was to be taken to the shrine to serve the keeper of the well as handmaid and live a maiden all her life.

Farro and Bobilla were sad to lose their daughter, though she was being so highly honoured. Ursa was very happy. At the shrine and the well she felt close to the Lord and his Mother. She loved to serve them; to watch the changing seasons for the times of their festivals and carry out their rites. When she was a child, she had given her heart to the Lord. She did not want a mortal man.

Nine years went by. The old keeper died. Ursa had taken charge of the shrine and the well, with Bobilla's youngest daughter as her handmaid, when Ælfrun came again. This time, the queen came with her, to drink the holy water and make an offering to the Mother at her shrine.

Irminburg did not look as if she needed healing. She was strong and well-fleshed, still very handsome though she was past forty. She looked stern; she did not smile when Ursa came to greet her, though she stared hard.

After she had drunk the water, she changed. Her face beamed; she said she had never felt better in her life, she would let the whole kingdom know how much she owed to the Mother. She called her servants to bring her thank-offering but took it into her own hands to give to Ursa.

It was a large box, heavy and clinking with metal inside, marked with a Thurs-rune on the lid to ward off evil.

Speaking loudly enough for the whole village to hear, the queen told Ursa to place the box in the shrine and keep the key herself. It was full of priceless treasures, though too little for what she owed the Mother. Next year, she would bring even more precious offerings. She patted Ursa's cheek, then gave her a jewelled headband and pins for her veil, as a token of her good will.

The queen talked of little else but her treasure and her gifts for the rest of her stay. As they rode back towards Lug's Dun, Ælfrun looked curiously at her sister, who was still in high spirits.

'That wasn't very wise of you, Irminburg, to say so much about the treasure and the gifts you were going to bring. You're not usually so careless. Anyone would think you wanted the shrine to be raided.'

Irminburg smiled.

'The Lady can look after her own if she chooses. – and how she chooses.'

Halga first heard about the treasure-house when he went off raiding early next spring. What pricked his curiosity was that the traders and exiles who spoke about it – they were all Saxons – told him nothing willingly.

A couple of seamen waiting for the next tide were talking loudly and eagerly about it till they saw he was listening nearby. They fell abruptly silent, then started talking about something else. He came across a Saxon exile sitting lonely on an ale-bench. They shared a drink; Halga steered the talk towards the treasure-house, only to have the Saxon veer away as they got near it.

This secrecy made him more eager. He kept a sharp look-out for Saxons and picked up every crumb of news they dropped in his path.

Once, in a brothel in Bononia, he thought he was going to hear the full story. A Saxon gleeman started a tale about a golden lady, bright with jewels, who lived in a stone hall, the ancient work of giants, by the sea, hidden behind Queen Irminburg's shield-wall. The queen had given –

The gleeman's fingers lost their place on the harp-strings. His mouth gaped but no sound came out. There were two Saxon seamen by the door; their hands were on their knife-hilts. They scowled at the wretched gleeman, told him to stop his raven's croaking and give them a bawdy song or they would slit his throat. When they left, without having a girl, they took the gleeman with them.

Halga did not give up easily. He went on gathering hints about the treasure-house while he traded and raided up and down the Narrow Seas, till he thought he knew the truth and why the Saxons were so shy of owning to it.

There was a holy well at a rich Christian shrine in Queen Irminburg's land, on the coast somewhere near the islands. Both the queen, who belonged to Woden, and her sister, the high priestess of Freo, had been healed by the holy water. They had been giving the gods' treasures to the Christians and joining in their rites, though they were trying to keep this shameful truth hidden from decent folk. They had spies along the coast, ready to kill anyone who talked abroad about their evil deeds.

Halga made up his mind to raid this Roman church and take the stolen treasure. Even he would never have dared to rob a house of the gods, especially Freo or Woden, as he knew they would destroy him in revenge. But Roman Christians were anyone's game – and as they had already profaned the treasure, he would be serving the gods by helping himself.

So, taking the bait that had been carefully laid for him, he brought his ships quietly among the islands, beached them in a lonely inlet and led his men through the woods to the farmlands.

They found no rich Roman villa; only a cluster of serfs' huts. They herded the farm-folk inside the stockade, trussed them up for the time being and went in search of the shrine. That was a poor little place too, though very neat and decked out with leaves and flowers ready to welcome Eostre. Clearly, it belonged to Freo. They could not even help themselves to a sip from her well without asking.

Halga's men began to curse all Saxons. Those trolls' bastards had been playing a game with them. They would be laughing-stocks all round the Narrow Seas for letting themselves be tricked to this barren spot on a fool's errand.

'Or decoyed here to our deaths.'

Halga's face was grim.

'Take our ships while we're ashore, then cut us off on land. Three rich cargoes for Queen Irminburg's gold-hoard. Let's be off. Six of you run back to the village and kill the lot of them. If Woden lets us cut ourselves out of the trap, I'll make him a better offering when we get home.'

Ursa was in the shrine, pressed against the door, listening. Behind her eyes, she was watching Farro and Bobilla, her brothers and sisters, all her dear kinsfolk lying helpless under the butchers' knives and axes. She knew that the time had come for her to share in the Lord's sacrifice. She must lay down her life for her friends.

The raiders looked round when they heard the door open. A tall woman was coming towards them, carrying a box with a key lying on the lid. Her golden plaits were fastened up with jewelled pins under a gold headband. She walked like a queen or a goddess; she must be the priestess of the shrine. Halga was going to tell her not to be frightened, they would do her no harm. Seeing that she was not in the least afraid of them, he saved his breath and waited for her to speak.

'This well and oratory belong to the Mother of the Lord. I am the keeper.'

She held out the box.

'If you swear that none of my poor folk will be killed or enslaved or robbed, I'll give you this treasure for their ransom, with the Mother's blessing and my prayers for you –'

She paused and drew her breath.

' – and I offer myself in the Lord's name for the sacrifice.'

Halga thought she was offering him a sign of peace: inviting him to take the Bealdor's part in the Spring Marriage she was clearly about to celebrate to bless the crops and the young stock. It would safeguard his men from attack; the Saxons could not kill a Spring Lord. Also, it was a high honour for a man when a priestess chose him to mate with her. He could be sure of a lucky year.

This priestess was very good to look at. She was as tall as himself, long-limbed and full-breasted. Her height and dignity made her seem older than he was, but her skin was smooth, her eyes were clear, her lips were red and soft. She could not have been many years past twenty.

He forgave the Saxons. Their gleeman had told a true tale. There was indeed a golden lady, bright with jewels, dwelling in a stone hall by the sea.

He smiled.

'That's a fair offer from a very fair lady. We'll carry out the rite down by the shore, if you don't mind. I want to be near my ships, and we can bless the sea as well as the land while we're at it. I've got some wine aboard; I'll send some up to your folk when we let them loose, so they can have a good merry-making. I swear we'll keep your terms – by the way, what's your name?'

'Ursa.'

'*Yrse*'. Halga tried to say it. It sounded strange on his lips, not like a Saxon name. Maybe her folk were Romwealas.

They swore their oaths to each other. Ursa called a terrified girl, her sister Ingund, from the shrine, took her hand and walked beside Halga down to the ships.

Where the trees thinned out near the shore-line, the seamen hacked down leafy branches and built a booth on a patch of soft grass. Ingund's terror had left her when she found that the seamen were in a good mood and did not mean to kill anyone for the time being. She gathered flowers to strew the grass inside the booth, then wove crowns for the Spring Lord and Lady.

The seamen unloaded their wine. Halga and Ursa drank to each other. The wine, the first she had ever tasted, warmed Ursa's heart. She felt the life flowing so strongly in her veins, she could hardly believe she was to lose it so soon. She made herself think of the chalice her Lord had blessed, of sharing in his sacrifice, of women martyrs going singing to their deaths. Halga was thinking of the pleasures to come. He took her hand, led her into the booth and laid her down, thanking Freo for her bounty.

During his years as a rover, Halga had tumbled country girls, hired skilful portqueans in Gaulish taverns, glutted himself with war-captives and enjoyed several risky but amusing adventures with noblemen's wives. He had never come across a woman like Ursa before. She gave herself up to him like a seeress going into a trance. He thought: *She's taking me as it I were the Bealdor himself!*

Then he knew the truth: because The Lady's priestess had chosen him and willingly given herself to him, for that time and place he *was* the Bealdor, with all the life of the spring in his flesh and blood. He had never felt such joy.

When he was resting at last with his head against her breasts, she said quietly, 'May I ask you –'

'Anything! You can have my share of the cargo! I'll sack a Roman city for you –'

' – how I'm going to die?'

He was not quite sure he had heard aright. He propped himself up on his elbow to look at her. She smiled at him.

'I'm willing to die – but sometimes the body struggles when it's taken unawares. If I know what sort of death I shall meet, I can be quiet and seemly when it comes.'

'What makes you think you're going to die?'

'I offered myself as a sacrifice instead of my kinsfolk, my life for theirs.'

Halga was struck by her calm cheerfulness as well as her courage. Here was the treasure he had been seeking.

'I'm not going to kill you. What a waste of a fine woman! Besides, you offered me your life, not your death. I'm going to make you my wife – I'll never find a better.'

Halga wanted to catch the evening tide and be out of Saxon waters by moonlight. While most of the crews worked on the ships, he sent a group up to the village, with a gift of wine and some spices, to let the farm-folk loose. Ingund went with them but came back to the shore to tell Ursa they were all safe and to bid her farewell.

Halga had given the box of treasure to his bride, to be part of her morning-gift. Unluckily for both of them, Ursa was completely honest. She handed the box to Ingund and told her to put it back in the shrine.

King Healfdene was surprised when his youngest son came back from sea so early in the year, with a Welsh wife he had carried off somewhere on the coast of Gaul.

He was not angry. He had just pledged himself to a good match for Hroðgar with the daughter of King Helm of the Wulfings. This lady was praised by the scops for being as wise and gracious as she was beautiful. As Halga was just turned eighteen, his father had not been in such a hurry to find him a wife.

Halga said cheerfully that he'd saved his father the trouble, like the good son he was. He'd found himself the best wife in the world; he'd brought her home to leave her in his father's care while he went off again to find her a dowry.

He could always talk his father into a good mood. He held his wedding feast for a fortnight, then put out to sea. When his ships came into haven in the autumn, loaded with loot, he found that Ursa was with child.

During that summer, the king had grown to like and respect his son's wife. His queen was dead; he was glad to have a woman in charge of his household again. Ursa was sensible and kept good order. Though she was only a village girl, her life as keeper of the holy well had given her dignity. She could make folk obey her without needing to try. Halga had told him that she had been ready to die for her kinsfolk; he was proud of his daughter-in-law's courage. Above all, he liked the girl for herself; she suited his moods, he was at ease in her company. When she bore him a fine grandson, he felt that even the Wulfing princess, King Helm's daughter, could never be dearer to him than Ursa.

For Halga, she was like a fruit-tree grafted into his stock. They were one in body, mind and heart. He began to say he would leave sea-roving in a year or two so that he could spend more time with her. Healfdene meant to give him Jutland to rule.

Next year, just after harvest, when Ursa was looking out every day for Halga's return, a Saxon ship put into the haven.

Her master came up to the royal stronghold with an escort from the coastguard. He had a message for the king.

Queen Irminburg of Rhinemouth was on her way back from visiting her kin in the old Saxon homelands. She sent her greetings to King Healfdene and would be thankful for his hospitality.

Healfdene smiled. If Queen Irminburg had been visiting the old Saxon homelands, her crew was badly off-course. He guessed that she had taken ship meaning to visit him. He thought he knew why.

He was the most powerful king in the north; also he was now a widower. She was a widow, getting on in years, with land-hungry tribes on her borders and unruly warriors to keep in hand. For all her pride, she would need a strong man to help her and would likely feel easier with one she had already known and tried.

The Rhinemouth, with its islands and haven and the old Roman road to the south, would be useful to have in his grasp. And if Irminburg was still anything like the woman he had lain with once, a friendly alliance with her would bring him some pleasure as well as profit. '*The third game wins the match*'.

He sent the Saxon ship-master back to the haven with his greetings to the queen and a hearty welcome to stay as long as she liked. He told Ursa to prepare a guest-hall for her and order a lavish feast for her crewmen and warriors.

Before she let Healfdene see her, Irminburg took trouble with her looks and her dress, to show herself at her best. When she was not smiling, her face was now harder and more worn but she was all smiles at their meeting. She held herself upright and her hair seemed as red as ever. Ample robes of purple Roman cloth, embroidered with gold, hid whatever the years had added or taken from her shape. She was still a very fine-looking woman.

If she knew Ursa, she gave no sign. She called her *Lady Yrse* in the Danish way; she was friendly and grateful to her for her welcome. Ursa waited on her in the guest-hall while her men feasted with Healfdene and his household.

When a servant told him that the women had finished their meal, Healfdene left the feast and sent word that he would like to talk to the queen unless she was too weary. Irminburg said she would be glad to see him; she led the way to her bedroom. Ursa had wine brought in. The queen smilingly asked her to stay and share it with them; the maids could wait outside in the hall.

Healfdene drank to their meeting, then asked after the state of her kingdom.

'It's half a lifetime since my ships put in at Rhinemouth. We don't get any younger. So you never married again after Garðrist died. What will you do for an heir?'

'My nephew, Ælle. My sister, the priestess, bore him to Woden. I brought him up to be king. He's everything I could wish. We plan to move into Britain soon – the Franks have taken all the good land this side of the Narrow Seas.'

Healfdene saw his dreams of an alliance drift away like the smoke from the hearth-fire.

'So what brings you to the north?'

'A mother's feelings. I wanted to find out for myself how well our daughter here –' she smiled at Ursa '– was settled before I went overseas.'

Silence.

Ursa was still as a stone. Healfdene's lips felt stiff; he licked them to find if his mouth would move. His voice seemed to have died in his throat. Irminburg watched his face with enjoyment.

'Remember the game you played with me, last time we met, down in the hollow by the oak-tree? And the box of treasure you gave me to pay for your lodging? You left another keepsake with me, to make sure I wouldn't forget you.'

Ursa had given a start when the box was mentioned; her hands clenched, then she was still again.

'You'd cut a thurs-rune on the box-lid. I worked that out in the end: a half-D for Healfdene. When you took the Danish kingdom and made a name for yourself in the world, I knew who you were and where to find you.'

'You planned this!'

'And made it happen. I had fine sport, luring your son along the coast till he fell into my trap.'

'Using your own daughter as a bait!'

'If you want to win board games, you must be ready to sacrifice your own pieces to take your enemy's king. I won the first game with you, then I lost a game. '*The third game wins the match*'.'

She looked at Ursa.

'You were my best piece, daughter. I let you be taken but you won me the match.'

Ursa said nothing. She was staring at the fire, sipping her wine, a dutiful hostess waiting for the talk to end so that she could say goodnight and go to bed. Irminburg was disappointed. She had been looking forward to shrieks, tears, curses and reproaches thrown at Healfdene, watching him grovel to her to keep her mouth shut on the story.

'You're very quiet, my dear. It must be a great shock to learn you've had a child by your brother.'

Ursa did not look shocked, just unconcerned.

'I'm not very interested in board games. I find them a waste of time, I can't understand how folk can keep going over and over the moves they made, or should have made. Still, I always wish to keep my guests happy. Would you like me to send for a board and a set of pieces? One of my maids plays quite well. Or is there anything else I can get you? More wine? Sweetmeats?'

Irminburg looked taken aback. Healfdene was proud of Ursa. With bitter amusement, he watched her making the same move against her mother as Irminburg had used against him last time they met. She was blocking the queen's triumph by a total lack of interest.

'Is that all you have to say when you meet your mother? You owe me a child's duty, remember!'

'I owe you nothing. You haven't been my mother since the day you pushed me out of your body. Bobilla is my mother; she gave me her care and her love. You gave me nothing but birth and that was unwilling.'

'I gave you a gold headband and some jewelled hair-pins. And I gave you your name – Ursa was a bitch I had at that time.'

Healfdene cursed and raised his arm to hit her, though she was his guest. Irminburg did not flinch and he managed to hold back the blow.

'That was an honour. Ursa was the best huntress I ever had, she never lost a scent and always brought down my quarry for me. I really cared for that dog.'

She smiled at her daughter.

'And I'll take good care of you too, once I've got you home with me.'

Ursa stared at her.

'I always meant to fetch you back, if my plan worked. You can't stay here as your brother's wife, you won't even want to face him, now you know the truth. The king looks sick at the sight of you already – and how will you enjoy taking your place beside your new sister-in-law in front of all the women, once everybody knows who you are? But don't be afraid, I'll look after you. You've done everything I wanted. And there's no need to be angry with me about the past, I'll make it up to you. I'll give you a dowry and find you a husband –'

Ursa stood up.

'Don't take any trouble, my lady. I can take care of myself. This is the last time I'll be under the same roof with you. I'll never come inside any house that holds you. I'm not angry – just careful of the company I choose. I don't want to be seen with a bawd.'

Healfdene laughed, making the sound as loud and jeering as he could. Before Irminburg could speak, Ursa opened the hall door, called the maids, told them to attend the queen and wished her goodnight. Healfdene followed her out but Ursa kept her own women round her as she went away to her bower. He dared not risk trying to talk to her.

Next morning, Healfdene and Irminburg said the right words to each other in front of their servants at the leave-taking. Ursa did not appear, nor did the queen ask after her. The guests were escorted to the haven and put out to sea. The shore-folk were still watching the Saxon vessel rowing away when Halga's ships were sighted, making for land. A messenger rode up the royal stronghold with the news. Ursa sent the king a rune-stave scratched with the words *Tell him.*

She was sitting on her bed, staring at her son Hroðulf asleep in his cradle when Halga rushed in. He signed to her women to leave them alone. They ran off, laughing at his eagerness to have his wife to himself after months at sea.

Ursa got to her feet when she saw him. He caught her in his arms and they clung to each other for a while, bodies and mouths pressed together as if they were one flesh. Then she broke free, pushing him away and turning her head aside.

'No, don't! It's deadly sin, we mustn't –'

'You're my wife.'

'I'm your sister. We should never –'

'Half-sister. And we didn't know – how could we? Tribes go wandering all over Middle Earth. Think what happens every time a war-band sacks a township, or a crew of sea-rovers comes into port! Brothers and sisters must be lying with each other every day without knowing each other.'

'So long as we didn't know, we were guiltless. Our child was true-born. But everything has changed now.'

'We're the same man and woman we were yesterday.'

'I cannot be my brother's wife.'

'Sigemund –'

'Sigemund and his sister were the last of the Wælsings. She gave her body to him so they would have an heir to avenge their murdered kin. And she had to change shapes with a witch before she lay with him, otherwise he couldn't have done it. The world knows what evil came of that mating. Halga, I love you, and I'll always be true to you but I *cannot* lie with my brother.'

'Will not. You've always been able enough, even that first time when you thought I was going to cut your throat as soon as I'd finished with you. Do you think I'll believe that a woman like you could be frightened – or frozen – by the sound of a word?'

He caught hold of her again, meaning to throw her on the bed and then prove to her how wrong she was. Even as he touched her, he knew his flesh would not obey him. Ursa made no move, either to struggle or to embrace him. Each felt the other's heart beating while they stared hopelessly at each other. Then he let go of her and went away.

He rode back to the haven and ordered the shipwrights to make his ships ready for sea again. He was in wild spirits. He sat and drank with the seamen. He swore it was a shame to waste such fine weather, it would not break for weeks yet. He had a mind to make one more voyage before winter set in; he asked if there were any bold lads within earshot, not ready to beach themselves yetawhile. There were so many, he could have manned his ships three times over.

He set off eastwards, making for Wendish waters. He never came back.

When Halga's ships had gone, Ursa asked to speak to the king. He was in the room behind the royal hall; Hroðgar was with him. Ursa asked calmly if he would let her leave his kingdom.

'Thought better of your mother's offer, have you?'

'Better! I'll never see her again. If I go away now, it's likely that your other son will come home sooner.'

'And what about your own son? Have you thought about him?'

'I have to trust that you will look after his welfare. He's your grandson – twice over.'

She could not keep her voice quite steady; her face was pale and careworn. Healfdene was bitterly sorry for her; it was not fair that she had to pay her parents' gaming debts. He wanted to say; *I'll adopt him!* but he had to think of his heir. What would become of Hroðgar, say eighteen years hence, with an adopted brother just come to manhood while he was ageing and his sons maybe still boys?

Hroðgar said quietly, 'I'll take care of Hroðulf for you, sister.'

He had always called Ursa '*sister*' from the time Halga brought her home as a wife, so the word held no poison for her coming from his mouth. He smiled at her.

'I know my bride is generous and good-hearted. We'll bring him up as our own child.'

Ursa clasped his out-stretched hand. There were tears in her eyes but she blinked them away and held her head up as she turned to leave. Healfdene asked her where she was going.

'The weather's so good, traders are still setting out. If I can, I'll take a place on one of your ships bound for Gaul. Maybe I'll find a house of Christian women who are handmaids of the Lord. I'm not a maiden but they might take me in as a widow. Or a serving-woman. I might even get to Rome. It doesn't matter where I go – I've no home anywhere.'

Healfdene suddenly slammed his fist down on the table. He was furious with pity for her.

'This is your home ! We're your kin. You're the mother of my grandson. You've done nothing wrong. There's no need for you to send yourself into exile and I won't let you do it! You'll stay here, just as if –'

– just as if none of this had happened.

Healfdene managed to shut his mouth on the words. What was done could never be undone. Each deed became a part of yourself, so you could never be rid of it. He cursed himself for having even thought of offering childish comfort to a woman like Ursa.

The silence grew heavy. He wished she would stop staring at him and say something. She did.

' – just as if I were your daughter.'

'Ane sweorde
merce gemærde wið Myrgingum
bi Fifeldore; heoldon forð siþþan
Engle ond Swæfe swa hit Offa geslog.'

Widsið

(With his lone sword he fixed the border against the Myrgings at Monster-Gate; ever since, the English and the Swabians have kept it as Offa won it.)

III Alone at Monster-Gate

In the old days, Wærmund son of Wihtlæg, Woden-born, was ruling in Angeln. This was before the Angelcynn went away overseas to the west.

Wærmund was a very great man. He was so great in size and strength that he seemed to be giant-born as well as god-born. He was even greater in courage, truth and generosity. The farming-folk obeyed him because he gave them fair dealing and kept them safe from raiders. His warriors were devoted to him because he led them to victory and plunder. The scops who made poems about him said that his gold-hoard was as vast as a mountain and his gifts flowed out of it like a river. He was a good king.

He had ruled for a long time; he had three surviving sons come to manhood. All these princes had inherited a good share of their father's strength and spirit. Luckily, they seemed to be good friends. The eldest showed no distrust of his brothers; the younger ones showed no envy. The eldest was lately married to a Jutish princess. Soon there would be grandchildren to carry on the royal line.

So Wærmund had good cause to be proud and happy. When he looked ahead, as a wise man must, to his coming old age and death, he was content to think of his sons guarding and guiding the Angelcynn in his place. Life had done well by him and he had done well with his life.

But Wyrd goes ever as she must. A life cannot be judged till it is over. Wærmund had many more years of kingship to endure before stronger hands took it from him.

His eldest son was killed horse-breaking before he had got his young wife with child. The second son dutifully took his brother's place and his widow. He was killed the same year, fighting off a Myrging raid in the southern borderlands. Then a wet summer, a ruined harvest and a bitter winter brought hunger and weakness to the farm-folk.

When the raiding season was over, and folk were keeping Mothers' Night at the dark heart of midwinter, the Myrgings attacked again. They struck at Angeln in mockery and contempt, to show that they could do as they liked on English land. They did not win much loot – there was not much to be had that year – but they came, they burned and they went home again without being stopped or punished. They boasted about it. Other tribes took note.

The Jutish king sent for his twice-widowed sister to come home before she could be married to her second brother-in-law. He thought that Wyrd had turned against the English. They were marked out for bad luck and he wanted no share of it.

When the warm weather came, fever came with it. Many folk died. Wærmund lost his last son and also his queen, his wise and faithful companion. He was alone, an ageing, childless king. There were too many nobles in Angeln linked to the royal house by marriage and descent, all ready to start a civil war as soon as he died or lost control of his war-band.

He sent envoys with precious gifts to his neighbour, the king of the Wærnas. The embassy came back with the king's daughter, a quiet, gracious girl. She was proud to be King Wærmund's bride; she truly wished to be a good queen to the English. She offered many sacrifices and gave rich gifts to the gods. She prayed that she might bear a prince who would be as great a man as his father.

It looked as if the gods had granted her prayer. She was soon with child; she grew so great and heavy that her every move was a struggle. Her women whispered among themselves. They were afraid the king's enemies had hired a sorcerer to cast runes against the queen's childbearing, to make her litter a dozen tiny creatures at one birth, all too weak to draw breath. When her time came, though, it was clear that she was carrying one child, so big that it could only force its way out into the light after a long struggle.

The queen bore her terrible labour with great courage. She would not let herself scream aloud, bringing her child to birth to the sounds of pain and fear. She made her women sing ballads about the deeds of gods and heroes; she joined in the singing while she could. Near the end, she could only moan and gasp for breath, but she kept as quiet as possible.

Her courage – and her prayers and gifts to the gods – seemed to be rewarded. She gave the English a prince, a big healthy boy, strong and likely to thrive. She did not enjoy her triumph and the king's gratitude for long. She had given too much of herself to her son's making, flesh, blood and spirit.

What was left of her life flickered for a little while, then went out.

Care for his last child first taught Wærmund to dread death. He had no wish to marry again. His heir must have no half-brothers to envy him, to be used as gaming pieces against him by nobles greedy for power. The king felt very old; he told himself grimly that he must try to stay alive and hold the land until Prince Offa had grown to manhood, able to handle weapons and rule warriors.

Meanwhile, though, Prince Offa belonged with his wet-nurses. He must be placed under the care of some high-born lady, the ruler of a great household, who knew how to guard a child's well-being.

Luckily, Wærmund's most powerful kinsman was the one he trusted and liked best, with good reason. Earl Freawine held the southern march against the Myrgings. They were troublesome folk to have over the border, restless and defiant. They were not a large or powerful tribe but they had the mighty nation of the Swabians at their back. The Myrgings were an off-shoot of the Swabians; they claimed the high-king as their lord and protector when it suited them. Most of the time, though, they did as they liked.

Freawine was a stern lord, unbroken in battle, rock-like in faith. He would make a good foster-father for the prince, to teach him warriors' honour and sword-play. His wife was well-born and wise. Also, he had two lusty sons, Wigheard and Cedd, just growing up to manhood. They would be guards, play-fellows and, later, brothers-in-arms to their prince.

So Offa, his nurses and servants were sent south with rich gifts for Earl Freawine and his lady.

Offa was well cared-for in his new home and grew at a great rate. His appetite was as big as everything else about him; he sucked like a young bull-calf. He was a good baby in that he hardly ever cried – but he hardly ever laughed either. His nurses claimed that he knew his mother had died to give him life. When he was awake, he stared hard at the world around him. He pushed and kicked out lustily whenever he was unwrapped from his swaddling-clouts. His body was flawless; every woman in the household doted on him. Yet weeks, months, a year passed, then two, and still he had not started to babble, however much his nurses coaxed him to talk.

When he first arrived, Wigheard and Cedd had come to their mother's bower to look at him. They had dangled their arm-rings and jewelled belt-buckles within reach of his fingers. They got no response but a solemn wide-eyed stare. They decided he was feeble-minded.

'He's an old man's get,' said Wigheard, a worldly-wise man of fourteen. 'They're always lacking somewhere – body, brain or heart.'

His mother cried out in protest.

'Offa's not stupid – look at his eyes! He's taking in everything we do and say. He'll talk when he's ready.'

'He'll be none the worse if he grows up to think before he speaks,' said Earl Freawine. 'That's a lesson you'd do well to learn, young Wiga.'

Freawine's sons had mixed feelings about having the young prince in their household. They were proud that the king had singled out their family for the trust. Wigheard was old enough to see that their father was now second man in the kingdom. He would be first man if Wærmund died before Offa was fit to rule.

Wigheard had already decided that Offa would never be fit to rule. He looked ahead twelve years, when Offa would be a man. By then, Wærmund would surely be dead and Freawine would be old.

Wigheard had no doubt that he would be the next king. His grandmother had been old King Wihtlæg's sister. He was too proud to harbour any thought that seemed like planned treachery. He told himself that idiots cannot rule. Angeln would need a strong-minded, warlike king.

Cedd was two years younger than his brother. His life was driven by two powerful forces: his hero-worship of Wiga and a burning wish to match him, if not out-do him. He followed Wiga zestfully into every scrape.

Both youths were ready to swagger around the tun as Prince Offa's picked champions. They were unwilling to give up any of their own amusements for his sake. When their father told them to stay at home from the first great hunting party of autumn and keep guard over the prince, they would have rebelled if they dared. Cedd could only curse over his lost sport; Wiga had other ideas how to pass their time pleasantly.

He had lately bought a Hunnish bow from a passing trader. That strange half-demon race was supreme in archery. Their bows were cunningly-made of horn, wood and sinew, with a double curve above and below the grip, so that though they seemed short, they had a longer draw and a much greater force than self bows. But Hunnish bows need skilled handling. Wiga did not want to make his first attempts with it in public, for the household to jeer at. He told Cedd they would go and practise on the water-fowl down by the river. There was no fear that their father would see or hear of them; he had ridden off to the heath-lands.

'He'll hear we flouted his orders. He told us we weren't to leave Offa.'

'We won't leave him. We'll take him with us.'

'You're mad.'

'He'll be no trouble. He always sleeps like a log after his morning feed.'

'His nurse won't let us take him out.'

'Eanswið always sleeps like a log too, after she's fed him. We'll get the maid to bring him out under her cloak.'

'She wouldn't dare.'

'She will if I tell her to. I can make Leofrun do anything I want.'

Wiga stuck his thumbs in his belt and straddled his legs, grinning.

Leofrun was scared but did as she was told. They made their way out of the tun, unseen, through the herb-patch and the orchard. They were soon hidden in the skirts of the forest.

The woods sloped down towards the river-bank. The land there was sour and marshy, unfit for crops or cattle. They did not expect to meet anyone. Then their path came out into a patch of open ground, where a man was at work.

He was undoing the carcass of a boar; its head was already off. Nearby stood a foundered horse, its head drooping. The man heard a twig crack; he looked round, then got to his feet, gripping his bloody hand-seax. Wiga and Cedd stood watching him. Leofrun drew back among the bushes, clutching Offa.

The stranger was a tall, powerfully-built man, dressed in plain workmanlike clothes of leather and dark wool. A knowing eye would have seen that his gear and his horse were of good quality. Young Wiga still judged a man's rank by his jewellery and embroidered borders, so he thought this one must be a churl. He noted that the stranger's hair was drawn back and knotted on the crown of his head, in the fashion of the Swabians, also their allies and hangers-on. Worst of all, however tall Wiga drew himself up, the stranger could look down on him. Wiga lost his temper.

'You Myrgings are stupid. You can't remember which side of the river you live on. I'll have to teach you another lesson.'

The stranger looked more amused than angry.

'You should have explained that to the boar when he crossed the water. I expect you can talk boarish. It's too late to argue with him now. As for me, no quarry of mine can go where I don't follow.'

The Myrging laughed, but pleasantly enough, so that his words could be taken as a joke rather than a challenge if his listeners chose. He was alone, not taking part in a raid. He had simply been unwilling to lose his quarry, a feeling that any hunter could share. Also, he had tackled it single-handed, so he must be brave as well as skilful.

An older man, more sure of himself, would have decided to take the words as a joke, joined in the laugh, perhaps invited the hunter home with him for food and rest before he crossed the river again.

Wiga had only just taken arms; he was not as sure of himself as he made out. He thought the Myrging was sneering at him in front of his younger brother and his girl.

'That's why you're going to end like your quarry, in the same place!' He drew his sword.

The hunter looked down on him with some kindliness for his pluck.

'Go home, pup. I don't want to hurt you. Fighting's for warriors. Run along and play with the other children.'

He glanced at Cedd, Leofrun and baby Offa, clearly putting Wigheard with them. Wiga nearly choked with fury.

'Yes, fighting is for warriors. Weaklings are only big-mouthed. Fight me if you dare. Dare or not, I'm going to kill you for treading on my land.'

Cedd moved closer to his brother, ready to keep his side and back. The hunter shifted his seax to his left hand and drew his sword.

'If that's your choice, you'd better come on together, for both your sakes. I'm more than a match for the pair of you.'

'No! Stay where you are, Cedd. Don't you dare interfere. I claim single combat. He's mine!'

He hurled himself at the Myrging.

At first, it was clear that the hunter meant to play with him for a while, then disarm him – maybe give him a drubbing on the backside with the flat of his sword to teach him not to pester his elders.

It is not easy to play with a strong, agile youngster, killing-mad and armed with a good sword. In a few seconds the Myrging was fighting in earnest. His strength and reach, his greater skill and experience gave him the mastery. Wigheard knew he had met his master; he was hitting out in mindless rage, then tripped and fell heavily, dropping his sword. If the Myrging had not paused in mid-stroke, he could have skewered him.

Cedd watched in anguish, torn apart by shame and honour. By refusing the stranger's offer to fight both at once, by claiming single combat, Wigheard had made it impossible for Cedd to join in on his brother's side. The Myrging had no fear that he would; more than once he had turned his back on Cedd, in perfect faith that Cedd would not lift a hand against him. No warrior could do so; he would kill his own honour with the first blow.

So he must just stand there, watch his brother being killed and do nothing? What sort of honour was that?

Anyway, when Wiga was dead, he would have to challenge the Myrging, to avenge his brother. He'd be killed too – if Wiga couldn't beat him, nobody could. And then, what would become of Offa?

If the Myrging wasn't blood-drunk enough to kill him and Leofrun at once – if Leofrun had time to say who the child was – what a trophy he would be for the Myrgings to gloat over, while they decided whether to sell him to a trader, keep him as a thrall, or make Wærmund humble himself begging them to take ransom.

Father and mother would be disgraced for ever – left to face Wærmund's fury with no sons to protect them –

Father had ordered them to guard Offa above all things – surely he'd want them to do anything, however dreadful –

– Anyway, I haven't taken sword yet – I'm not a warrior – I'm not bound by –

Wiga was on his feet again, breathless and unsteady but still refusing to yield. He threw himself at his enemy like a madman. Once again, his blows were parried, his sword knocked from his hand, he was beaten to the ground. The Myrging was angry now. He kicked Wiga's sword out of his reach and stooped over him.

'Go to Hel, then, if that's what you want – I wish Her joy of you.'

Before he could strike the death-blow, Cedd's hand-seax went into his back with all the force of Cedd's arm behind it. He crashed down spewing blood, twitched and was still.

Wigheard slowly got up. Neither brother spoke; they both knew what had happened was unspeakable. Wiga took his own seax; he went behind a thicket of alders and began cutting turfs. Cedd joined him. When they had cleared enough ground, they hollowed out a grave.

Luckily, the Myrging had fallen forwards; they did not have to look him in the face. They spread his cloak alongside him, rolled him onto it and wrapped it tightly around him. They carried him to the grave and laid him out in it as decently as they could, with his hunting spear, his sword and his seax beside him. They piled the earth over him and laid the turfs, stamping them down and scattering fallen leaves over them.

They dealt with the boar more briefly by dragging it a good way in the opposite direction and leaving it where the undergrowth was thickest. There would only be scattered bones left of it by morning.

They did not want another tell-tale corpse to hide, so they dragged and beat the horse down to the river and stoned it away from the bank. The current was strong; the wretched beast was swept a good way downstream before it started trying to swim.

When they got back to the glade among the alders, Leofrun was still standing like a tree-stump. She stared at them. Her cloak had fallen open. Offa was awake now, he was sitting up in her arms. He stared at them too.

Cedd hated the girl for having watched them.

'Best cut her throat and bury her too. We'll say she ran off to amuse herself and left the child.'

'Leofrun won't talk.' Wiga smiled at her terrified face. 'She's a good girl. She'll say no more about it than *he* will.'

He jerked his thumb at Offa.

'Can we be sure he won't tell when he starts to talk? Remember how mother said he takes in everything we do –'

'I don't believe that. He just gapes like an idiot. Even if he should talk about it – if he ever talks! – we'll just talk him down. We'll say he must have had a dream about a story Leofrun told to amuse him.'

Long before they came home, they had been missed and searched for. Wiga boldly outfaced the resentment of the guards, the outcry from Eanswið the nurse, the anger of his mother.

Father had told them not to leave Offa; they hadn't left Offa for a single minute. They had taken him to watch them trying the Hunnish bow, as a treat. They thought it would be good for him to see men's pastimes instead of spending the whole day with women. Wiga's clothes were bloody and torn because he had gone up a tree after a wild cat and had fallen off a branch when it sprang at him. No he wasn't hurt, only a few scratches. They had been doing their best; they thought folk would be pleased with them. All right, they promised not to do anything like it again.

They kept their word.

When winter was over and traders could travel again, they brought a strange story across the Eider. The Myrgings had lost their king, Eadgils. He had out-ridden his hunting companions, going after a huge boar that had killed his hounds and two of his men before breaking out of the ring that was baying him. Eadgils often boasted that he never let a quarry escape him, however far he had to follow it or what wild land he had to cross. Not one of his men was surprised that he had not come back by sunset. They only began to search on the second day. They never saw their king again.

A while later, a Myrging fisherman had found what was left of a drowned horse in the mud, far down towards Eidermouth. It had fine trappings; the fisher took them to his chief, who recognised the designs on the metal-work. Perhaps the king had been lured to his death by a water-demon that had taken the shape of a boar to bring him into the river and drown him. The Eider was known as 'Fifel-dor', the Monster-Gate, because of the otherworld horrors that swam inland from the ocean with the sea-fogs and the raging winter gales.

Some of the Myrgings were inclined to blame the English for the loss of their king. That was because they blamed the English for most of their troubles. They had no idea that Eadgils had crossed into Angeln; they suspected he had caught an English raiding party on his borderland and attacked them single-handed. Yet no Myrging had seen or suffered from raiders. No word came out of Angeln boasting of a king-slaying.

No word about Eadgils' death came from Angeln because no such word was spoken. Leofrun kept her mouth shut. She got a brooch from Wiga; also, next summer, a baby. Offa never spoke a word about what he had seen, through all the years of his childhood, because he never spoke at all. The king's only son was a dumb idiot.

Freawine's household shut their minds to the fact as long as they could. The lady still insisted that Offa understood everything that was said and done around him. Eanswið and the other womenservants told each other about children they knew who had not said a word till they were three years old – or even four – then talked all the better when they did begin. No one knew a story about a child who had not spoken till he was five – six – seven, half way to manhood. No one had ever heard Offa speak one human word. After he stopped making baby-noises, his silence was unbroken.

They gathered healing herbs at the due times with many incantations; they brewed potions for him to drink and made salves to rub on his throat. They said charms over him, engraved loosening runes on amulets to hang round his neck, offered sacrifices and gave treasures to the gods. Nothing they did could win or buy a voice for Offa.

Earl Freawine and his lady grieved for their king and for the boy. He was the image of a prince, tall and strong as a young Thunor, with handsome features and clear grey eyes. He had always been active and healthy; he could swim like a fish, even when the Eider was ice-cold and swollen with melted snow. He followed every hunt – only chaining would have kept him at home – running tirelessly beside Freawine's horse. He must have had some animal sense, he was good at tracking and turning game; he seemed fearless. In the tun, he squatted patiently for hours, watching the young warriors at their weapon-play. He would have made a fine hound.

For some years there was little trouble from the Myrgings. Eadgils had left sons; the eldest was old enough and fit to rule but there were uncles and cousins who thought themselves fitter. There was civil war, with a savage kinslaying among the nobles of royal blood.

Wærmund was glad of the respite. If he had been younger, he would have been raiding beyond the Eider and taking tribute from the Myrgings. Angeln seemed as strong as ever, but only because it had not been attacked; it could no longer make its power felt beyond its borders.

The king was still respected by most of his own folk. He believed that his counsellors and his war-band would be faithful, even at a last stand. But there was no longer the old intense rivalry to join his household. Foreign champions did not offer their services to him now. The younger English nobles were going away to other lands, to serve more warlike kings who offered the chance of winning honour and plunder. He heard of some who were with the Jutes, the Danes, the Frisians, the Franks. He guessed by what he did not hear about some others that they had gone to the Swabians.

The glory of Angeln was fading into twilight. Darkness was coming even sooner on Wærmund. His eyes were failing. Offa was now nearly fourteen, young to be a king but old enough, if he had good counsel. He sent for his heir.

Freawine had warned the king long ago that Offa was sluggish and unwilling to put himself forward. Pity had kept him from telling the father just how backward his son was. Also, he had kept hoping that some sorcerer would find a cure for the dumbness or that the gods would give the boy a voice.

So, wishing the king nothing but well, Freawine made the death of his hope more painful when it came. If Offa had been feeble or deformed, the sense of loss would have been less bitter. He looked all that an æðeling should be. At the first meeting, it seemed to Wærmund's fading eyes that his long-dead eldest son had come back from his grave-mound to help his father in the hour of need.

Then the old king learned that this last son was a mute. He took the blow as bravely as he had borne all the others that life had dealt him. He settled Offa quietly in a hall of his own inside the royal tun, with a guard of trusted old warriors. Eanswið, who was devoted to him, kept the house.

Wærmund could not stop folk talking. Soon, gloating voices across the Myrging border were spreading the tale that the English æðeling was a drooling idiot, a man of fourteen still in the keeping of his wet-nurse. He knew that the Myrgings would attack soon.

The Myrgings now had a stronger power to back them. In exchange for help in wiping out his kin, the new chief, Meaca, had taken King Witta of the Swabians as his overlord. The Myrgings no longer had a kingdom; Meaca was holding the land for King Witta and took his orders. He paid tribute; his younger brother Mearcweard was a hostage among the Swabians, serving in the king's war-band.

Meaca was willing to pay this price for being chief man among his own people and for the hope of bringing Angeln down. King Witta's eyes were looking north; he had picked Angeln as his next prey, with the Myrgings as his hunting-hounds.

Wærmund told his council that a blind man could not rule. Freawine would be the next king, with Wigheard as his heir. In return for the kingship, Freawine must adopt Offa as his son and promise to protect him.

At midwinter, the Myrgings tried another surprise attack, not a raid this time; they struck with all their force. Freawine was ready for them and brought them to a standstill when they had only got a little way north of the Eider. But he was slain, with Cedd at his side. Wigheard, fighting with the battle-fury of Woden, rallied his men, broke the Myrging host and drove them headlong back through the river. Two days later he died of his wounds.

Meaca called on his overlord to protect the Myrgings against further English attacks and make them pay wergild for the blood they had shed. King Witta promised his help.

Wærmund told the boy who guided his steps to lead him to the war-chest, take out a sword and put the hilt in his hand. He tried two or three for weight, balance and ease of grip, found one to his liking and sheathed it in his empty scabbard. The boy was puzzled but said nothing. No one questioned Wærmund's actions, even when he was old and blind.

When he first knew that he was losing his sight, Wærmund had taken his own sword and gone out alone from the royal tun. The sword was Weland's work; it was precious, not so much for the wrought gold and garnets that gleamed on its hilt but for its strength and cutting edge. Its name was Stedefæst, because it could be trusted to cut through anything in its way, however hard, at a single blow.

Wærmund had made up his mind that King Witta would never lay hands on Stedefæst as a prize of war, to boast about in his own tun or, worse, give away as a reward to his Myrging henchmen.

He went far out to the desolate moorland, to one of the grave-mounds of the ancient kings, so long dead that even the scops did not know their names. Hawthorns covered the hill-side. The barrow was girdled with nettles, brambles grew thickly all over it but the huge stones at the entrance could still be seen.

He could not open the mound by himself. He walked east from the portal till he came to an old thorn tree and buried his sword at its foot. Then he went back, counting his paces, to the stone blocking the entrance to the barrow. Lifting the bramble-fronds aside, he scratched ↑ with his seax – the sign of Tiw, the bravest and most faithful of the gods, who had sacrificed his sword-hand to keep his word. Underneath, he cut the thorn rune Þ and a mark for each pace. So he left Stedefæst under the protection of the Sword God. Any weapon from the war-chest would do for his last stand, when the Swabians came across the Eider.

The first Swabians to cross the Eider carried green branches. They called themselves envoys, coming in peace and offering friendship. Their manners were insolent. They swaggered into the king's hall like conquerors. Their spokesman was Mearcweard the Myrging. He was widely known and feared for his swordsmanship. He often said that no living man had fought with him; it was his favourite joke.

'King Witta is merciful. He'll let you spend the rest of your days as chief, if you take him as overlord and pay tribute. Your folk can go on living in Angeln to farm the land. Also, you must swear never to lift a hand against his kinsmen, the Myrgings. You must give us all the land up to ten miles north of the Eider, to keep our borders safe from your thieving. And you must pay us whatever wergild we set for our blood you have shed.'

He grinned at the scowling faces of Wærmund's men.

'If you don't like the terms, send a champion of royal blood to meet me by the Eider this day week and settle the matter once and for all. The king will be on the southern bank by then with his warriors. He'll expect an answer – fight or yield. What do you say?'

Wærmund waited inside his darkness, listening.

In the old days, the hall would have been shaking to the roar of warriors trying to shout each other down, all claiming the right to take up the challenge.

No one spoke.

Wærmund's men were loyal, willing to die with their king. But for too long, their thoughts had been fixed on a hopeless last stand. Their spirits were not ready to challenge Wyrd at a moment's notice.

The silence only lasted a moment, long enough to bring Wærmund's heart near to breaking. Slowly, he got to his feet. He spoke out into the darkness towards the jeering voice.

All my life I've led my people. My strength has ebbed and my eyes are dark, but I am still the king. I only fight my equals. Tell King Witta I'll meet him in combat, if he'll stand to exchange blows with me.'

Mearcweard guffawed; his companions joined in the laugh.

'You're in your dotage! King Witta wouldn't stoop to strike you. Even if you could see what you're doing, there isn't enough blood in your carcass to redden his sword-blade. You've wasted enough of my time. You've heard your orders. Obey them.'

Without the courtesy of leavetaking, he turned to go.

'Not so fast, Myrging. You haven't got our answer to take back to your master.'

Mearcweard stopped abruptly, glaring round for the speaker. He did not like the sound of '*your master*'.

The words had come from a broad-shouldered man sitting near the door. He was well-dressed but his lowly place showed he was not of much account. Also, he was very young; he could barely have finished his weapon-training. He was likely showing-off in front of the older men, trusting that no foreign warrior would take a challenge from him and that his own folk would never let such a raw lad step forward in their name.

The youngster spoke again. His voice was level and slow, as if he thought of each word on its own before he said it.

'Tell your king to gather his tribute somewhere else, unless he wants it in spears, or a sword through his guts. That's all he – or you – will ever get from Angeln.'

Mearcweard sneered. 'Lip-courage! Stop yapping at my heels or you'll get kicked. You know very well I'd never agree to meet you in single combat.'

'Don't be afraid. I'm not asking you to meet me in single combat. I want a fair fight, so I'll let you bring a friend.'

Mearcweard nearly choked on the insult. A few seconds passed before he could answer.

'Very well, you young whelp. You'll get what you've asked for.'

The envoys left. No one else moved or spoke.

Then Wærmund said, 'Who answered for Angeln?'

The household was almost dumbstruck. He heard someone clear his throat and mutter, ' Your son, lord.'

'Don't mock me. Whoever he is, he spoke like an æðeling and he shall have an æðeling's place. Let him come to the high table.'

Heavy footsteps strode towards him. The slow voice spoke again, near at hand.

'I am your son.'

Wærmund reached out into the darkness. His hands touched a big, firm-fleshed trunk, broad shoulders, muscular arms. His finger-tips drew a face he had seen a little while before he went blind. He clutched Offa's arms and rested his head for a moment on Offa's shoulder. Offa felt him shudder and gasp once; he put his arms round his father. Neither wept.

The king straightened and stepped back from his son's embrace. His face was stern.

'Why? Why have you kept this terrible silence, Offa? How could you do it?'

The household had been asking themselves the same question. They listened intently.

'When I was a child, I watched two English fight a Myrging. He'd come into Angeln by chance, following a boar he was hunting. He offered to take on the two of them together but they chose single combat. Then, when he'd got one of them down, the other stabbed him in the back.'

Offa stopped. The household waited, puzzled, for him to go on. He seemed to believe he had said all that was needed to explain himself.

In his blindness, Wærmund's other senses had sharpened. He could hear in the tones of a voice what the speaker was not saying in words. He had even learned to hear what was said in the silences between words. He listened now to Offa's silence.

The Myrgings had not raided Freawine's land during Offa's childhood. If they had, the prince would never have been taken from the women's bower to watch the fighting. But King Eadgils had ridden out hunting and had never been seen again.

Wærmund had no trouble guessing the names of Offa's two childhood companions who had killed Eadgils against all the laws of honour. He saw the terrible choice that Offa had to make while he was too young for such a burden. If he spoke of other things and never mentioned the killing, he would have made himself a partner in it. If he spoke about the killing, he would betray his foster-brothers and shame Freawine. So he had decided not to speak at all.

That was not the worst. A brave and generous man, a king, lay in an unmarked grave, without honour in dying and without his rites. Offa could not right that wrong, so he had buried himself in a living grave, without respect or friendship.

And now, after paying his childhood as wergild for Eadgils, he had pledged himself to go alone against two champions, to wipe out the disgrace on his folk.

There was nothing Wærmund could do to ransom Offa's lost youth. He must do his best to safeguard the rest of his son's life, short though it must be. He had one week.

'We'd better start your weapon-training,' was all he said.

They hunted through their precious store of mail-shirts for one to fit Offa. Most were clearly too small. He burst the links of the two they forced on him, just by trying to breathe. Only his father matched him in size. Wærmund ordered his own mail to be brought out. That masterpiece of smith's work was unwrapped from the oiled cloths in which it had lain for years. They got his arms in without straining. Offa said patiently that the byrnie would serve him very well. Wærmund passed his hands over his son's body and found that he was slightly hunching his shoulders and hollowing his chest.

'Cut it open down the left side and fasten it with straps. He'll have to cover the gap with his shield.'

The best swordsman in the war-band began to teach Offa the simplest lessons of sword-play, not to swing wildly, wasting his strength, missing his blows and leaving himself wide open to his enemy. The swordsman was used to callow boys threshing about; he got a surprise.

Offa had spent years watching Freawine's young warriors at their weapon-training, storing up every word and move. He knew how to hold a sword and where to aim his strokes. But he was desperately slow.

The swordsman struggled to find words to let Wærmund see something he himself had never seen before.

'Watching him is like listening to a scop reciting a lay about some old hero-fight. Offa's strong enough to kill a man with one blow and he knows just how to do it. But it's all thought-out, like a scop choosing the best words and linking them together. He takes too much time over it.'

Offa had too little time.

'Well, if he knows what to do with a sword, set two or three men on to him at once,' said Wærmund grimly. 'Don't give him time to think.'

There was another deadly flaw in Offa's swordsmanship, as well as his habit of stopping to think out every move. He could kill a man with one blow; he could also destroy a sword at one blow, he struck with such force. If he did not kill his man at once, he would likely leave himself weaponless.

'There was a sword worthy of him,' said Wærmund '– if I can still find it – if the rust hasn't eaten it already in its grave'.

He told them, as best he could, the way he had gone out on to the moors with Stedefæst. They found the barrow at last; his fingers groped for the runes on the stone. They counted the paces till they came to the right tree; his fingers scrabbled among its roots. They dug where he told them and Stedefæst was lifted into the light. The blade was already rusted; the swordsmith promised to do his best with it.

Wærmund forbade Offa to practise with it. 'If Stedefæst is broken before the deathblow, there's not another sword on Middle Earth that can help you.'

Messengers from Angeln had already gone to King Witta, to fix the meeting-place, on an island in the Eider between the English and Myrging lands. At that place the current rushed so fiercely through the Monster-Gate that there was neither bridge nor ford. The island could only be reached by boat, so there would be no danger that either side could get sudden help from friends on the river-bank.

The English envoys pledged themselves, in the name of King Wærmund and the Angelcynn, to keep the terms. If their man lost, they would yield their borderlands up to ten miles north of the Eider and pay wergild to the Myrgings. If he won, they would keep their lands and take as much wergild from the Myrgings as the Myrgings had claimed from them. They would also take hostages for peace-keeping. The fight would take place under the eyes and judgement of the Swabian king.

Witta was a shrewd man. He noted that the English had slightly shifted the moot-point from his claim of overlordship to a quarrel between English and Myrgings, with himself as the wise fair-minded judge. He liked the part. He felt he was heir to the dignity of the Roman Kaisers in the old times. He let the terms pass. Whatever the English said would make no difference. Everyone knew how the fight must end.

When Wærmund and Offa came down to the ferry-boat, both banks of the Eider were crowded where they overlooked the island. King Witta's high seat had been brought on a wagon; he sat there enthroned, looking over the heads of his warband. The Myrgings had come in throngs to cheer for the death of the English prince and the humbling of Angeln. On the English side, a good many nobles and warriors had come, heavy-hearted, out of loyalty to Wærmund. The farming folk were keeping well away, guessing that the Myrgings would be across the river once Offa fell.

Some strangers had arrived – Wærnas, Jutes, Frisians – drawn by curiosity, pity, or the sheer huntsman's joy of seeing a creature bayed and done to death. There were wild stories about Offa going from mouth to mouth, to give spice to the entertainment. Was he really a lack-wit? A mute? Was that huge young warrior really the old king's son – or Thunor in his shape, come to help the English? Even the members of Wærmund's own household, who had seen him and spoken with him, did not know what to make of Offa or what to expect of him.

Wærmund reached for his son's sword-hand, to touch it in farewell. He found it was holding a drawn sword; he cried out in alarm.

'That's not Stedefæst! What have you done with him?'

'He's in my scabbard, behind my shield.'

Offa sounded more cheerful than Wærmund had ever heard him.

'I mean to fight fair. There's no reason why I shouldn't be fair to myself as well as to the Myrgings. I can only use one sword and hit one of them at a time. Even if I've got a weapon for each of them, I'll still be holding our border single-handed.'

He stepped into the ferry-boat. Wærmund's boy led the king to his own chosen place. A stream came down into the Eider, just north of the island. It was wide and swift enough to need a foot-bridge. When they stood on the bridge, the boy would have a clear view of the fight and could describe it to his lord, undisturbed by shouts and scuffling.

Wærmund had another reason for placing himself on the bridge and telling the rest of his household to stand aloof on the bank, but he had not spoken about that.

The ferry-boat's prow grounded on the island. Offa stepped ashore; the ferryman pushed off, leaving him alone against his enemies. The two were already waiting for him. They did not budge, leaving him to walk forward and put himself within reach of their swords.

Meaca had come with his brother; he was looking forward to killing Wærmund's son with no risk to himself. When the English heard who the second swordsman was, they spat. Even some of the Myrgings, who had come to yell for his victory, muttered that no one could make a better second at a child-killing than Meaca. He had already slaughtered his kinsman Eadgils' sons.

The Myrgings struck at once. Offa parried their blades with his shield. He made no attempt to strike back. The brothers grinned at each other. So the rumours were true; old Wærmund's last get couldn't handle a sword. They set out to wear him down and bewilder him under a hail of blows. Fairly soon, one of them would get behind him, or his left arm would droop from the strain of their battering. Then they could run him through.

Wærmund had no need to listen to his boy. The sound of swords meeting a shield, never sword on sword; the roar of cheering from the south bank, the glum silence on the English side told him what was happening. He began to edge towards the far end of the bridge, where an eddy from the current swirling downstream had scooped out a deep pool. When Offa fell, so would he.

But it was taking the Myrgings a long time to tire Offa and break his guard. As a child he had run beside Freawine's horse, or raced ahead with the hounds in full cry, because no one had dared to let him ride. He stood in the ring when the quarry was brought to bay, alert to dodge at the last moment of safety, when the boar charged or the stag swung its antlers. Now, his big lungs were still breathing easily. In spite of his size and weight, he was quick enough to block the Myrgings' every move.

So they began to goad him, to draw his attention from their swords to their words, to make him so angry that he rushed at them and started to flail with his sword-arm.

They called him a mooncalf, an old man's sapless get, without the wit to wipe his nose or his backside, let alone use a sword. They told him his mother had made up for her husband's withered tail-tree by whoring with etins in the forest to get herself with child. That was why Offa was such a monstrous sackful of offal, he'd split her to the navel being born.

Offa had spent his childhood listening to Freawine's men talking about him. That had been worse, because they had not meant to hurt him or even knew he heard. They simply thought he was born a lack-wit and that being lack-witted meant being deaf as well as dumb. There was nothing the Myrgings could say now that could get through his guard.

The brothers had slackened their attacks to have breath for their insults. Offa used the respite planning how to separate the pair and deciding which he would take first. He chose Mearcweard, as the more dangerous, likely to give most trouble. Destroying Mearcweard might cost two swords; he would rather tackle Meaca, if he had to do it with only his shield and his bodily strength.

Having made up his mind, he joined in the talk.

'When I told you to bring a friend, Mearcweard, I didn't know you hadn't got any – that you'd have to beg your elder brother to stand up for you, just when he thought he'd found a use for you. He was glad enough to pack you off to the Swabians as a hostage. But you're not giving your new master much return either today, for the food and straw he allows you.'

Offa took in everything he saw. He had noted how much Mearcweard hated the word '*master*' and guessed that he resented being held as a hostage, was bitter that his brother had handed him over, even though he had no choice.

The words were spoken flatly, without much interest. Offa's tone said clearly that Mearcweard was not worth the trouble of losing one's temper. He stood looking at Mearcweard, bored, his unused sword dangling from his fingers.

Mearcweard could not stand him. He charged. Offa seemed taken aback, unable to move. Mearcweard swung his sword up, ready to hack through Offa's right shoulder and take off his sword-arm. For a moment, his own right side was unguarded.

In that moment, Offa stepped neatly to the left to avoid him, but struck out at the same time with a back-handed slash as Mearcweard, unable to check or change direction, hurtled past. Offa had placed his blow; the blade went in under the rib-cage, slicing through mail, flesh and guts. When it met the spine it was shattered but so was Mearcweard's back. He crashed to the ground.

Wærmund heard his boy cry out. The cry – almost a shriek – echoed all around him from the English bank. He stepped towards the edge of the bridge.

The boy yelled, 'Mearcweard's down! He's killed Mearcweard!' then, terrified, 'Take care, my lord – *step back!*'

Wærmund tottered – then felt hands clutching him. He was shaking but he let himself be guided. A small hand gripped his and kept hold of it. He knew he would have to take the boy with him if he drowned himself.

On the island, Meaca stared at his brother's body, struggling with his shock, his grief for the one man he had trusted – and with his fear. He had never tackled an enemy before without armed companions to back him.

He looked uneasily at Offa, who was watching him with no sign of triumph.

'There's your younger brother, down in the dirt where you belong. You got out of the womb in front of him, but you've skulked behind him ever since.'

Offa was holding Meaca's eyes, so that he was no longer looking down at his brother's body. He shifted his position very slightly back towards his right. Meaca, frozen by his cold voice, did not notice.

'You'd always rather let others do your killing for you, so they say. Yes, I know you slew King Eadgils' sons, but that was at a friendly meeting. They didn't have their swords.'

'And neither have you!'

Meaca pointed his own weapon at the fragment of blade, broken off near the hilt that Offa was still holding. He laughed as he darted in to the kill. Offa dropped his useless weapon. Meaca lunged forward. Offa chose his moment to draw Stedefæst; the gold and garnets on the hilt flamed across Meaca's eyes in the noon-day sun.

Meaca stumbled. He had killed his kin, it was just that his kin should help Offa to kill him. He tripped over Mearcweard's feet and spitted himself on Stedefæst.

King Witta, glad to show himself unconcerned in the Myrgings' defeat, played his part as fair-minded judge of the combat and forbade any more fighting. He sent some of his men to fetch the corpses and hand them over to their own people. The Myrgings would not be needing another chief; he would take care of their land. He would deal with the English another time.

When Wærmund's men came for Offa, they found him by the southern shore of the island, drawing Stedefæst's blade through the Eider. He lifted the glittering sword, clean of Meaca's blood, to greet them.

'I've just drawn our border. The boundary-line stays here.'

'Ne læt þu þec siþþan siþes getwæfan,
lade gelettan lifgendne monn.
Ongin mere secan, mæwes eþel,
onsite sænacan, þæt þu suð heonan
ofer merelade monnan findest.'

The Husband's Message

(From now on, don't let any living man hold you back from
the journey or block your way. Set out and make for the
sea, the gull's home, and board a ship so that over the
seaway, southwards from here, you may find your man.)

IV Rune-Riddle

Seafarers coming in from the west saw a line of islands and sand dunes. Behind that was a low coastline where the earth seemed to be melting into the water, a land of marshes and meres with ridges of drier heath beyond.

Folk who were jealous of the Frisians' skill in ship-building and trading, or who had come up against their stubborn courage in holding on to their gains, said that the Frisians spent so much time in their ships because they were drier there than in Frisia. They said that the Frisians had to live on top of their middens to get up out of the mud. They added that Frisians were born with webbed feet.

The men aboard the Saxon ship coming into the mouth of the Ems saw a coast so like the one they had left behind, that landing was almost like home-coming. The king of the East Saxons wanted to marry the Frisian king's sister. He had sent precious gifts in the care of his youngest brother to show how much he valued the alliance. He had also sent two of his wisest counsellors to do the talking when the bargaining started.

The strangers had been watched since they came within sight of the Frisian coast. As they passed between two of the islands that lay across the mouth of the Ems, a warship rounded the point to their starboard and followed them up river. When they came into the haven, the coastguard was already waiting for them, with a large and well-armed band of warriors behind him.

Young Prince Sigewulf grinned approvingly.

'Nobody's likely to catch the Frisians off-guard!'

The counsellors, Lord Ealdhelm and Lord Hereberht, looked at each other behind his back but said nothing.

In answer to the coastguard's challenge, they named themselves and said they came in peace with a message for King Frealaf. The coastguard let them land; he was polite but wary. He put watchmen aboard their ship, promising that it would be kept safe and seaworthy for them, but set out with most of his men to see them on their way inland towards the royal stronghold. Prince Sigewulf glanced back towards the river. The Frisian warship was pulling away toward the islands at the river-mouth.

The track was raised on a causeway above the flat boggy land. A mile or so ahead they could see a low hill crowned with a stockade. As they got nearer they could see that the hill was steep, flat-topped and so perfectly round that it must have been man-made.

Another band of warriors came down from the stronghold to meet them. Once more, they told their names and their errand. The coastguard and his men turned back to the haven. The Saxons went up the steep ramp to the gate, still politely shepherded, still under guard.

Inside the stockade, they noted all the signs of wealth and power – the roomy stables and storehouses, the work-huts, guest-halls and bowers. Towering over every other building was the king's great hall, high-gabled, with a deep porch and wide doors, all handsomely carved.

One of the hall-thanes was waiting inside the porch to greet them and learn their names, so that he could announce them to the king and bring permission for them to enter. Meanwhile, they stacked their spears and shields in the porch and sat down on the benches to wait.

Prince Sigewulf was nearest the open door. He glanced inside, careful not to crane his head too far in case the Frisians saw him gaping.

Everything inside the lofty hall was fresh and new, from the feasters' shirts and cloaks to the rushes on the floor. The carved beams and bench-ends, painted and picked out in gold, the white-plastered walls, the embroidered hangings, the emblazoned shields set up behind the feasters – all seemed to have just come from the craftsmen's hands.

He looked at the feasters, the king's hearth-companions. These noblemen of the royal bodyguard all looked new as well. They were hardly more than boys, almost too young to bear weapons or to stand in a shield-wall – except for a group of old men sitting at the top of the hall near the royal gift-stool. They were so old it seemed cruel to have called them to the king's council.

He turned to Lord Hereberht at his side.

'That's a strange company in there – nobody but grandfathers and grandsons. Where's the *duguð*? Why aren't there any battle-hardened fighting men in the king's hearth-troop?'

Hereberht sighed.

'You won't see them here. You'd have to go to the urnfield. That's where their ashes are, round the barrow that was raised over King Finn's pyre. It's five years since they were seen in hall. They died with their king when the Danes sacked Finnesburh.'

Sigewulf's eyes opened wide with excitement. He stared around in wonder as if he were looking at the Roman Emperor's palace.

'This is *Finnesburh*?'

'No! Keep your voice down, lord. Finnesburh is no more. You must never let King Frealaf or any of his people hear you say that name. While we're here, forget you ever heard the scops singing about it.'

Just then, the hall-thane came back to lead them in and present them to the king. Prince Sigewulf, walking at the head of the group on his first errand of state, was very careful of his dignity, uncomfortably aware of the Frisians staring at him. When he came face to face with King Frealaf, he had to fight with himself not to show how shocked he was.

Why, he's a child – he must be years younger than I am – he's not even as old as those boy-soldiers in his bodyguard. He's far too young to rule, even with the help of his grey-beards –

It was lucky he had learned his speech and practised it with Lord Hereberht; his lips went on saying it smoothly, without much help from his mind.

The king welcomed his guests to his court; he hoped that their visit would be as pleasant to them as it was to him. His manner was easy and graceful, he seemed truly glad that the East Saxons were to feast with him in his hall. He spoke mostly to Prince Sigewulf; he smiled and their glances met. Sigewulf felt cold. His skin crawled on the nape of his neck as if his hairs were bristling.

What was looking at him was not a child. He wondered if it had ever been young – whether it was a changeling, an elf or a thurs ages old before ever it stole into a human body. Even when Sigewulf had finished reciting his greetings and was seated in the place of honour, it was a long time before the fire's heat, the roast meat and the mead made him feel at ease.

Five years ago, Frealaf had been a human child – a boy wild with excitement because his Danish uncle Hnæf, his mother's brother, had come to Finnesburh for a Yule-tide visit. He admired and liked Hnæf, who was handsome and generous as well as a great fighter, like all the Scylding House.

With Hnæf came Friðuwulf, King Finn's elder son. Hnæf had fostered his nephew and trained him in arms. Frealaf loved his elder brother without envy or resentment. The pair had already planned their future: Friðuwulf was to be the greatest king that had ever ruled Frisia, greater even than their father. Frealaf was going to be the captain of his war-band.

It was wonderful to have Friðuwulf home again, a man of fourteen, at ease among the warriors. Even more wonderful to Frealaf was the presence in Finnesburh of Hnæf's hearth-companions, the finest fighting-men of the age. There was Sigeferð, prince of the Secgan, with the Danish lords Guðlaf and Oslaf. Greatest of all was the Jutish champion, leader of the companions, Hengest himself.

Hengest was already famous throughout Germania, not just for his courage (all Hnæf's men had courage or they would not have been his companions) but for his skill as a leader. It was said of him that he fought like a German hero and thought like a Roman general. Above all, Hengest was known for his *treow*, his unbreakable loyalty to his pledged word. Most men, and even some women, will absolve themselves from their oaths in a tight corner. Everyone believed that Hengest would smash his way through the gates of Hel's stronghold to keep a promise.

When Frealaf saw Hnæf's men strolling around Finnesburh, practising weapon-play, drinking in the hall, he felt as if the heroes of the old stories – Sigemund, Ðeodric, Offa – had come to honour his father with their company. He tagged after them like a puppy, eavesdropped to catch their talk, treasured every scrap of their casual, good-humoured notice. He worshipped Hengest in those days. He was going to be like Hengest when he grew up. He would have trusted Hengest with his life; but then, so would everyone else in his family.

And then . . .

There was some old feud, forgotten by all but themselves, between the Jutes in Finn's household and the Jutes in Hnæf's bodyguard. After some time of brooding and resentment, which they did not dare to show in front of Finn, the feud broke out again violently, with a treacherous night attack on the guests' hall. Finn's night-guard, thinking that foreign raiders had broken into the stronghold, rushed towards the shouting and the clash of arms. In the confusion, some of them were killed by Hnæf's men. Soon the whole royal household was drawn in to the battle at the doors of the guest-hall.

Frealaf woke up into a nightmare of flaring torches, clashing weapons, shouts and screams. He learned that his uncle had been killed by his father's men; that his brother had died on Hengest's sword, as the Jute stood over Hnæf's body. He heard his mother wailing over their corpses. He stood with her, watching them burning side by side on the same pyre, their heads crumbling, their wounds bursting open, blood spurting and sizzling as the flames bit into them.

A wound was torn in his spirit, as deep as the wound Hengest's sword had torn in Friðuwulf's breast. So the marsh demons, who always lurk round the homesteads in winter or wet weather, got inside him. Soon he was raving with fever. What he shrieked about Hnæf and Friðuwulf in his delirium was enough to break the uneasy truce that had been patched up between Finn and Hengest, after each had realised that the other was not guilty of starting the fray and that neither side could win.

Finn did not want any more trouble; Queen Hildeburh could not face another death in her family. So their daughter Freawynn took her brother away to the woman who had nursed her as a baby. This woman was very skilled in charms and herb-lore; also she lived on the heathland, where the marsh demons did not haunt.

At first it seemed as if the marsh demons had travelled inland with Frealaf. He seemed to have gone beyond the help of charms and herbs. He lay by the hearth, shivering and burning, talking to the demons. Every clank of the cauldron chain was the clash of arms at Finnesburh. The smoke and flames on the hearth rose from the pyre where his uncle and his brother were crumbling to ashes. Then, one dreadful time when only Freawynn was with him, a demon took Hengest's shape and came bodily into the house.

He could not move or cry out. There was such a roaring in his head that he could not hear what the demon said to Freawynn, who sprang up to confront it. The demon drew a sword – Hengest's sword – Frealaf thought: *here is death*. But the creature did not strike; it only dragged the sword-point through the ashes on the hearth-stone. That was worse; it was marking out death-runes, drawing out some hideous curse that would bind them till the end of time. Terror came over him like a breaking wave: he drowned in it.

When he came to himself, the demon had gone and so had the fever. He was soaking in his own sweat, pleasantly warm. There was no one in the house but Freawynn, standing gazing down at the hearth, idly brushing her foot across the ashes.

Spring was coming. He was getting stronger, beginning to want his home – until one day his father's counsellors, the old chiefs of Frisia, who had been wintering in their own strongholds, came grim-faced to visit him. They told him that the Danes had come to take the price of Hnæf's blood, that Hengest had avenged his lord, that Finn was dead with all his hearth-companions, that Finnesburh was a burnt-out ruin and that he was king of Frisia.

Frealaf knew that they did not want him as king – who in their senses would want an eight-year-old king? But he was Finn's son, Woden-born. More to the point, they already had trouble with the Danes and the Jutes: they would be having trouble with every tribe within raiding distance of their borders it they started fighting among themselves. So the chiefs held together. Frealaf was taken in hand and trained in war and statecraft by the grim old earl who had once led his grandfather's war-band.

So now, here he was, a man of nearly fourteen, a king in his fine new hall with his fine new companions. And all the time, behind his eyes, he was alone in the blackened ruins of Finnesburh among the corpses of his kin.

A richly-dressed woman, gleaming with golden ornaments, came to the dais and offered the mead-cup to the king with formal courtesy; he took it with formal thanks. Then she went to the king's visitors, to his counsellors and companions, each in due order. She had a greeting for every man as if he alone were her guest and she felt specially honoured by his coming. Hereberht whispered to Sigewulf that this woman was Freawynn, the king's sister.

She was a good deal older than her brother; she was Finn's first-born. Now, past her twentieth year, she was verging on middle-age. She was still very fair to look at, fair enough for the eyes of the young companions to follow her progress round the hall with pleasure and the stirrings of hopeful lust. They knew she had made a solemn vow that she would never take any other man as her lord until her brother had taken the rule of his kingdom into his own hands. Now she was free of her vow and could make up for lost time.

The Saxon guests also watched her with interest; they were looking at her as their future queen. She had taken the trouble to learn their names from one of the servants; they were pleased with her dignity and gracious manners.

The only eyes in the hall that did not look at Freawynn with pleasure were her brother's. By taking him to her nurse five years ago, she had certainly saved his life. She had cared for him devotedly ever since. But she looked too much like her mother, Danish Hildeburh.

Frealaf never spoke about his mother; it hurt him to think about her but he could not keep her out of his mind. The Danish avengers had taken her back to her own country. Had she been dragged away from his father's body, struggling and screaming like a war-captive? Or had she gone with her people willingly, because she could only see Finn and his men as her brother's killers who had got what they deserved? Worst thought of all, had she known the raid was coming, plotted it with Hengest, spent the rest of that blood-stained winter gloating at the thought of it? Had she welcomed the raiders into Finnesburh? He would never know because he would never ask.

Freawynn shared the same flesh and blood. She sensed that, behind his determined courtesy, her brother could hardly bear the sight of her. She was wise enough to understand why, and strong enough to pity him. She kept out of his way as much as possible, except on state occasions like this, when they were both armoured in their formal duties. Freawynn had not had much joy during the last five years.

Her duties in the mead-hall were now over; the men had settled down to the serious drinking. She signed to her maids and led them back to her own bower. A trader was waiting for her there, with bales of bright silks, stiffly-embroidered brocades and cobweb-fine linens from the Greek lands in the south. She was known among the merchants as a lavish buyer. Frealaf liked her to go splendid, to adorn his hall, to show off Frisia's wealth and power; also, and mostly, to soothe his guilt for loathing her.

Freawynn always had a welcome for traders, for their news as well as their goods. She was eager to know what was going on around Middle Earth: what great deeds were being done by which heroes; what exiles were carving themselves new kingdoms out of the ruins of the Roman Empire.

The trader chattered away, praising his wares, waving his arms like a juggler, unfurling his silks like banners, making great play with his tally-sticks. When the haggling was over and he took his leave, he was very insistent that she should lay her brocade carefully in her chest herself, smoothing it flat with her own hands; on no account should she let her maids soil it with their greasy paws.

She took his advice. As she gathered up the shining length, she saw with some amusement that, in spite of all his warnings to her to take care of the stuff, he had left one of his tally-sticks caught up in a fold. She drew it out carefully to avoid snagging the gold thread, glanced at it carelessly - and then sat staring at the five runes cut into the wood, her lips moving as she traced the marks with her finger-tip:

ᛋ ᚱ ᛠ ᚹ ᛗ

'Sigel . . . Rad . . . Ear . . . Wynn . . . Mon . . .'

This was not a merchant's tally-stick. The rune-letters did not spell a word. The rune-names - sun, road, ocean, joy, man - made no sense. They were cunning runes, they kept their secret; they had no message for chance readers.

Freawynn was not a chance reader. She had seen these runes set in the same order before - drawn with a sword's point in the ashes of her foster-mother's hearth. They were carved in her mind; she thought she heard them whispering to her:

'Sun-road. That's west, the sun travels west - no, south-west now, it's still early spring. Ocean. South-west from here across the ocean means Britain - the south-eastern point of Britain - Jutish Britain. That's where Joy is to be found' - *if I can still feel joy at my age!* - ' and a Man who would be joyful to see you.'

After five years? If he still remembers what I looked like then, he wouldn't know me if he saw me now. It's his own good name he's in love with, his 'treow', not me any more. He was thinking of his honour when he cut those runes.

Did he think he only had to crook his finger and whistle and I'd come running?

No. Let me at least be just. He's done what he swore he would do. It would never cross his mind that I would not or

*could not keep my word to him. A great chance a woman would
have of finding joy if she set out to look for it on her own!
Though I daresay I'd find a man soon enough – and rape and
slavery, if I wasn't lucky enough to get killed struggling.*

*If ever I go to Britain, it'll be better for me to go with a fleet
of Frisian ships and an escort of Saxon nobles, to be queen of
the East Saxons. That would be a new life for me, fit for a great
king's daughter. Frealaf can rule without me now; he's old
beyond his years, poor lad, and the chiefs have a habit of
loyalty to him. I'm the last relic of Finnesburh; he'll be glad to be
rid of me.*

That truth could still hurt. She winced, clenching her fingers
against the pain, and the rune-stave dug into her palm. She
opened her hand and read the runes again.

*And you, my lord, can boast that you kept true to your vow,
as usual. When you've waited long enough for me in vain, you
can claim your freedom from it. You can say I was the one who
broke faith.*

She threw the tally-stick into the fire and watched it burn.
Then she locked the brocade in the chest where she kept her
treasures: her jewels, her robes of state and, hidden at the
bottom, a leather bag. There, wrapped in oiled cloth, lay the
shirt of ring-mail and the sword that she had ordered her
father's weapon-smith to make in secret, as a New Year's gift
to Friðuwulf. He had never lived to see them.

The fire was smoking; she complained that it was making
her eyes water. She set her maids singing how the god Thunor
had disguised himself as The Lady and gone as a bride to trick
the king of the Frost Giants. This lay was ribald and very
funny. Freawynn laughed so much that her eyes watered even
more.

A few days later, Freawynn came to her brother while he
was hearing petitions in the great hall. Her favourite maid, who
was her foster-sister, came with her. The girl had her face
muffled in the end of her head-rail; she could be heard
whimpering pitifully inside the folds.

Freawynn made her carefully-prepared speech. Every word
of it was true, as her brother would find out when he checked
what she said. She would not lie to him to save her life.

Her faithful old nurse had been summoned to go on a
journey with no return. She would not be seen much longer in
the home where she had lived so long. Naturally, the poor
woman wanted her daughter with her in these last days.

Freawynn too had vowed not to be parted from her while there was breath in her body. She asked the king's leave to go from the court.

Politely hiding his pleasure at her absence, the king told her to take her own time and to choose her own escort. She was soon on her way, with her leather travelling bag, her foster-sister and the girl's two brothers, who were grooms in the king's stable.

Near the southern border of Frisia, at one of the Rhine mouths, there was a great haven, busy and loud with shipwrights hammering, merchants chaffering, travellers singing at the ale-booths, shouts from aboard ship to hurry stragglers ashore. One boat was just about to cast off, coasting south to Frankland. A little group of plainly-dressed folk, just arrived at the waterside in a hurry, stood haggling with the shipman for a passage in her.

Their leader was a slight young man in thick shabby clothes like a ploughman's. He was well-born, though; the shipman noted that there were warrior's braids under his hood, not a churl's crop; the tip of a battered old scabbard hung below the edge of his travelling cape; when he moved, there was the unmistakable clink of a mail-shirt. With him was a pretty young woman, his wife; a haggish old one, her mother; two sturdy servants.

The shipman judged his passenger to be the youngest son of some free-born land-holder who had too many mouths to feed on his farm. He thought the lad had better have stayed at home, even so. He'd have a hard time finding his fortune among the Franks with those four to look after as well as himself. Still, that was not the shipman's worry; they had paid for their passage.

North across the Narrow Sea from Frankland, there was a coastline of white cliffs and a Roman harbour where the Frankish merchants unloaded their wares. A Roman road, straight as a sword's edge, led inland to a Roman city, Cantwarabyrig, guarded by huge stone walls that had been built by giants in ancient times.

There was a new lord in Cantwarabyrig, a great warrior, stern but just. He kept good order in the city and all around, which made a pleasant change for the Cantware. He had spent the morning hearing law-suits in his pillared hall, which had once been the forum basilica. Now, the hearing was over. The claimants and their oath-helpers had gone away. The lord had withdrawn to his private chamber; the hall was being set out for the feast. Some of the war-band were lounging in the ante-room, whiling away the last hour of waiting.

A stranger hurried in, a new-comer to Cantwarabyrig. He was too late for the hearing, though he had only delayed long enough to take lodging for his women-folk and servants at an ale-house just inside the city gate and to ask the way to the lord's hall. He did not know he had missed his time. He tried to go into the hall but the warriors were crowding so close around the doorway that he could not push past. They turned to stare at him, scowling at his impudence.

The stranger was only a beardless boy in a shabby hooded cloak, stained with salt water. He had been through a rough time lately; he was limping, there was deep bruising round one of his eyes and on the cheekbone, the hand holding the edges of his cloak together had a nasty gash over the knuckles. He was no one important.

'So where d'you think you're going, young capon?'

The lad said quietly that he had come to take service with the lord of Cantwarabyrig. The warriors howled with laughter.

'Does your mother know you're out on your own?'

'Run away and play with your own little spear!'

'Can you manage to keep it erect for long?'

'Tried sticking it in anyone?'

'If you want free food and a job around the hall,' said the biggest man with the loudest voice, 'you'd do better to offer yourself as a fool or a tumbler, help kill some time for us – and time's all you're ever likely to kill, Pretty-face.'

The lad looked coolly at them.

'I see I've made a mistake. Sun must have got into my eyes. I thought I was talking to some of the lord's companions, not to some of his swine . . .herds.'

He stepped back, raising his voice to catch their attention before they could get their hands on him.

'But since you're all in a merry mood, I'll swap you a riddle for a forfeit. If you guess right, my forfeit will be to clear off – and the man who finds the answer first can give me a buffet as I go. But if you can't guess right, your forfeit will be to get out of my way and let me into the hall.'

The chance of clouting the self-assured little bastard at his own invitation was too tempting to refuse.

'Let's hear the riddle, then.'

'Tell me – what word is spelled Sigel, Rad, Ear, Wynn, Mon?'

There was a short pause while they tried saying *sreawm*. But of course, there was a catch in the question or it would not be a riddle.

'*Day!* The sun's road across the sky takes a day to travel.'

'What about the rest of it – the sea, the joy, the man?'

Another pause.

'It's a mead-hall at sunset! Look – the *sun* takes the *road* west and sets in the *ocean*, right? That's the time *men* sit in the hall and *enjoy* themselves drinking.'

They were sure that must be right. The clever one grinned at the lad, clenching his fist and choosing the place to hit him where it would hurt most. The lad laughed in his face.

'The rune said *one man* – and what sort of joy would he feel, alone in a deserted hall? Anyway, I asked you to give me a word, not a recitation. What's the word?'

The biggest man lost his temper.

'There isn't a word. It's just a jumble of runes. Own up, you slinking cub, you just made that nonsense up to trick your way into the hall!'

They closed in on him, cursing; but by now they were making so much noise that everyone inside the hall was looking towards the doorway. The lord had come in at the far end; he was frowning and asking what in Hel's name was going on down there. The hall-thane moved purposefully towards the jostling huddle, followed by four guards.

Word was brought back to the lord that a stranger had challenged the door-keepers to let him into the hall if they could not answer his riddle.

'Well, could they?'

No, they could not.

'Then let him come in.'

The lord took his place again on the gift-stool. 'Folk who make bargains should pay what they owe.'

The hall-thane signed to one of his guards to take any seax or knife that the stranger might have about him. He threw back his cape to show a very fine byrnie of ring-mail. From his battered old scabbard he drew a magnificent sword. In the westering sunlight its hilt flamed with gold and garnets; the serpent-patterns flickered along its blade.

Only a Woden-born prince had a right to own such a sword. The warriors stared at the shabby figure walking slowly up the hall. Who – or what – was he? He was limping, and he brought a sword fit for the gods. Could he be Weland, come to offer his services to the greatest swordsman of the age?

But that eye! – and he was wearing a hood! – and asked riddles that no one could answer! If it was the Shape-shifter, the Gallows-Rider, the Master of Death-Runes, what – or who – had he come for?

In spite of their courage and their well-tested devotion to their lord, his hearth-companions drew away from the dais as the eerie stranger came past.

Alone at the gift-stool, the Lord Hengest called up all his strength of will to sit calm and unmoving as he watched Friðuwulf's ghost coming towards him.

He had loved Hnæf's foster-son, had taught the boy his own swordsman's skills – and then put his own sword through Friðuwulf's breast when he headed the last desperate charge at the door of Finn's guest-hall. Hengest was barring the way, standing over Hnæf's body, cut down by Finn's men.

Hengest had set himself a price for Friðuwulf's blood, since no one else was strong enough to demand or force it from him. He had banished himself from Germany, made himself a homeless exile. He had kept nothing of his former life except his sword and armour – and one vow, that he had made in happier times. But if Friðuwulf could not rest under his mound without a higher bloodprice, he would pay it. Hengest believed that folk should pay what they owe.

The ghost of his past stood in front of the dais, staring at him. Hengest stared back, stony-faced.

'Ask me your riddle and name the forfeit you demand.'

'There is none,' whispered the ghost. 'If you've no word to give me, I'll go away and never trouble you again. What word do you spell Sigel, Rad, Ear, Wynn, Mon?'

Silence.

The folk in the hall held their breath; then stared in amazement as Hengest stood up and held out his hands to the stranger in glad welcome.

'The same word as you do, Freawynn. Our word is *treow*'.

'nu is se dæg cumen
þæt þu scealt aninga oðer twega:
lif forleosan, oððe langne dom
agan mid eldum, Ælfheres sunu.'

Waldere

(Now the day has come, son of Ælfhere, when you must meet one of two fates: lose your life or win lasting fame among men.)

V Rhinegold

The Lord Attila, Master of the World and Scourge of God, sent his spokesmen to the Emperors of East Rome and West Rome. They brought the same message to Constantinople and to Ravenna:

'Attila, my master and your master, has sent me to tell you to get your palace ready for him.'

However, not even the Lord Attila could lead his horsemen east and west at the same time. He made up his mind to bring down the eastern half of the Empire first. It was richer and nearer.

Meanwhile, he did not want the western Emperor to use the respite hiring German mercenaries or making alliances with the German kingdoms in Gaul and Spain. He sent his spokesmen to these kings of the west with orders to pay him yearly tribute and to send him their eldest sons, the heirs to their kingdoms, as hostages for their good faith. If the tribute was refused, he would come himself and take it. If ever the payment stopped, the hostage would be impaled.

For all the kings knew, Attila's horsemen were already waiting to come down on them 'like a snowstorm from the high mountains.' Their speed was as horrifying as their pitiless savagery. Each king decided that it would be cheaper to pay the Huns to leave them alone.

As to handing over their sons, though, each king cheated Attila as best he could.

Cheating Attila came easiest to Gifica, king of the Burgundians. He had a step-son.

When he led his folk across the Rhine eight years ago and set up his rule in the frontier town of Borbetomagus, the Vandals had already passed through, wrecking as they went. Gifica and his Burgundians came in as federates. The Roman government in Gaul – what was left of it – let them take the district on the understanding that they would hold it against all other comers. The Roman citizens already living there were resentful of their new protectors but helpless, for the time being, to be rid of them.

Soon afterwards, Gifica married a Roman noblewoman with large estates, hoping to get a stronger hold on his unwilling subjects with the help of his queen. Lady Justina was a widow; her first husband had died fighting the Vandals. She had two children: a girl of nine years and a boy of five. Most kings would have seen to it that these children died fairly soon, before the boy was old enough to make trouble, or the girl could breed a claimant to her father's estates.

Gifica was a just man and, when he was off the battlefield, good-humoured. He respected his queen and wanted his home life to be cheerful. He took his step-children into his household and treated them kindly. The girl would marry one of his nobles; the boy would inherit a good share of his father's land.

When Romans did not hate or despise Germans, they often thought higher of them than of their own people. They admired the barbarians for their splendid bodies, their courage and fighting skills, their frank hearty manners, above all for the strong bonds of love and loyalty between the chiefs and their war-bands.

Little Quintinus Constans could hardly remember his father. He grew up devoted to Gifica, who had not beggared or enslaved him but treated him as a son. With all the fearsome determination of his Roman soul, he set out to make himself into a Burgundian warrior. He would be the king's loyal hearth-companion, a faithful elder kinsman and shield-friend to his baby half-brother Guðhere. In his dreams, he held the Burgundian shield-wall from breaking in a last stand or died heading the last charge in some great battle that would be sung till the end of the world.

Constans was sturdy; not very tall but with big bones and powerful muscles. He had his mother's black eyes and hair. Thick eyebrows, nearly meeting over a nose that grew more like an eagle's beak as he got older, made him look as if he was always frowning.

The Burgundian warriors' sons who lived, played and fought with him in the king's household all treated him with respect. He was serious but not bad-tempered. Also, he could out-do them at any feat of arms. They called him '*Hæg-ðorn*' because he was like a hawthorn hedge – spiky and unbreakable if you tried to beat him down but a trustworthy barrier between you and your enemies.

Constans was proud of his by-name. It was a compliment; also it made him feel Burgundian born. In time, no one used his Roman name any more. He was 'Hagena', even to his mother.

When Gifica was told of the Hunnic threat, he sent for his step-son. He talked to the boy, man-to-man, a king taking counsel with his trustiest warrior. Would Hagena undertake this dangerous task and go to the Huns in his young brother's place? Would he live up to his name and make himself a thorn-hedge indeed, standing alone between his folk and their Hunnic foes?

Hagena would.

He bound himself to be true to Guðhere, his future king, as long as he lived. He swore to shield him from every danger at the cost of his own life. No other cause would ever count for more with him than the claims of his brother and his lord. He called on all the gods and powers of the three worlds to bear witness to his vow.

Guðhere was now seven years old. He was brought in to hear the oath-taking. He never took his eyes off Hagena. He could not understand all that was going on but he did gather that his dark rather frightening elder brother now belonged to him and for all time to come would have to do whatever he wanted.

Gifica wept with pride – and relief – at his step-son's truth and goodness. Hagena was smiling.

Tolosa was the Visigoths' royal stronghold, far away in south-west Gaul. Rumour of Attila's demands arrived ahead of Attila's horsemen. King Theodrid had time to make his plans.

He was not short of heirs. He had six sons and three of them had already come to manhood. He was still unwilling to send his eldest as a hostage to Attila. He knew that once Thorismund was out of the way, his brothers would start plotting against each other for the kingship. As a matter of course, they would join forces to murder Thorismund if Attila ever let him come home. Thorismund knew his brothers. If ever he did come home, he would likely bring a troop of Hunnic mercenaries with him.

King Theodrid did not want his kingdom torn apart. Before Attila's messengers arrived, he summoned Ælfhere's widow to court and told her to bring her eldest son.

Ælfhere had been one of his nobles, a fine warrior, brave and open-handed – too open-handed and much too fond of gambling. Wyrd was kind to him; she let him die in battle, fighting heroically beside his king. His debts were so many that his widow could not meet them even if she beggared herself. She dreaded that her family might be sold into slavery by the creditors. In desperation, she appealed to the king.

Theodrid welcomed her kindly but he looked most at her son while he listened to her tale of woe. Waldere was a fine-looking lad, about ten years old, a true Goth, tall and long-limbed, with thick corn-gold hair. The king noted that he was neither timid nor swaggering when he came among strangers. He looked folk straight in the eye and waited quietly while he sized them up. He showed promise of being a good war-leader; he had a princely air. That thought made the king smile as he offered his terms.

If the Lady Galswinth would let him adopt Waldere as a son, if Waldere would agree to go to Attila's court as a hostage, if he would take an oath never to own that he was not Theodrid's off-spring, then the king would take care of Waldere's family as if they were his own kin. His sisters would have noble marriages; his brothers would have places in the royal household now, with estates to come; his mother would be wealthy all her days – to say nothing of the honours, the riches, the lands that would be Waldere's when he came home.

Waldere watched the king's smiling face. He knew that this last bribe was an afterthought. The king did not believe he would ever come home.

But Waldere knew also that King Theodrid never went back on his sworn word. If he did what the king wanted, his family would be royally cared for.

He glanced at his mother's worn face. In his mind's eye he saw his younger brothers and sisters, hungry and shabby as serfs. Ever since his father's death had made him the man of the family, he had been trying to think what he could do to save them all from ruin. Now he knew.

'I'll do it,' he said.

The war-leader Chlodovech had brought about his brothers' deaths some time ago. He was ruling alone over all the Franks west of the Rhine. Then Attila sent his demands and Chlodovech learned, like his brothers, how it felt to be caught in a trap.

His first-born and only son, Merovech, was still at the breast. He had come after seven years of miscarriages, still-births and boys who had died of fever, lung-disease or the bloody flux before they had lived a year.

Chlodovech cursed himself for not sending his wife back to her family years ago and taking another queen. But she was a Thuringian princess; that folk made bad enemies. Also, he had hoped to use a son of hers, in time to come, against her kin and take Thuringia. So he had kept her.

His patience had been rewarded when Merovech was born and lasted through his first summer and winter. The boy was sturdy and full of life, the king's most precious treasure. And now that treasure was demanded by the Huns.

It was not likely that Merovech could live through the fearsome journey to the east. If he did survive the road to Attila's camp, he certainly would not last long after he reached it.

Huns were not fully human. Their forefathers had been spawned by hel-runing Gothic witches, coupling with trolls in the eastern wastelands. Whenever the Huns took a Roman city, it was known that they cut open every childing woman they caught and ate the unborn babies. Chlodovech foresaw little Merovech served as a tasty morsel to Attila – yet if he refused to send his heir, the Huns would come and destroy the whole Frankish race, Merovech among them.

The king had several other sons, by his mistresses and slave-girls. None of them had the makings of a prince. He would have sent any promising lads to be fostered among his nobles and brought up to be war-leaders, so that if need be he could have chosen an heir from among them. He knew he could not hope to pass one of his bastards off on Attila as a royal Frank. Also, he could not be sure of any one of them not to blab the truth as soon as he got to Hunland, from fear or stupidity or the hope of gain.

He could not make any of his cousins give him one of their sons to go instead of Merovech. He knew his kinsmen. They would turn on him at the first hint of need or weakness.

For some days, Chlodovech brooded by himself over ways of saving his son without openly defying the Huns. He could see none. The time for thinking was almost past. He sent for a few of his counsellors, old shield-friends he could trust. They came to the Roman merchant's house in Turnacum that he had taken as his palace. They were led into a small room facing the inner courtyard. The king sent the servants out of earshot.

They talked over the chances of finding someone fit to take Merovech's place, the risk of being caught trying to cheat Attila. At last, the king said gloomily that he could see no way out but to send Merovech to the Huns. He must leave it to Wyrd – now that the queen's bad luck in rearing boys seemed to be broken – that he would soon get another living child.

'You've already got another living child.'

None of the counsellors had said a word. Whoever had spoken was at the king's back. He swung round, gripping the hilt of his hand-seax. There was nothing behind him except a weapon-chest. He bent over it, then reached into the space between the chest and the wall. He pulled up a thin arm, then dragged out the scrawny body of his daughter Hildegyð. He glared at her.

'You skulking bitch! How dare you come spying in here!'

She glared back at him.

'I've a right to know what's happening! I'm your eldest child. You always talk as if Merovech were the only one. What about me?'

'Are you stupid as well as shameless? You've overheard all we said. You know it's no concern of yours. Attila wants my son.'

'He wants your eldest, your heir. I'm the eldest. I was your heir till Merovech was born. If he dies on the journey – you said yourself he'd surely die on the journey – I'll be your heir again.'

She smiled, sure of herself.

'I know you've made plans about that, long ago. I heard you once telling Lord Guntram that I'd have to marry cousin Charibert's son. You said he was a young swine but the best of the herd.'

'You hear too much for your own good. One of these days I'll slice your ears off. And if you speak so much as a word of what you've heard today, I'll break your jaw and you won't speak again in a hurry. Now get out, you've wasted enough of my time. If you can't help, don't hinder.'

She gasped as if he had struck her there and then, but stood her ground.

'Why can't I help you? I'd give my life –'

'Because you're not a boy. I need a boy.'

'I'm as good as any boy! I'm as strong as a boy. You let me ride with you and hunt with you. Often and often you've said you wished I was your son!'

Her father's face softened.

'Wishing won't change you into a boy, Hildegyð.'

'I could pretend to be a boy.'

He looked at her with sudden interest. She was eight years old, thin and wiry, with fair skin tanned by days spent out of doors. Her eyes were amber-brown but her hair was so light it shone more silver than golden. In her hunting tunic and breeches, she looked more like a boy than a girl. Men of the god-born Frankish royal house wore their hair uncut. A stranger to his court, seeing her riding beside him, would take her for a Frankish prince.

The girl basked in her father's notice. It was the first time he had really looked at her since Merovech was born. She was desperate to take first place with him again, to show him she was worth more to him than her brother.

'Remember the wolf-hunt last winter? I kept up with you all the way, didn't I? You kissed me after the kill and said I was fit to ride the Wild Hunt with Woden.'

He nodded. He had always made a pet of her. He had been happy even when she was born, pleased to know his wife was fertile, glad that a girl had come first to open the gate for his sons and make their passage easier. He had been proud of her strength and fearless courage. He had looked forward to the time when he would have a son like her. During the last few years he had kept her by him to show his gloating kinsmen that he could get a living child out of his queen. Then Merovech had come and he stopped thinking about her.

'I can hold the Huns off from our kingdom for you. Merovech couldn't do that!'

It would be a good four years till she showed as a woman and started bleeding – possibly five, she was so thin and boyish. In four years' time the Huns might have started fighting among themselves – or some of their subject tribes might have turned on them – or the Romans might have bribed someone to kill Attila. Anyway, if she could trick the Huns for four years, he would have built up his power in Gaul till he was strong enough to face them.

'Can I trust you to keep the secret?'

'Trust me! I'll keep it to my death.'

The Huns would kill her, of course, as soon as they found out how she had tricked them. Better to lose one girl, though, than his kingdom and his son. Still, it was a pity; she was a fine girl, fit to ride with Woden –

He would vow her to Woden, send her to her death in Hunland as a sacrifice for his kingdom and his royal race. Woden would chose his time to take her. And if she went

willingly, offered herself, that would make her a more precious
gift to the god.

'Are you quite sure you want to do this for me, my darling?'

'More than all the treasure in the world!'

He held out his arms. She ran to him and he held her tight.
She was sobbing for joy.

Each of the three hostages set out on the journey to Attila's
court in a glow of pride and self-satisfaction. That glow had
faded from all of them long before they reached Augusta, the
frontier city far up the Rhine, where Attila's troops had come
to meet them. As they rode further from home, they thought
less about the folk they had left behind and more about the
Huns who were waiting for them. There was plenty to think
about, all of it unpleasant.

Huns were vile creatures, sprung from Hel. They and their
uncanny horses could move with more than mortal speed, so
no warrior of merely human flesh and blood could fight
against them.

Huns were so hideous that the very sight of them would
freeze a brave man numb with fear. Their faces were shapeless,
their skulls were deformed, their skins were the same colour as
their filthy linen.

Huns were beastlike in their habits. They never washed or
changed their clothes till the stuff fell to bits, rotted by their
sweat. They did not know how to cook; they carried raw meat
on their saddles between their thighs till it was crushed and
warmed by their body heat, then they tore and ate it.

Huns could not walk like humankind, because they lived on
the backs of their horses – and probably mated with them, too.
They had picked up their speech from the dwarves or the Dark
Elves; it was not like any tongue of mortal man.

Their cruelty was unspeakable – which did not stop folk
speaking about it in sickening detail.

The hostages were relieved to find that the warriors who
met them in Augusta were Ostrogoths. They were Attila's most
faithful allies, but at least they were Germans.

The three hostages eyed each other, stiff and wary, like
young dogs of different breeds. Their tribes had already
clashed bloodily, more than once, since they moved into Gaul.
Huns were ogres in fireside tales but neighbours were everyday
enemies.

They were dismayed when Valamir, the chieftain
commanding the Goths, told their escorts to go back home.

The escorts protested that they could not go against their kings' orders to stay with their charges. The Franks refused to budge. They said that King Chlodovech had made them swear an oath to guard and serve their young prince Hildebrand. Rather than desert him, they would die where they stood.

Valamir shrugged.

'Just as you like about that. But Prince Hildebrand's coming with me and you're not, whether you go home or stay here for ever. It's my job to guard him now and my life to pay if I fail. As for servants to wait on him, Attila's got so many the boy won't even have to lift his food to his mouth if he doesn't want to. So you needn't worry about him.'

Valamir had the tribute of three kingdoms to guard, as well as their three princes. He had brought a large troop of heavily-armed Gothic cavalry with him. The escorts stopped arguing and left.

Attila had taken some thought for the comfort of his hostages. He had sent a large Hunnic travelling-wagon with a tented top, well-furnished with mattresses and pillows, embroidered coverlets and fur rugs. The hostages were surprised that the Huns enjoyed such luxury. However, they preferred to ride their horses. Valamir let them have their way, but he made them keep near the wagon, with the Gothic horsemen all round them. Also, he took charge of their knives.

After some hours, they stopped to stretch their legs and empty their bladders. At home, riding or hunting with their friends, the boys would cheerfully have pissed beside the track. Among strangers and under guard, their sense of dignity – with some shyness and a feeling of wariness that was on the edge of fear – took them into the bushes.

Waldere and Hagena stopped as soon as they were screened from the highway. The young Frank went on until he was hidden among the trees. He was so long out of sight and sound that Waldere went after him. Hildebrand was such a little lad; he could only just have started his weapon-training. He might have forgotten the way he had taken, pushing through the undergrowth, and gone wandering deeper and deeper into the forest, lost and frightened.

It was some time before Waldere caught sight of him, squatting among the ferns. The Frank saw him at the same moment, hurriedly pulling up his breeches while scrambling to his feet. He was not quite quick enough. Waldere gaped with shock.

'You're a girl!'

'I'm not! Don't tell lies. I'm not!'

Waldere shook his head.

'You're wasting your breath. I've got five younger sisters.'

'Don't tell anyone! You'd no right to come spying on me!'

Hagena's voice made them both jump. He had come in search of them; he looked vexed.

'No one's spying on you, little fool. Why did you come so far from the road? You'll have Valamir beating the bushes for us – then we'll all be shut up in that wagon for the rest of the way.'

Waldere turned to Hagena for help and advice. He was older; he looked like a grown man, he was so grave and thoughtful.

'The Frank's a girl.'

Hagena's eyes opened wide. He stepped up to Hildegyð, stared at her, then began to scold.

'Has your father gone out of his mind, trying to play a stupid trick on Attila, of all people? He could slaughter the whole Frankish race for the insult. Lucky we've only come a morning's ride on our way. Valamir will be furious at having to turn back again. He'll take it out on us as well, because of you.'

'You're not going to tell Valamir about me – you can't! My brother's only a baby – he'll die if the Huns take him away. I told my father I'd come in his place, till he's a man like you. I gave father my word I'd never betray the secret: I said he could trust me. Now, you're going to break my word, that I swore I'd keep till death! You've no right!'

She was sobbing with fury. Her great heroic deed, meant to win back her father's heart and keep it for ever, was going to end in shameful failure after only a few hours. Worse, it was going to end as a ribald joke. Men would guffaw about her on the ale-benches.

The boys were touched by her love for her little brother but they still thought she had taken on a hopeless task.

'It's no use, you know.' Hagena spoke more kindly. 'You'd have to give the secret away in time. You couldn't stop yourself, because you can't stop yourself growing into a woman. And when Attila knows you've been making a fool of him –'

He bit his lip. Waldere suddenly felt sick. When Attila found that he had been tricked by the king of the Franks, he would ask questions about the other two hostages. Each boy knew that he also was a cheat.

Hildegyð saw the guilt and fear on their faces. She read it as treachery to herself.

'You mean to betray me.'

She stooped to pick up her cloak, as if she had given over pleading and was going back to the road. She took her brooch – but instead of fastening the cloak at her shoulder, she hurled herself at Hagena, driving the long pin at one of his eyes.

'You'll never live to see the day you do it!'

Hagena jumped back, tripped and went sprawling helplessly. Waldere gripped Hildegyð's right wrist as she stabbed downwards at Hagena's face. She twisted, kicked, stamped on his foot, tried to claw his eyes with her free hand but he held her at arm's length, tightening his grip till her fingers went numb and she dropped the brooch.

At once, she lowered her head and fixed her teeth in his arm, breaking the skin and drawing blood. Hagena had got to his feet and came at her to throttle her. In spite of his pain, Waldere pulled her behind him, still with her teeth in his arm, and fended Hagena off with his other hand.

'Stop this, both of you! We mustn't fight. We've got to stand together against the Huns. Otherwise we'll ruin ourselves and our folk. We've got to keep faith with each other!'

Hagena stared. Hildegyð's mouth opened in surprise; she stopped biting and struggling. They looked at each other. Visigoth, Burgundian, Frank. Their folk were enemies. Their truth belonged to their own folk. Each had the same thought: how could they trust the other two to keep faith?

'We must swear to be as true to each other as if we were blood-kin,' said Waldere. 'We must make ourselves blood-kin.'

He picked up Hildegyð's brooch and drew the dagger-sharp pin along his arm, where blood was already oozing from her teeth-marks, till he had made a deep scratch.

'We'll drink from each other's wounds, so we'll all share the same blood. And when we drink, we'll take an oath to each other –' He thought for a moment. 'We'll say '*I swear, in the sight of the sun and the hearing of the gods, that I will be true to you my sister, to you my brother, and that no other oath or law or love will ever come between us.*'

Hagena looked worried and unwilling. He was thinking of his oath to Gifica.

'Only as long as we're hostages. I won't swear to any oath that might make me break faith with my king.'

Hildegyð sneered at him.

'Don't worry. Once you're home you're welcome to try making war on us Franks – and we'll thrash you!'

'Stop that! All right, Hagena – '*until I am back in my own land.*' Will that do?'

Hagena nodded. He and Hildegyð slashed their arms; they all licked up each other's blood and repeated Waldere's words that bound them to each other. Before the boys made their vows to Hildegyð they asked her name so that they could take their oath to her true self.

'And now, we must forget we've ever heard it,' said Hagena. 'She's got to be Hildebrand, even when we're by ourselves, or we might use her girl's name when we're in company.'

At that moment, they heard someone coming. Valamir appeared through the bushes, looking angry and suspicious. Hildegyð was pinning her cloak at the shoulder; he saw blood trickling down her arm.

'What Hel's mischief have you been up to?'

Hildegyð looked him straight in the eyes.

'I dropped my brooch. They were helping me look for it. I caught my arm on the pin while I was groping for it in the ferns.'

Valamir grunted and turned back towards the road. As they followed him, Hildegyð winked at her new brothers.

After they had made their pact, the hostages began to enjoy the journey. They had allies; they were seeing the world, setting off to have adventures and make a great name for themselves. Valamir was glad that they were cheerful and gave him no trouble, so he was good-humoured and easy-going with them and saw that they were as comfortable as possible.

They were travelling eastwards with the Danube, following the Roman frontier road. The Western Empire still held that part of the line, though the ill-paid frontier troops had taken their women and children into the forts with them and spent more time farming than patrolling the borderlands. Traders still came to the larger towns and the inns were still open.

Latin was Hagena's mother-tongue; his mother had made him talk it to her and read it with her priest. Now, he talked to local folk at the inns and forts; he took care to learn the name of every place they passed through. He also counted the number of days they travelled and tried to find out how far they went each day. He made pictures in his mind of the mountains and rivers they saw; he went past them again in memory each night before he went to sleep. He did not mean to be lost in the strange land he was going to, unable to find his way back.

He tried to make Waldere and Hildegyð learn their road home as well; he was already taking on the duties of an elder brother. But they took his lessons as a game. When they made mistakes, they only laughed at each other.

At last, the Danube turned south. They came to Aquincum and found it in ruins, almost deserted. They crossed the river and went on eastwards, into the wasteland.

The plain was bare and almost colourless as if had been hammered flat by giants. The sun stared down at them from a cloudless sky. Between the emptiness above and the emptiness all round, they shrank to insects. They felt their spirits withering. Two day's ride from the Danube, the horizon had vanished, except where a faint smudge of mountains to the north reminded them of the world they had lost. Elsewhere, the plain seemed to stretch to the ends of the earth.

They were not all alone in this strange land. Great herds of cattle, horses and sheep moved slowly across the grassland. Sometimes they came to clusters of peasant huts near wells. Once they were ferried, wagons and all, across a great river on rafts. And they caught their first sight of Huns.

During the last week of their journey, they had spent most of the time in their wagon, because they could not bear to look at the desolation outside. So they only caught glimpses of the horsemen who galloped up out of nowhere, exchanged a few words with Valamir, then sped away again.

They had enough time to see that these riders were not dressed in filthy rags, as folk said at home. Still, they were glad they could not see the riders' faces under their furred caps. It was bad enough having to look at their mounts. Nothing they had ever heard about the Huns' horses came anywhere near their monstrous ugliness. That was probably true about the Huns as well.

Waldere had the Gothic love of fine horseflesh. He almost worshipped the beautiful Libyans that the Romans bred for chariot-racing. One of his dreams was that some day he might be rich enough to own one. After his first sight of the hideous creatures from the east, he spoke his disgust at their great hook-nosed heads and bulging eyes, their huge rib-cages and skinny loins, long bodies and short legs. Surely they had been sired by trolls, not stallions.

Valamir laughed at him.

'When you know them better, you'll talk more sense. Hun horses are worth their weight in gold. They've carried the Huns to victory. They're as hard as rock. They don't need cosseting; they can be left out on the pasture all year round, come frost or snow, There's not an ounce of spare flesh on them. Those short legs can move like a whirlwind. Barrel chests mean big lungs – they can keep going for ever. And they've got sensible minds in those big heads of theirs. They don't panic. I heard a Roman horse-doctor say that when you learn to read their looks, there's beauty in their ugliness.'

The hostages, all keen riders, listened to Valamir with interest. His next piece of news was even more interesting, but it made their hearts sink. They were near the end of their travels. Tomorrow he would hand them over to Attila.

Along the way, Valamir had spoken about Attila's '*camp*', his '*palace*' and his '*stronghold*'. They were not sure whether these were three different places. They thought of their own kings' halls, built where enemies could not easily get at them, on high rocks or girdled with marshes or hidden deep in forests. They all knew Roman towns, with their thick stone walls and towers, the palaces and villas where some of their own kings and chiefs now preferred to live. Nothing they had ever seen or heard of in stories could have prepared them for what they found at their journey's end.

The Huns were nomads. They carried their tents, along with the rest of their household gear, in their wagons and set them up wherever they chose to stop for a while. Many of the households and clans who had followed Attila's grandfather and uncles into Europe still chose to live in their tents because they hated houses. Those folk who were ordered into Attila's presence, or who came to beg favours, also camped within reach of him.

However, some of the Hun lords had taken a fancy to the great timber halls where the German kings lived, who were Attila's subjects and allies. They had got Gothic craftsmen to build halls for them too, adorned with fine carving. These halls, with their bowers, out-houses and fenced enclosures, stood here and there among the wagons and tents. Lesser folk, peasants and war-captives, had put up flimsy huts of mud and straw wherever they could. This clutter of households had been set down on the plain with no attempt to defend it. There was not even a fence or a ditch to mark where the settlement began. Huns did not defend themselves in that way. Their defence was in the speed of their attacks and the terror of their name.

Valamir led his party along a rough track towards the middle of the settlement. Here the ground rose slightly. On top of the mound – it could not be called a hill – was the largest enclosure they had seen. The wooden fence had been cut to look as if there were turrets set all round it but these were only decorations. At the gate, Valamir told the hostages to get down from the wagon. Their baggage was taken out; the carts carrying the tribute were unloaded.

The hostages followed Valamir through the gateway. Attila's palace was in front of them, in the centre of the enclosure. Around its porch was the crowd that always waits outside a king's hall – bodyguards, petitioners, loungers, servants. Standing on the porch step was a man who blazed in the sunlight every time he moved.

They did not expect that Attila himself would be waiting to welcome them. This must be his hall-thane, some great lord of the royal household. They stared at him, bracing themselves for the dread moment when they would have to see the Scourge of God himself.

The Hun lord was wearing a wide-sleeved cloak and breeches of felt that were tucked into soft leather boots. The cloak hung open to show a tunic of heavy eastern silk, bright as a kingfisher's tail. Each garment was thickly embroidered with coloured threads, gold braid and crystal beads, in patterns of dragons coiling among flowery branches. Everything he wore, from the diadem on his neatly-cut hair to the latchets on his boots, was trimmed with plaques and tags of wrought gold.

To German eyes he was short, though broad-shouldered and powerfully built, but he carried himself well. His hair was jet-black, so were his eyes, deep-set above high cheekbones; his skin was swarthy. He was not so very different from the Romans in Gaul. He was not only human but lordly – unlike the creature sitting by his side.

This one was the Hun out of the tales and nightmares – the squat figure, the huge round head tapering up to a narrow cone of skull, the small eyes like slits in the folds of yellowish flesh, the flattened nose. His clothes were clean, but drab-coloured and without ornament. He wore no sword, so he was a churl.

So the Huns in the stories, that made folk shiver at their firesides just to hear about them, must be the common soldiers of the horde, not the nobles.

They wondered why such a man was sitting in the presence of his lord. Perhaps he was a reeve, or a tax-collector, telling over his accounts, though he had no tablets or abacus on his lap.

Then they saw Valamir kneeling in front of the seat. The creature squatting there was Attila.

Valamir was talking Hunnic but they heard their names. The huge head turned to look at them. In that moment, they knew why Attila did not need embroidered clothes and jewelled weapons to show his power and terrify those he dealt with. He was Power and Terror.

Attila spoke to them in Gothic. There was no expression on his face, his voice was low and toneless.

'So your fathers have sent you to me, as pledges of peace in return for tribute. They shall have peace, so long as they pay the tribute. I keep faith with those who keep faith with me.'

Suddenly, he struck the arms of his chair and screamed at them.

'But I will not be defied! I will not be cheated! If anyone tries to play me false, he'll have no more tribute to pay! I'll destroy him and everyone of his blood!'

The three young tricksters felt sick with fear, for their people as well as for themselves. They felt sure that their guilt was written on their faces. They tried to look Attila boldly in the eyes, as if there was nothing to hide.

Attila could see that they were frightened; he had meant to frighten them. He could also see that they were struggling not to show it.

He smiled.

'Your fathers have put you in my keeping. I am your father now. I will treat you as my sons.'

He put his hand on the arm of the nobleman standing beside him.'

'This is Onegêsh, my chief captain. He is training my sons in weapons and horsemanship. You will live in his household and obey him, as they do. But today, you will break bread with me and eat my salt.'

By now, they were bewildered. They went where they were taken and did as they were told. Servants led them to a small bower near by, where they washed, combed their hair and put on their best tunics, brooches and arm-rings.

Onegêsh came and led them back to the palace. Inside, it was richly decorated with carvings and embroidered hangings, like the hall of any German king. There were no long benches or trestle tables, though. The Hun lords, splendidly dressed like Onegêsh, were sitting on chairs along each side of the hall. Attila was on a couch in the middle. He was wearing the same drab clothes.

Their new master took the seat to the right of Attila's couch. They learned later that this was the place of honour. They followed Onegêsh like sheep and sat next to him. Today, they were being specially favoured.

Then there was a long ceremony of toasting. Attila drank to Onegêsh, who stood up at once and stayed on his feet till the king had handed his own cup back to his cup-bearer. Then Onegêsh led the company in drinking to Attila, who did not rise. Onegêsh drank from a goblet of wrought gold, set with jewels. Hagena suspected it was a chalice looted from a wealthy church. Attila's own cup was made of plain wood.

Next, the king drank to the hostages, one after the other, and they drank back to him. Onegêsh and the cup-bearers signed to them and prodded them gently to show when they should stand, when they should drink, when they should sit. Their goblets were filled with wine, which they were not used to drinking. They began to feel giddy; it was mid-afternoon and they had not eaten since early morning. They were worried because there were no tables in the hall. They remembered what the Huns were said to do with meat – and what had Attila meant by saying he would make them eat bread and salt?

At last, when the healths had gone round the hall, a procession of servants brought in tables, one for every three or four guests in the Roman style. The table-ware was gold and silver, looted from eastern cities. The platters were loaded with meat and fish of every kind, fragrant with costly spices, cooked with rich sauces and unexpected stuffings, served with freshly-baked bread to mop up the gravy. Along with their other loot, the Huns had helped themselves to skilled cooks.

Only Attila ate plain roast meat, served on a wooden trencher.

A boy about Hagena's age was sitting on the edge of Attila's couch, as far away from the king as possible. Two younger lads were sitting in front of the couch. Onegêsh murmured that these were three of the king's sons. The princes kept their heads bent and their eyes lowered. Attila treated his two younger sons as if they were invisible. Once or twice he said a word to the eldest; even then the boy did not look up.

Attila had said he would treat them as if they were his sons. They wondered what he did to freeze the life and joy out of them.

When all the food had been eaten and the tables cleared, they thought the feast was over. Everyone stood up and there was another round of toasting. Then everyone sat down again. The tables were set with a second course of dishes, differently and even more elaborately cooked. When these were eaten, the same drinking ritual followed. Then a third course, mostly sweetmeats, was brought in.

Evening was falling; the torches were being lit. By now, the hostages could hardly see straight or sit up in their chairs. Onegêsh gave some orders. Servants took their hands and led them quietly outside. Litters had been brought for them; they were carried through the dusk out of Attila's courtyard to another enclosure some distance away. They were taken into a hall that gleamed with embroidered hangings. The floor was spread with carpets and furs; silken mattresses had been laid out with cushions and coverlets. The servants unlaced and drew off their shoes but the hostages had dropped down and fallen asleep before they could be undressed.

When they woke up next morning in the House of Princes, their minds were still hazy. Their bewilderment lasted somewhat longer than the wine-fumes in their heads but also passed in time. At first, all their surprises were pleasant ones.

They met Ellak, the king's eldest son by the queen. When he was not frozen under his father's eyes, he was merry and ready to make friends. His younger brother, Dengizikh, was pudgier and looked sullen but was only shy. The third prince, Ultzindur, was a half-brother by one of Attila's other wives. He was polite but his eyes were wary.

The hostages were to sleep in the same hall as the princes and share their education. They all ate in Onegêsh's hall. His chief wife, the Lady Ai-yaruk, made much of the newcomers. Most Huns liked children, other folks' as well as their own, so they were in a fair way to be spoiled. As nearly everyone in the camp spoke Gothic as well as Hunnic, they could talk freely to their companions and understand what was being said to them.

There seemed to be as many Germans as Huns in Attila's following – Ostrogoths, Gepids, Heruls, Rugians. These did not see themselves as conquered races. They shared Attila's victories and loot; they shone in his glory. Not all of them were subjects or hostages. Some were exiles who had put themselves under Attila's protection against feuding kinsfolk or Roman assassins.

It was startling to learn that folk could feel safer with Attila than they did at home.

Another surprise was the amount of dealing, open as well as secret, that went on all the time between the Huns and the two Roman governments of East and West. Attila had Latin secretaries to handle his affairs with the Empire. One of these, Constantius, had been sent to him, at his own request, by Flavius Aëtius, the Roman commander in Gaul. When Aëtius was young, he had lived with the Huns and learned their fighting skills. He was said to prefer them to Romans and Germans as reliable troops. He often hired them, with the Hun kings' goodwill, as mercenaries.

Onegêsh saw to the hostages' weapon-training, in both Hunnic and Gothic styles of fighting. Hagena and Waldere already knew something about foot-combat with spears and swords. Hildegyð took to it with zest.

They began to ride the wiry little steppe horses and to understand why Valamir thought they were worth their weight in gold. They tried to handle the terrible, double-curved Hunnic bows. Only Hildegyð was ever really at ease with them. She proved a skilful archer; in time, she even mastered the trick of shooting backwards from the saddle while going at the gallop – and hitting her target.

The older men watched them with interest, assessing what they would be like as warriors when they grew up. Waldere showed promise of being a champion, like the god-born heroes of old. There was a lordly magnificence in his fighting, yet he could be prudent, using his enemy's weak points as well as his own weapons. Hagena fought like a Roman, reasonable and self-controlled, but sometimes he took unexpected risks that caught his opponent by surprise. The little Frank fought like a demon. If the three friends kept together, they would be unbeatable.

Everyone was struck by the powerful bond between the hostages. It was touching to see the care the two older boys showed for the youngest. They stood guard over him all the time, shadowed his every movement. When they camped out after a day's hunting, they slept one on each side of him.

The Roman, Constantius, wondered whether Hagena and Waldere were lovers and which of them had the boy, or whether they shared him. He could not be sure. Whatever was between them, their friendship never showed any signs of strain.

Meanwhile, the three had begun to feel at home among the Huns and had grown used to the sight of them. Huns were broad-shouldered and thin-flanked, deft and nimble in their movements. Golden skins could be as delicate as white ones; black hair could be as glossy as silk; slanting black eyes could shine as bright and kindly as blue or grey ones.

The three might have said the same about Huns as Valamir did about their horses: that their 'ugliness' was really beautiful. But by now they had stopped talking about *the Huns*; they only thought of Ellak, Onegêsh, Lady Ai-yaruk and their other friends.

They spent their days in mock-combats, horse-breaking or following the hunt. Their evenings were passed in feasting, listening to hero-tales and laughing at the antics of mimes and buffoons. They were very happy.

One day, Onegêsh took them hunting with him near the marshes down by the Körös. The hounds found a boar among the tangled willow thickets. The huntsmen cast about till they were sure they had him within their ring. Onegêsh ordered the youngsters to fall back before the bushes were beaten to rouse the quarry out. They were not strong or skilled enough to be faced with a charging boar.

The three made as if to obey; instead they rode round to the far side of the ring. They quietly took their station behind one of the Gothic nobles, a tall man mounted on a big German horse, hoping he would not notice them. He was one of the exiles, a prince of the god-born Amaling line, who had been driven from his own land by a savage family feud. Attila respected and liked him; Prince Đeodric was one of his greatest captains.

The three arrived just in time. The hounds had been working through the thicket. Suddenly the boar broke cover almost under their noses and tried to dash through the line of waiting men. The creature was huge but moved with such terrifying speed that it was on them before they had time to ready themselves. It brought down two foot-followers in its rush, swerved and slashed open the foreleg of Ðeodric's horse as it hurtled past. The horse screamed, reared then fell, bringing Ðeodric down with it. He lay still.

At that moment the leading hounds came out of the thicket. The boar, fresh and full of fight, turned to meet them. Ðeodric was lying in its path, crippled or stunned.

Waldere jumped from his saddle, grabbed Ðeodric's boar-spear and stood barring its way. He remembered what to do: he took the spear-shaft close to his side, holding it well forward with his left hand, gripping near the butt with his right. As the boar came at him, he dropped to one knee and aimed the spear-point inside its shoulder-blade, under its shields of hide. He struck true and with all his force but he was not yet strong enough to drive home a death blow.

The boar tried to break the spear or make Waldere let it go. Waldere was dragged around and battered against the ground. Only the length of the shaft held the boar away from him, so he hung on grimly, though he felt his arms were being pulled out of their sockets and his bones were being splintered. Hagena and Hildegyð had drawn their hunting-knives; they ran to Waldere, dodging round to keep near him and avoid the boar, ready to strike if it broke Waldere's hold. They all knew they could only fend off death for a few seconds more.

That was time enough. Ðeodric had rolled over and drawn his sword. As Waldere held the boar on his spear, Ðeodric drove his blade into its throat. Meanwhile the hounds had come up and flung themselves at its hindquarters. Other huntsmen had closed in with their spears and finished it off.

Waldere's left shoulder-blade was out and three of his ribs were broken. He was carried back to the House of Princes, where a Greek doctor set his bones and a Hunnic shaman gave him herbal potions and a charm against fever. So long as he was bed-ridden, Hildegyð, Hagena and Ellak kept him company at his bedside. Attila sent him a jewelled goblet to drink his potions. Lady Ai-yaruk sent platefuls of delicacies to tempt his appetite. Onegêsh ordered teams of mimes and jugglers to amuse him.

Prince Ðeodric came himself. He carried a sheathed sword with a richly jewelled hilt.

'They say that a gift-sword cuts friendship unless the giver takes a gift in return –'

He smiled at Waldere.

'– but you've already given me my life. Even Mimming is a small return for your generous courage.'

He drew the sword. The blade was even more wonderful than the hilt. Mimming was a seax. His single edge was honed so fine that it could have cut a hair in half lengthwise. His back was broad to give a crushing weight to his blows; his blade was damascened with serpent-patterns.

'Weland's masterwork.'

'It's a gift for a king,' said Ellak, without envy.

'It was meant as a gift for a friend – the dearest friend and truest companion I ever had. He came and rescued me when I was trapped in a dark and fearsome place.'

Suddenly Ðeodric's strong face looked haggard with grief.

Waldere had been ready to pour out his gratitude and joy for the wonderful gift. Now, he could not think what to say.

Ellak asked gently, 'He died, then – your friend – before you could give him the sword?'

'No. Vidigoia is still alive. He fights in the ranks of those who want me dead.'

Hildegyð looked furious. 'The filthy traitor!'

Ðeodric sighed. 'The one who most wants me dead is my uncle. He claims to be my king. Vidia might claim that *I* am the traitor, while he stays loyal to his lord.'

He touched Waldere's hand. 'I shall be glad to think that you've got Mimming. Wear him at your right side in case your longsword breaks in battle. May he always serve you faithfully – and may all your friendships hold firm.'

'They will.' Hildegyð smiled triumphantly. 'Nothing will ever part us, except death!'

Hildegyð meant what she said. She would gladly have died fighting to save Waldere and Hagena, or to avenge them. Yet the passing of time and the changes of the moon made her the first to leave the fellowship.

Seasons changed, years passed. Hildegyð began to feel out of sorts. She scorned illness; she refused to believe that any elf or ill-wisher could have so much power over her. She forced her body to carry out its usual tasks, while her limbs felt like lead, her bones ached, she grew more weary every day and sleep did not refresh her.

Then, one morning at first light, she woke with a start. Someone had stabbed her in the belly while she slept; her guts were pouring out of her. Before she could stop herself, she screamed.

Waldere and Hagena opened their eyes to see her sitting up with her coverlets thrown back. Her eyes were wide with shock. She was staring at the blood trickling down her legs.

Waldere said, 'You've turned into a woman.'

Hagena said, 'I warned you –'

'I haven't, I haven't! Don't give me away! You promised me you'd never tell –'

She had already given herself away. Ellak and his brother had woken up; the servants hurried to her bedside; the hall-thane who had charge of the princes' household came to see what was amiss. Hildegyð was wrapped in cloaks and carried off to Onegêsh. Her blood-stained coverlets and mattress were taken away to be burned before they could bring bad luck on the men.

Waldere and Hagena dressed hurriedly and went after her, followed by Ellak. The guards told them that Onegêsh had gone to Attila. Hildegyð was in Lady Ai-yaruk's hall and they were not allowed to enter. They kept watch outside her door, refusing to budge until they had seen Hildegyð.

It was not long before Attila appeared, his face like a thunder-cloud, with Onegêsh at his side. They were followed by some of his officers who had been with him when he heard the news. The doors were opened for Attila. The boys slipped inside after him. Attila had scowled at them as he passed but said nothing.

Lady Ai-yaruk was standing by a couch where Hildegyð lay. She had been washed, padded against her bleeding and dressed in a flowing woman's robe of crimson silk. She tried to raise herself from her cushions as Attila loomed over her.

'Don't move. Can you think of anything to say to save your life? Are you going to plead that your father forced you to cheat me?'

She reared her head like a wild young falcon going to strike at his eyes with its beak.

'How have we cheated you? You asked him for his eldest child, his heir.'

'I ordered him to send me his eldest son.'

'He's only got one son. When your message came, he was a baby at the breast. If he'd been sent, he'd have died on the way and I'd still be the heir.'

Attila scowled at the other two hostages.

'You knew about this. All these years you've been my guests, you've known she's been fooling me and you held your tongues. You're as guilty as she is – you're partners in the lie.'

They thought their last hour had come.

Hagena said calmly, 'We'd found out her secret long before we sat as guests at your table. We had sworn not to betray her to anyone and we don't break our word.'

Waldere added, 'We took an oath in our blood.'

Hildegyð stood up, her back as straight as a lance.

'This matter is between you and me only, Attila. I stand here for my father.'

'A woman cannot stand for a man.'

'A Hun woman can't – or a Roman – or a Greek –' Hildegyð was too angry to care what she said '– but don't dare tell me what I can't do! I'm a Frank, a free German! I'm a shield-maiden. We're Woden's daughters – the waelcyrian, the choosers of the slain! We decide which warriors can go and live with Woden in the Hall of the Heroes – and which will go to Hel!'

She stopped to get her breath. Her eyes were gleaming with pride and triumph; she had been carried away by the picture of herself riding the storm-wind over a battlefield. In another moment she would be telling Attila where she would send him. Waldere and Hagena were cold with fear for her.

'That is the truth, Lord King.'

Constantius the secretary had come with Attila. He was worried. Governor Aëtius did not want the Franks destroyed by the Huns just yet. He was planning to use them against the Goths. Constantius had to back up Hildegyð's claims but without showing his own interest and concern. He spoke as coolly as if he were making conversation at a feast.

'One of the striking things our Roman travellers noticed about the Germans, when we first met them centuries ago, was the way they reverence their women. *'Inesse sanctum aliquid'* as Tacitus says, *'they believe that there is something innately holy in women and that they have prophetic powers.'* And he remarked how much they hate sending their young noblewomen as hostages.'

Hildegyð nodded.

'Father didn't want to send me but I told him it was best, just for the time being. I shan't stay here much longer. Merovech is old enough to travel now. Father will send him to you and I'll go home to help him rule the Franks.'

'Maybe.' Attila smiled grimly. 'But meanwhile he's left his most precious treasure in my hands. I must be sure to keep it safe. I'll put you in the care of my queen.'

He went away, followed by his secretary and his lords. Onegêsh had a litter brought for Hildegyð. She was carried away to the queen's palace. She was too proud to cry out or weep but as the curtains were drawn around her, she looked at Waldere and Hagena. Her eyes pleaded: *Don't desert me!*'

They begged Ellak to help them get to her. He had been deeply interested to see Hildebrand suddenly change into Princess Hildegyð. Even in his father's presence, he had never taken his eyes off her.

Ellak told them that while she was bleeding no man would be allowed to come near her. When she was fit to be seen, he would take them with him to visit her in his mother's hall.

Attila had many wives but Erekan was his queen. She was a Hun princess and had borne him three sons. Her dignity was part of his own pride in himself and he made his other women honour and serve her.

Erekan was a very beautiful woman; Attila still enjoyed her body. Also she was shrewd and strong-minded, so he respected her and listened to her advice. She had a large household and a great hall of her own, where she entertained ambassadors and received gifts from the Roman Emperors and the Great King of Persia. Afterwards, in bed, she would take their characters to pieces and discuss with Attila how far to trust them.

Ellak led his friends into a scented room, its floors spread with patterned carpets, its walls hung with embroidered cloth. The queen's couch was on a dais, where she was reclining among a pile of cushions. A half-circle of women sat on the floor in front of her – well-born Hun girls whom she was bringing up, with some of Attila's lesser wives. They were embroidering the brightly coloured stripes and borders that the Huns used to decorate their clothes.

Hildegyð was sitting at the foot of the queen's couch, listlessly stitching beads on to a linen band, taking her first lesson in women's work. She was wearing a long tunic of finest lawn, under a wide-sleeved robe of pale blue silk, embroidered with peacocks that glittered as she moved, with the light from thousands of tiny crystals. Her hair was coiled and pinned up under a veil, bound with a gold diadem set with almandines. She looked strange; she was already distant from her friends.

When Hildegyð had first been carried into the queen's house and dressed in women's clothes, she had felt as frantic as a wild creature suddenly shut inside a cage. She had passed most of her nights weeping with rage, pulling her coverlet round her head and pressing it against her mouth in case the women heard her. If Erekan had been strict with her, or the other women had mocked, she might have taken a knife to them.

But the Hun women were kind. Erekan treated her with respect and wisely kept her on a loose rein. The other women admired her; they were also in awe of her, as a warrior-woman who was going to be queen over the warriors in her own land.

Hildegyð enjoyed being admired and feared. She was also too proud to like being bested at any skill. She forced herself to make neat embroidery stitches, to sing the girls' songs and move gracefully through the steps of their dances. If she still wept sometimes at night for the loss of freedom and brotherhood, she let no one share her grief.

Her blood-brothers did not leave her alone in the women's world. Ellak brought them with him whenever he came to the queen's hall, which he now did very often. They met his youngest brother Ernak, who was still with the women but would soon be coming to join the young warriors in Onegêsh's household.

Ernak was the only one of his children for whom Attila showed any tenderness. He treated Ellak with the respect due to a promising war-leader of noble blood. He was indifferent to the others. But he brightened whenever he saw Ernak. He would keep the boy beside him in the crook of his arm, stoke his cheek and let him chatter.

Ellak offered to take his little brother out riding with his two friends, if Hildegyð would come as well to see they did not tire the child or run him into any danger. These rides gave her a taste of her old freedom, a chance to fly hawks and to use her bow.

At first, Waldere would bring a sword for her, so that she could fence with him or Ellak, as she used to do in the old days. She soon gave up trying. She had lost her skill for want of daily practice. She felt she had gone soft; she could see that the other two were trying not to hurt her or to disarm her too soon.

Hagena refused to let her fight with him. He did not even want her to come out riding with them so very often. He was more Roman than he cared to admit to himself. He made it clear to her that these pastimes were not fitting for a modest maiden and that she had no place in men's company. She was no longer one of the brotherhood.

Hagena was the next to go.

The secretary Constantius had a liking for him, because he spoke good Latin and was interested in statecraft. A letter came to Constantius from Gaul. One piece of news in it made him seek for a chance to talk to Hagena in private.

Gifica was dead. Guðhere was king of the Burgundians. It was being said that at the feast after his king-making, he had boasted he would send no more gold to Hunland.

'Don't let anyone know I told you,' said Constantius. 'I shan't repeat it to Attila. It's only hearsay at the moment. You'd better be out of Attila's reach when he learns it's true. I suggest you make for Ravenna. With your Latin and your Hunnic military training, you could easily enlist in the army.'

Hagena thanked the secretary; then went away by himself to brood over what he had heard. He said nothing to his two friends but they could see there was a shadow on him and demanded to share his trouble. He told them, under their old oath of silence and secrecy.

Hildegyð was shocked and angry.

'You mean your younger brother's stolen your kingdom?'

'And wants to goad Attila into killing you for him.' Waldere looked sick.

Hildegyð gripped Hagena's arm.

'You must appeal to Attila! Guðhere's turned against him as well as you. Ask him for a troop of Huns to win your kingdom back. They could collect the tribute at the same time.'

Hagena shook his head.

'It isn't my kingdom. I'm not even a Burgundian, my father was a Roman lord. King Gifica married my mother after she was widowed. He was a kind step-father to me and my sister. I swore I'd always be true to him and his son. Guðhere's my king now, as well as my half-brother. I won't do anything to harm him, even to save my life.'

'Not even after the harm he's done to you?'

'He was only a child when he last saw me. I can't mean much to him, if anything. He may not even know I'm still alive – perhaps that's why he never sent to tell me about Gifica's death.'

'You must get away at once! It's not far to the Danube frontier. You can easily pass as a Roman –' Waldere checked and laughed at himself '– of course, you *are* a Roman! Pretend to be a merchant, say you were being chased by brigands so you left your goods and fled to save your life.'

Hagena said nothing. His face was stony with misery. Hildegyð shook his arm.

'Do you want Attila to kill you?'

'I don't want him to kill you. He knows we tell each other everything. If I disappear and then the Burgundian tribute doesn't arrive, he'll think Guðhere plotted with me to defy him. I'd be out of reach, so he'd torture you to death for keeping silence.'

They knew this was true. Waldere tried to think what they could do. He wished he could ask Prince Ðeodric for counsel – or even protection, as Attila liked and valued him so highly. But Ðeodric had gone away, to fight for his kingdom, perhaps to kill his friend Vidigoia or die on his sword. They would have to help themselves out of their danger. Suddenly, he made up his mind.

'We must quarrel! We must quarrel so bitterly that the whole camp knows about it. We'll turn against you, we won't speak to each other or keep each other's company. Then you can go off on your own.'

'But what shall we quarrel about?' asked Hildegyð.

'What we've nearly quarrelled about already. Hagena thinks it's wrong for you to come out riding with us now you're a grown woman. Quarrel with him about that, Hildegyð – insult him and I'll back you. Then Hagena can be angry with both of us. Go on, play a scene, like the jesters at the feasts.'

They stared at each other. It was hard for friends to quarrel in cold blood.

Hagena said slowly, 'It's time you stopped trying to be a man, Hildegyð. You make a disgusting show of yourself, and you're a burden to us, you spoil our sport.'

'How am I a burden? I never lose my hawks. I keep up with the riders as well as any man.'

'You can only keep up because we rein back to stay with you. It was the same with your sword-fighting. I've watched Waldere and Ellak trying not to get the better of you, in case you burst into tears. Women are all alike. If a pearl dropped out of your ear-ring, you'd stop a hunt in full cry to make them look for it.'

'That's not fair, Hagena! The only time Hildegyð ever dropped out of a hunt was to help you when you fell off your horse.'

Hildegyð burst into jeering laughter. Hagena's face was flushed and sullen.

'My horse caught his leg among the tree-roots and I fell with him. That was just bad luck, it could happen to anyone.'

'Not to anyone who knows enough to sit a horse and look where he's going. Would you like me to give you a lesson?'

'You're the one who needs a lesson, Hildegyð. You need to learn to act like a high-born maiden, not a camp whore. A good woman holds her tongue, keeps her place and doesn't meddle in men's affairs.'

'How could you know what a good *woman* does, Hagena – or a camp whore either? And will you ever be man enough to teach me?'

Someone guffawed. They looked round. Ellak and Dengizikh had come looking for them and had heard most of the scene. They, and their servants, were grinning with enjoyment. Ellak bowed to Hildegyð.

'Don't be vexed, princess. I'll be happy to ride with you whenever you like.'

Hagena scowled at him.

'I wonder if your father would be happy to know you spend your days dawdling at a woman's skirts. I've better ways to use my time.'

He turned his back on them. Hildegyð was trembling with anger. Waldere looked wretched. Ellak and Dengizikh told the story all round the camp as a huge joke, but the quarrel had been too bitter to die down at once. Hildegyð would not even try to make peace with Hagena; Waldere would not refuse to let her ride with him. They spent most of their time with Ellak and his brothers.

Hagena took to hunting by himself, on the plains, in the marshes between the Tisza and the Körös, away to the north among the Carpathian foot-hills. Once he came back with a boar's head; once with a dead wolf lying across his horse's shoulders. Hildegyð's taunts seemed to be goading him to prove his manhood by harsher and harsher tests. He would sleep out alone in the wild for nights before he returned to camp. Then one day he rode out and did not come back.

They hunted for him far and wide but no trace of his body, or his horse, was ever found. It was believed that a wild beast had got him or that he had been drowned in the marshes.

Next spring, the Burgundians sent no tribute. Attila said quietly that he would go to visit King Guðhere and settle the matter once and for all. However, he did not set out for the Rhine that year; he was too busy in the east.

The Emperor had made a truce with the Great King of Persia. Attila meant to strike them both hard before they could turn their armies against him. Also, the Akatzirs of the eastern steppes had rebelled against his overlordship. He was fairly certain that the Emperor had bribed them lavishly to turn on him. The Akatzirs were more dangerous than the Roman troops because they were a Hunnic tribe and fought in the Hunnic style, with hailstorms of arrows and bewildering charges.

Attila was sending Ellak against them, with orders to thrash them and then rule them. Onegêsh was going with him to advise him on his first campaign. Ellak picked Waldere as one of his chief captains.

Not long before the war-host set off, Ellak went hawking with his friends for the last time. Waldere was puzzled by Hildegyð's behaviour. She seemed to be trying to prove that what Hagena had said against huntresses was true. She insisted on bringing out a half-trained hawk, though everyone told her she would lose it.

And so it happened. As soon as she let her hawk fly, it wheeled away from the river bank, where the water fowl were rising in flocks, and headed for the nearest trees. Hildegyð galloped after it, calling to Waldere to come and help her recapture it. He followed, impatient at the loss of his sport. In his mind he could hear Hagena saying: *I told you so!*

When they were well-screened from the river bank, she drew rein and waited for him to catch up.

'I warned you, Hildegyð –'

'And now it's my turn to warn you. I threw away my hawk and made myself a laughing-stock so that I could talk to you in secret.'

He forgot about the hawk.

'What's wrong?'

'It isn't easy to cheat Attila. He keeps spies along the Danube and the Rhine, they tell him who comes and goes.

Hagena got back to his own land. He's at King Guðhere's court.'

For a moment he was radiant with joy; then he felt cold.

'That's wonderful news – does Attila suspect we knew about his escape?'

'No. He thinks Hagena foisted a quarrel on us so that he could get away by himself.'

'How do you know all this?'

'I listened to him telling the Queen.'

He stared at her; she stared back defiantly.

'You know Erekan has put me in charge of her household. She trusts me more than Attila's wives – she knows I won't try to seduce him away from her. I can come and go as I please at all hours.'

'Does she know you come and go as you please behind her bed-curtains?'

'Waldere, we're being kept here as hostages. I won't be treated as a mindless chattel. We've a right to know what they're planning to do with us.'

'What are they planning?'

'Attila doesn't want to lose you as well as Hagena. Folk would think his power was waning if his hostages could take themselves off whenever they chose. And he values you as a warrior. You're one of his finest war-leaders. In a few years you could step into Onegêsh's place. He doesn't want you fighting in the ranks of his enemies. Erekan said they must bind you to them for ever, make you into a Hun. You must have a Hun wife and get Hun children, so you'll never go back to your own people even when your father dies. They're going to give you Onegêsh's youngest daughter.'

Waldere was stunned. As Onegêsh's son-in-law, he would be exiled in Hunland for life. Yet to refuse the offered bride would drive Attila into a rage of suspicion. It would also be an insult to Onegêsh. Attila would likely kill him on both counts.

'They mean to hold the wedding feast before Ellak's host rides to war. Attila wants a great celebration to show he's sure of victory.'

'I can talk him into putting the wedding off until after the victory. I'll tell him I won't have the heart or the strength for fighting after bedding a beautiful girl.'

'But when you've won his battles and come back a famous hero, he'll be even more determined to make sure of you.'

Waldere sighed.

'At least, I'll have gained some time. I'll have to think of something else to stop him.'

'There's only one thing you can say to Attila to stop him giving you a wife. You must tell him you're already betrothed – to me. Listen, I've made a story for you. When we were young, our fathers bound themselves by oaths that we should be man and wife, to stop the ill-will between our peoples. They kept the betrothal a secret from everyone except their closest counsellors. If the Romans had got wind of it, they would have thought we were plotting to divide Gaul between us. They would have struck at us first. But I overheard my father talking to my mother about the betrothal, one day when I'd run away from my nurse and hidden in her bower –'

Waldere could not help smiling.

'– but I never said a word about it because I wanted to be a boy. I hated to think I'd be given to a husband and have to obey him. Then, when there was even more bad blood between your folk and mine, I hoped they'd forgotten about the betrothal or quietly broken it off. I've never mentioned it to you. But of course, when you tell me about Attila's proposal, I'll have to speak out for the sake of Ai-yaruk and Onegêsh. If you're already betrothed to me, their girl can never be your true wife and her children wouldn't be true-born.'

'Except that I'm not already betrothed to you.'

'We can do that now, make ourselves handfast to each other. That's why I got us away here by ourselves. Once I've taken gold from you and we've sworn our oaths to each other on iron, even Attila – even our own fathers couldn't make us wed anyone else while we kept faith. We'll be bound to each other for life.'

Waldere thought that their lives would not be very long once Chlodovech found out that his daughter had bound herself to the son of a poverty-stricken Visigoth, of no great name – and had told Attila a pack of lies about her betrothal. In any case, it would be a betrayal of her trust to let her bind herself to him without telling her the truth about his family. Yet he had sworn to King Theodrid that he would keep the secret.

She saw his doubt and unhappiness.

'You don't want me!'

'I don't want you binding yourself to me for life just to safeguard my freedom.'

'Your freedom is as dear to me as my own – dearer. I swore to you, years ago, that no other law or love would ever come between us. I let you drink my blood, remember? But if you're afraid of having me bound to you for life, you can always shelter behind Hagena's words: '*until I am back in my own land.*' Could you bear to be betrothed to me for that long?'

He could see that he had wounded her by the cold welcome he had given to her offer of herself. He did not want to hurt her any more. Hagena's words would shield her from the dangers of her reckless generosity. Trust a Roman to foresee how rashly-worded oaths could trap you!

Nevertheless, he hoped he would not need to let anyone know he was betrothed to Hildegyð. He would try every other excuse he could think of to avoid marrying Onegêsh's daughter before he led his troops against the Akatzirs. It would be the first time he fought against Huns; likely it would be his last.

If he lived through the war, he must try to get away like Hagena. His attempt would be far more dangerous. Attila would not easily let a second hostage escape; he would be hunted relentlessly. Still, whether he died shot through with Hun arrows or dragged down by a wolf-pack, Hildegyð would be free of her oath.

He pulled off one of his gold arm-rings and asked her formally if she would have it as a sign that she was willing to take him in wedlock. She put the ring on her own arm as a sign that she had accepted him. He drew Mimming and held him in a shaft of sunlight. They laid their fingers on the blade and swore to keep faith with each other as man and wife.

They had hardly finished the oath-taking when Ellak and some of his friends rode among the trees looking for them. Waldere was still holding Mimming. Ellak asked him, grinning, if he had been going to kill Hildegyð for spoiling his sport.

Next day, Attila called Waldere aside to talk with him in private. He flung his arm across the young man's shoulders and told him what a fine warrior he was. He should not be wasting his strength and his seed in slave-girls and peasants' daughters. It was time he married a noble wife and got sons who would be worthy of him. Onegêsh was ready to give him his youngest daughter. Attila himself would be his father and give the wedding-feast. No need to delay; he could be married and get his wife with child before he went to war.

Thanks to Hildegyð, Waldere had his answer ready. He showed surprise, joy, grateful devotion to Attila. He said he was afraid that having such a beautiful girl in his bed would blunt his fighting-edge. He would have spent all his strength before he joined battle; he would be dreaming he was still going into her when he ought to be thinking about bringing down Akatzir horsemen. Let him help to win victories for Attila and see his dear friend Ellak as lord of the Akatzirs. Then he would be free to do his duty to his bride.

Attila laughed, clapped him on the back and said he had the spirit of a Hun. There was no more talk about weddings for the time being. A few days later, Ellak's war-host rode to the east.

The fighting was savage and cost many lives. Their enemies were Huns, as swift, wily and ruthless as themselves. Waldere's horsemen had to strike far into the steppes. He had not known that Middle Earth was so wide. He saw strange rivers, seas, mountains; he learned strange names – Azov, Tanais, As-tal, Serai, Ural. Time and again he drew near the road to Hel-gate. Then, suddenly, the enemy grew tired of fighting. They had lost too many of their warriors; their chiefs were dead.

The Akatzirs were hard folk. They did not waste grief or memory on chiefs who died in lost battles. They were willing to take Ellak as their lord and follow him, so long as he led them to sack Persian cities and loot caravans on the Silk Road.

Onegêsh stayed with the new prince to see him firmly in power. Waldere took his troop back to Attila's stronghold. He met Attila himself, coming back loaded with booty from a raid into Greek lands and followed him to a triumphant home-coming.

As they rode into camp the well-born Hun girls, daughters of his lords and officers, came to meet the horsemen, dressed in their richest clothes, walking in rows under canopies of fine white linen singing Attila's praises. Hildegyð led the first group, glittering with jewels as if she were Queen Erekan's daughter. Her feet were moving and her mouth was uttering the song. Otherwise, she might have been a Roman statue decked out for a festival.

All during the welcome, the handing of wine-cups, the laughter and questions, the unloading of spoils and giving of presents, Hildegyð moved through the queen's house with the same stony dignity. Waldere could not win a look or a smile from her. He got her away at last by taking her to see his gift for her, a beautiful little Persian mare, that stood out like an ivory carving among the chuckle-headed Hunnic horses.

As soon as they were by themselves, he put his hands on her shoulders.

'Hildegyð, what's wrong?'

She held her head high as usual but looked at the ground so that he could not see her eyes. Her face gave no sign of thought or feeling.

'Ellak wants me. He's wanted me for some time, it seems. As soon as he's settled in his kingship, I'll be sent to him'

'That can't be true. Attila is always just to those who deal honestly with him. Your father sent you to him as a hostage for peace. You're here in trust. Attila will never hand you over as a concubine, even to his son.'

'As a wife. A chief wife, like Erekan. Ellak will make me Queen of the Akatzirs, far away in the deserts at the world's end. I'll never come back.'

'Dear, don't be angry, I'm not saying this to insult you. You know what Huns think about their blood. They'll take wives from every tribe they meet. But the chief wife has to be a Hun noblewoman. Attila wouldn't let Erekan's sons have anyone less, certainly not Ellak. He's the heir.'

'Ellak doesn't count. He's going to be killed soon.'

Waldere was shocked. He remembered that Attila had killed his own brother because he was jealous of his power.

'Murdered?'

'No. He's going to die in battle. Not just at once, in a few years' time. He'll never rule Attila's kingdom. The shaman read that on a shoulder-bone; then he went on a spirit-journey to see for himself. Attila is going to die in his bed at the height of his joy. His other sons will lose everything he and his forebears have won. That's why he can hardly bring himself to speak to them, he despises them so much. Ernak's the one who will win back the family glory. But because Ellak's a brave man and is going to die a hero, he can have anything he wants to make his time pass pleasantly. He wants me.'

'Your father –'

'Why should he complain when his daughter's chosen queen to Attila's eldest son?'

'But you said he wants you back. Your brother will surely be coming here next spring to take your place. He'll be as old now as you were when you came here.'

Her lips quivered. She made herself raise her eyelids and look him in the face. He could see that only her pride was holding her up.

'Waldere, I won't lie to you – or let you go on deceiving yourself. My brother will never come here to take my place. Father doesn't care what happens to me as long as Merovech and his kingship are safe. He stopped thinking about me from the moment Merovech was born. He's never sent me a word in all these years.'

She pressed her lips together to hold back a sob, then went on calmly.

'I'd have stabbed myself or jumped into the fire to win a look or a word of praise from him. I thought I could make him proud of me by offering to be his hostage. But I was just part of the price he was ready to pay to keep Merovech. For Merovech's sake he'd have strangled me himself as a gift to Woden, or bound me to a hurdle with his own hands to be drowned in the holy pool.'

In that case, King Chlodovech might be willing to give her to a seasoned warrior, who knew all the tricks of Hun fighting and had beaten Huns in battle. For all the danger he was going to bring upon himself by thwarting Attila's plans, Waldere suddenly felt light-hearted.

'Anyway, it's not for your father – or Attila – to say what becomes of you. You took your fate into your own hands when you betrothed yourself to me. I have first claim on you now before all mankind.'

She looked horrified.

'But I only did that to save you from being turned into a Hun. I never meant to drag you into my troubles. I can cut my own way out of them. I know a short road to freedom and the Huns won't catch me when I go.'

She smiled. Waldere knew she meant the length of her knife-blade. She laid her hand on his arm.

'You're not bound to me any longer, Waldere. Here and now I set you free from your oath.'

'You can't set yourself free from your own oath. You'd be mansworn if you broke it. You gave your word to be true to me and I'll hold you to it *till you win back to your own land*. I'll tell Attila you're my promised bride. If he sends you to Ellak, I'll go with you and challenge his claim at sword's point.'

She could not help laughing.

'You know what would happen to both of us if you said that. We'd better start planning our escape.'

'I've already planned that. And now, we've got to start planning a feast.'

Next day Waldere went to Attila and asked leave to hold a great feast for him, with all his lords and captains, in honour of Ellak's victory and the glory of the Huns. On the same day, Hildegyð would feast the Queen, the royal wives and the other high-born ladies. Attila was pleased at the flattery and gave his consent.

Erekan had always pampered Hildegyð. Now, she saw her as a daughter-in-law. She gave the girl a free hand with all her stores towards the feast. As Waldere had no wife to oversee his household, he needed Hildegyð's advice and help with his own plans. They were often seen with their heads together. Hildegyð went to and fro among the store-houses and helped herself to whatever she wanted.

The whole camp was looking forward to the feast. Waldere had let it be known that all the servers, attendants and cooks were to feast as well, when the noble guests had taken their fill. The common folk could share what was left. From the amount of food and drink Waldere had ordered, the left-overs alone would surely make a feast.

The day passed in unclouded pleasure. Attila rode out hunting in the early morning. He had great success and came back in a sunny temper with a sharp appetite. For once, he broke his custom and changed his hunting gear for royal robes. When he came across the courtyard, the sounds of singing, flutes and drums followed him from the Queen's house, where the revels were already beginning.

His great hall was bright as a rainbow with silk hangings. His lords, splendidly garbed and jewelled, rose to receive him. Waldere came forward with the cup of greeting. He was very plainly dressed like a servant. Attila stared in surprise. Waldere said, smiling, that he had awarded himself the place of highest honour – he was the king's cup-bearer for that day.

This was a novelty. The Huns were amused and touched. Attila showed his pleasure by draining the cup instead of merely tasting the wine. The nobles followed his lead every time the healths went round.

The tables were set and the food was carried in, piled high on gold and silver platters. The Greek cooks had out-done themselves inventing new sauces and stuffings; they had been lavish with eastern spices, especially pepper that the Huns loved above all flavours. Eating was thirsty work, but Waldere and his troop of cup-bearers kept the goblets filled to the brim with strong red wine all through the meal, as well as in the rounds of toasting that followed each course.

Minstrels came in. They sang of Ellak's victory – Attila's victories – the victories of his father Mundzuk – his uncle Ruga – his forebears Uldin and Kursikh. The Huns wept and cheered and drank to them all.

Mimes, buffoons and jugglers ran into the hall. The feasters shook with laughter at their lewd antics, stamped to applaud their skill. They roared themselves dry-mouthed and gulped more wine to quench their thirst.

By now, the whole camp was carousing. Waldere had sent casks of ale to all the homesteads and huts. For some time the hall-servants had been helping themselves in the porch and among the cooking-huts. The cup-bearers, except Waldere, were unsteady on their feet. Sometimes they poured the wine over the guests instead of into the goblets. As the guests were seeing double and feeling the floor sway under their feet like a raft on the Tisza, they did not notice. Many were already slumped in their seats and snoring; some had slipped to the ground. Attila had a wine-cup in each hand, he was calling healths and answering them himself, turn and turn about. Time and again, a man would stagger towards the door, fumbling at his breeches and lurch outside. These guests did not come back.

Far into the night, the torches and fires had burned out, untended. All was quiet in the camp, except the snoring. Here and there a shadow stirred – a dog skulking after scraps, or a mazed reveller trying to find his bed before he slept where he fell.

One shadow moved steadily through the camp, beyond the outlying huts and away across the plain towards the Tisza. A man, plainly clad in a dark felted coat and a furred cap. Likely some watchman who had stayed sober enough to give an eye to the beasts at pasture. The cattle were sleeping undisturbed. Now and then a horse snorted, or scrambled up and bounded away as the man passed nearby.

He drew near to a clump of willows, where another shadow moved to meet him – a young peasant or serving-boy armed with a bow and quiverful of arrows.

'Waldere? Is it safe to go now? Are you sure nobody followed you?'

He chuckled.

'Every man in the camp is as blind and deaf as a log of wood. They won't stir through most of tomorrow's daylight. Even when they do, they'll be too thick-headed to notice I've gone – they'll think I'm sleeping the wine off somewhere. What about the Queen and the rest of the women? Did you manage to make them dead-drunk too?'

Hildegyð shook her head.

'No. It didn't seem fair to Erekan and Ai-yaruk. I just gave them a sleeping-draught in their wine-cups. Once the mistresses were asleep, the slave-girls couldn't wait to fuddle themselves blind. I had all your gear packed ready. I got Lion and came away as soon as it was dark.'

She pointed to a couple of chests and a leather bundle under one of the trees. A spear and shield were propped against its trunk. A horse was standing by them as if on guard. This was Waldere's favourite, 'Lion', so named for his sandy hide and his courage. He was either the ugliest or the most beautiful mount ever foaled, according to one's view of Hunnic horse-flesh. Lion had the biggest hook-nose, the deepest chest, the most sinewy flanks, tireless legs and a great heart.

Waldere opened the bundle, which held his mail-shirt, his helmet and his swords. He put on the byrnie and the helmet, covering them with his coat and furred cap, belted on his long horseman's sword, and hung Mimming at his right hip.

Hildegyð had gone to buckle the chests on either side of Lion's saddle. Waldere bent to help her, swung one up and gasped with surprise at its weight.

'What have you got in here? Stepping-stones to cross the rivers?'

'No. Just what you told me to bring: cloaks, extra boots, bread and meat for tomorrow, fish hooks, some dried *fogas* in case you have bad luck with your fishing – and our wages.'

'Wages?'

'You've served Attila faithfully all these years, risked your life in his battles, helped to make his son a king. I've had charge of Erekan's household. You deserve a warrior's reward from him, I deserve a dowry from her. So I've paid us what I think we're worth. One for you –' she touched the lid of the chest he was holding; he saw it was marked with the ᛈ rune '– and one for me.' She pointed to the other chest, where ᚻ had been scratched.

Waldere shrugged. If Attila caught them, he would kill them anyway, for tricking him with the feast and running away. Whatever gold ingots or Roman coins Hildegyð had taken would not add much to their score.

He mounted Lion. Hildegyð handed him his spear, then jumped up behind him. They set out to find their way back to their homelands.

They knew that Attila had spies and informers on the Roman roads to Italy, and along the old frontier that followed the Danube and the Rhine. He would send orders to watch for them there. Yet their homes were beyond the Rhine and sooner or later they would have to cross it. They had only the faintest memories of the road they had travelled as children, Anyway, they would not dare to follow it since Hagena's escape.

Waldere's plan was to go north along the Tisza towards the Karpat mountains. Once they were hidden among the wooded uplands, they would turn westwards, trying to catch glimpses of the Danube valley to the south of them and following the same line. When they came to the upper reaches, they would set off northwest through Mirkwood, the ancient forest of Germania. However long it took them, they must come to the Rhine in the end. With luck, they would reach the river so far north that they would be near Hildegyð's folk and beyond Attila's ken.

They rode through the rest of that night and during the next day, with only the briefest stops for rest. They kept away from villages. The grass-lands seemed as deserted as ever. If any far-off herdsman glimpsed them, he would think nothing of a single horse passing in the distance. The hunt would not be up for another day and their hunters would not think of looking for them due north.

Even so, the fugitives felt naked to their enemies out on the plains. It was a relief when they reached the Karpat foot-hills and the forest wrapped them in its green cloak.

They travelled by night, steering by the stars, leading Lion and going quietly, following the deer-paths, keeping well away from any track that might take them into a village. When the sun rose, they withdrew into coverts, sleeping turn and turn about, while the other kept watch and Lion dozed or cropped the grass. They breakfasted at sunset and supped at dawn.

They lived mostly on fish, that Waldere caught and Hildegyð grilled. Fishing was a silent craft. Hunting made too much noise; they had not dared bring hawk or hound with them.

Waldere had believed that, even if they kept ahead of their hunters, they would have a grim struggle against weariness and hunger. He had been afraid for Hildegyð – her courage was as high as ever but she had been living soft in Queen Erekan's household for the last few years. The ordeal would surely be too much for her strength. Likely they would both die in the wasteland.

Yet the month he spent with her in the forest under the harvest moon was a time of hearts' ease such as they never knew again.

Sleep was warm and easy during the sunlit hours. At night, they walked through a green and silver world, sharing it with the forest creatures, who were not hungry at that time of year and let them be. A fine year had brought a harvest of nuts and berries to round off their meals. Hildegyð took her turns at leading Lion or keeping watch, light-footed and tireless. She was in high spirits, as if their desperate journey was a pastime.

One morning just before sunrise, she was sitting against a tree-trunk watching the light grow in the eastern sky. Waldere was stamping out the last embers of their small fire, so that there should be no thread of smoke rising from their hiding-place. Suddenly she laughed.

'This is like the old times, when we were brothers and warriors together. I thought those days were dead.'

She grinned at him. Her mouth was stained with blackberry juice. For a moment he saw her as the lad Hildebrand, five years ago.

'I can tell you now – when they first carried me away to Erekan and dressed me in skirts, I cried every night and bit my nails down to the quick, for grief and rage to be so trapped. I knew I could kill myself whenever I chose, but I never dared hope I'd live to enjoy my freedom again with you. We won't let anything part us a second time.'

Waldere smiled back at her but said nothing. Later, when he was keeping watch, he looked at her as she slept. She was curled up in her cloak on a pile of bracken. The sunlight dappling down on her through the leaves, made her braids gleam like silver.

When they reached the Frankish palace at Turnacum – Waldere was beginning to think '*when*' not '*if*' – she would no longer be a brother and a warrior. She would be Chlodovech's daughter, under the rule of her father and king. Chlodovech would not feel himself bound to uphold a betrothal that had been made in Hunland without his knowledge. He would give her in marriage as he chose.

Hildegyð sighed in her sleep and turned over towards him. He felt his body stirring. He could turn the betrothal into wedlock now, take her between sleep and waking, make the age-old excuse that her beauty and his longing had overpowered him. He could easily teach her to enjoy love-play; they were already dear to each other.

Yet he did not like the idea of taking Hildegyð unawares and without her full consent, even if her body took sides with him. And a greenwood marriage would be no surer tie than their betrothal. King Chlodovech could easily rid himself of an unwanted son-in-law. He might kill his daughter also, in case she had seed in her and bore a child to avenge her lover.

He must somehow make the Franks give her to him willingly. He would bring her to her father, still a maiden, as her rescuer and protector. Then he would offer to fight the king's champions for her hand. He would dare the twelve foremost warriors to face him in single combats, one after the other, in front of the king and all his folk. They could hardly hold back, with such odds in their favour. If they killed him, Hildegyð and her honour would be safe. If he won, it would be such a feat of arms that the king must welcome him as a fit husband for his daughter – or at any rate, be ashamed to go back on his word.

Till then, he would have to practise chastity. While he spent his nights tramping the hills or fishing and his days taking turns to keep guard, he thought he could manage to stay chaste a little longer yet.

The harvest moon waned; then the hunter's moon lighted their paths. Nights were longer and colder, though the days were still warm for sleeping. By now, they had come a long way north-west, though they had lost miles whenever they came to rivers, searching for fords because they did not dare go into villages to ask for a ferry-boat.

One night, near to full moon, they climbed the crest of a ridge and saw a river below, shining like a sword-blade. It was wider than any they had crossed before. At first, they both thought they had come to the Rhine. But this river was flowing due west.

'The Rhine doesn't flow as straight as a spear-shaft,' said Hildegyð. 'It bends east and west. It'll lead us north in the end if we follow it.'

They did so. Day was breaking; the sky was grey and the air was chill. The trees were thinning out. The ground was growing softer under their feet. They came into an open space and saw that the river they had been following flowed into one that was even wider, sweeping north with a strong current. They had reached the Rhine at last.

They would need a ferry to cross that great expanse of water. They could no longer avoid the risk of meeting strangers. There would be villages along the bank, that traded across the river with the Roman towns on the other side. Though they were tired and hungry after their night march, they went on but the going was hard. The bank was marshy and overgrown; there was no sign of a track.

The way ahead ended in a shallow creek. On the other side was a rough embankment of stones. A wide track led away to higher ground among the trees. A thread of smoke was rising there through the branches. By the embankment, its prow grounded in the mud, was a broad, flat-bottomed boat.

Waldere crossed the water first, testing each footstep with his spear-shaft. Hildegyð waded behind him, leading Lion. She looked at the boat, then across the Rhine.

'Couldn't we just take – borrow it?'

'No oars or paddles. Besides, we've no skill to cross a river as big as that. If we didn't come to grief, we'd be seen and chased. We'll have to rouse the ferryman and beg a passage.'

They went up the track towards the hearth-smoke. The ferryman had already been roused by the barking of his dogs; he was watching them from his doorway. He was a tall, sinewy old man with a skin like leather and a clamped suspicious face.

'Is that your boat down by the creek?'

'What if it is?'

'Will you ferry us across the river?'

'If you pay me.'

The ferryman looked at the jewels on Mimming's hilt, then at the chests Lion was carrying. He leered at Hildegyð, standing by Lion's head.

'You're not from these parts.'

'I'm a Goth, from the east.'

'So what are you doing here?'

Waldere thought it was high time to frighten the churl. He took a step towards him. The byrnie clinked under his coat.

'I won a fight. The man I killed had powerful kin. The chief listened to them, I couldn't afford the blood-price he set. So I've come to take service with the Franks –'

The ferryman glanced north, scowling evilly. So they had not come to Frankish land and were not among friends of the Franks.

'– or the Lord Aëtius.'

The ferryman spat. It seemed they were not under the Eagle's wings either. He did not think it wise to admit that he did not know where he was.

'Well, are you going to take us across?'

The ferryman grunted. He shouted for his boy, a rat-faced lad who had been listening behind the door, to bring the oars, yelled into the hut and was screeched at by a woman's voice, then led the way down to his boat.

As Lion was lifting one foreleg after the other over the side and humping himself aboard, the chests swung backwards, then forwards. They clinked. The ferryman and his boy glanced at them, then at their passengers, but said nothing.

The boatmen let the river take them downstream, with a stroke now and then to bring them towards the other side. Beyond midstream, a current drew them in to the far bank a mile or so northwards. Here there was a better landing-stage and a cobbled track leading inland. Remembering their childhood journey, they knew that the track would take them to a Roman road, to inns and walled towns, to chiefs who lived in Roman villas and called themselves federates of the Empire.

Waldere turned to settle with the ferryman.

'What do folk usually pay you?'

'With whatever they've got.'

He and the boy stared at the chests. Waldere had nothing to pay with but gold. If he let them see what was in the chests, they would bring their whole tribe after it, like hounds that have smelt the blood of a wounded stag.

'I'm an exile. I own nothing but my weapons. I can give you a day's food.'

He nodded to Hildegyð. She opened her leather bag and took out last night's catch, cleaned and wrapped in dock leaves. The ferryman flung out his arms towards the Rhine.

'He pays me in fish!'

'Caught and cleaned for you, all ready to cook. Our work pays for yours.'

'If I want fish I can get them out of the Rhine whenever I need them.'

'Not fish like this!'

Hildegyð reached to the bottom of her bag and brought out the *fogas*. The huge pike-perch had been gutted before smoking but its head had been left on. Having been smoked, it would keep for a long time. To please Hunnic taste, it had been pickled in spices before drying. Hildegyð lifted it up towards the ferryman and the boy. It stared at them with cold scorn.

'There's no fish like this in the west of Middle Earth. It lives in a great sea of fresh water away in the east. It's been soaked in spices brought from the far edge of the world. One pinch cost more than you could earn in a year! You must soak the flesh for a day and a night, then seethe it gently till it's tender. Then you can boast you've eaten a dish fit for Atti – an emperor's table!'

The ferryman looked sullen. 'Why can't you give me a jewel from your sword-hilt?'

Waldere drew Mimming.

'I always settle my debts with the blade, not the hilt. Be off! We're giving you more than your work's worth. If you don't like our fish, take it to your chief. It's fitter for a hall than a hut.'

Suddenly the ferryman smiled.

'Maybe I'll do that.'

Waldere wanted to be rid of his company. He mounted Lion; Hildegyð got up behind him; the tough little horse set off at a fast trot. After a while, she glanced back. The ferryman, carrying the fish, was trudging up the track behind them.

A mile or so further on, they came to the road. Where the track joined it, there were the ruins of a Roman guard-post and toll-station. The place was deserted, so was the road as far as they could see north and south. The ruins blocked the view along the track to the river.

'Get out of sight,' said Hildegyð. 'Stop when we're hidden and watch what he does.'

Once they were among the trees at the far side of the road, they dismounted and waited. When the ferryman came into sight at last, he stood still, looked up and down the road, listened for hoof-beats, then set off towards the north. Waldere laughed.

'So he's taken my advice. He's going to give the fish to his chief. I hope he gets paid for it.'

'He's going to tell his chief we're carrying two chests full of treasure. He'll get paid for that.'

'Lion will take us there before him. We'll tell the chief who we are and ask for shelter and protection. We're doing no harm in his land – and we can afford to give him a fine present for his hospitality.'

He turned to get Lion. Hildegyð clutched his arm.

'No! You saw that brute's look when you spoke of Franks. Whoever these folk are, they're my enemies. We must go south.'

'But the Franks are to the north, near the Rhine mouth. We'll have to cross this land to get to your father. I swore to keep faith with you till you were back in your own land. I haven't come so far to fail you now.'

'I won't risk your life just to save my pride. Yes, I wanted to see my father again. I wanted to tell him that though he'd never wasted a thought on my fate all these years, I'd got myself a prince for a husband and a queen's treasure for my dowry, without his help. For very shame, he'd have had to pay out treasure for treasure to you from his gold-hoard, to match my winnings. I was looking forward to watching his face while he did it. And I'd like to ride into Tolosa at the head of a great wedding procession, with an escort of Frankish nobles. But none of that is worth one drop of your blood. We'll go south. Your father will have to take me just as I am.'

'But I'm not –'

'I know you're not willing to go back when you think there's an enemy in front. But you swore to stick by me. I'm going south. We'll hide in those hills, then travel by night again, till we reach your kingdom.'

She jumped on Lion's back and rode off, so he had to follow her. In a while, she stopped to let him catch up. They headed south-westwards, till they were far away from the road and the river, among the forested heights.

The ferryman got a lift in a farm cart. Still, it was well past noon before he was set down in Borbetomagus. He made his way to the palace kitchen, showed the strange fish to the chief cook and told his tale.

The cook put the fish just as it was, stiff as a board, on to a silver platter. He went to the king's porch, spoke to the dish-thane, then carried the platter through the length of the great hall up to the high seat to present it to the king.

The feast was over but the scop had not yet begun to sing. The feasters were chatting to their nearest neighbours over their wine and ale.

The king had a very large following of Burgundian nobles, high-born exiles and visiting champions. Gifica had left his son a strong kingdom and a large gold-hoard. Guðhere was brave enough, rich enough and more than free-handed enough to attract warriors to his hall, all eager to serve him for daily feasts and splendid gifts of treasure. The royal gold-hoard was much smaller now. The king's chief counsellor was beginning to worry what would happen when there was nothing left of it. The king would have to win a great victory soon and bring home rich loot. Guðhere agreed. He meant to take the Frankish land to the north and force the Franks to pay him tribute.

The chief counsellor, Quintinus Constans Hagena, was sitting in the place of honour at the king's right hand. Guðhere had not remembered his half-brother with much childhood affection during their years apart. Still, when he stopped paying tribute to Attila, he had put Hagena's life in danger, so for his own honour's sake he had been forced to make him welcome when he came home.

Hagena was proving very useful. He knew Latin, so he could deal with Romans on equal terms and make sure that the king's secretaries and accountants were not cheating him. He could teach Hunnic battle-tricks to the war-band and entertain them in hall with stories about the Huns' wars in the east.

Guðhere stopped talking as the cook came up with the platter. He glanced at the dried fish with distaste.

'What's this?'

'It's just been brought as a gift for you, lord. The man who gave it said that only kings may eat it.'

'It looks as if it's just swum up from Hel,' said Æscrof, the eldest champion.

'It's come from Hunland,' said Hagena, quietly, 'and it's true that only the greatest folk eat it there.'

'Hunland!'

Guðhere was now sure the fish was poisoned.

'Bring the man here.'

The hall-guards brought in the ferryman; they stood close by to cut him down if he made a move against the king.

'Where did you get this fish?'

'It was given to me, lord. I had it from some folk I brought across the river this morning.'

'You ferried Huns over the Rhine?'

The ferryman looked scared.

'I couldn't tell they were Huns, lord. They looked just like humankind to me.'

'And they told you to bring this fish to the palace and make sure that only the king ate it?'

'No, lord! They gave it to me for their fee.' His voice was bitter. 'They said they'd got nothing else to pay me with, yet one of them had a seax in a jewelled sheath, worth a queen's bride-price. And they had two chests clinking with metal, packed to the lid with treasure, I'll stake my life on it. So I thought you ought to know such folk were in your land.'

Guðhere looked like a hound picking up a scent.

'How many came over the Rhine? Warriors?'

'Two, lord, or maybe three if one of them was a shape-shifter. Queer folk. The biggest man I've ever seen – he could have been one of Thunor's gets, if he wasn't Thunor himself. And the fairest serving-lad –'

The ferryman had felt safe from the moment he saw Guðhere's face when he said the word *'treasure'*, so he risked a wink.

'– put a gown on him and he could pass as one of The Lady's bower-maidens. And the ugliest horse off Hel's pastures – a scrawny, hook-nosed, barrel-chested brute with a sandy hide –'

'Waldere's come back from Hunland!'

Hagena had been listening to the fisherman's tale with growing excitement. His usually sombre face was alight with joy.

'That's Waldere and his horse, Lion! My friend, my blood-brother, Waldere the Visigoth and the Frankish princess, Hildegyð –'

'Chlodovech's daughter?'

Her name seemed to please Guðhere mightily. Then he looked puzzled.

'Where were they going?'

'There was no sight or word of them on the road here, lord. I think they went south, towards Waskenstein.'

'Making for Aquitania,' said Hagena.

'Without a word to you, their friend and blood-brother? And without greeting me, or asking my leave to pass through my land? I take that most unkindly.'

'If they've just made their way through Mirkwood from the east, it's likely they don't know where they are. It's a wonder they reached the Rhine.'

Hagena was smiling at old memories. 'When we first set out for Hunland in Valamir's wagon, I tried to teach them the way back. But they were only children, they took it as a game.'

'Then we must find them and bring them back here to feast with us,' said Guðhere jovially. 'It's a shame to my hospitality that your childhood friends should be skulking in the wastelands like wolves' heads. And their treasures – we must see that those are safely guarded.'

He looked towards the porch. 'It's nearly sunset, we can't go hunting them in the dark. Meet me at first light, Æscrof – and you, Cymen – Ecgfrið – Randwulf –' he named nine of his best champions '– fully armed and –'

'Fully armed?' Hagena looked surprised.

'The Huns may be on their track. It's a wonder Attila didn't come after you, brother, when you gave him the slip.' He sneered. 'He must have been afraid he'd meet my war-band. We might have to rescue Waldere tomorrow.'

He told the dish-thane to see that the ferryman had a meal, a bed and a gift. He promised the man a greater reward when Waldere, the princess and the treasure were all safe in the palace.

Later, when the drinking and the singing had ended for the night, he spoke his mind, apart with Æscrof.

'Any treasure that comes here from Hunland is mine by right. Two chestfuls is only a small part of the gold my father sent to Attila every year – still, it'll be useful. So will the girl. I'll make Chlodovech pay a good price to get her back, else I'll keep her as my whore.'

Hagena was teaching his eldest nephew to be a warrior. He had brought the boy to the palace to attend on him, to pick up the ways of a king's household: learn to ride and fight, watch the champions at their weapon-play, meet the great men of the kingdom and listen to the scops singing about the ancient heroes and the glory of the Burgundians.

Beadufrið was the son of his elder sister Quintinilla. King Gifica had made a good marriage for her to a Burgundian lord, before Hagena went away to Hunland. When he came home, he found her a widow with five children.

Hagena had an austere, lonely spirit. He had never been close friends with anyone save Waldere. He took no interest or pleasure in the company of women. He had thought, without much zest, that if ever he came home to his father's estates he would have to marry to get an heir. He was pleased to find that he had a ready-made family and need not burden himself with a wife. Young Beada was brave and truthful, with a temper as sunny as his hair. He was just the son Hagena would have prayed for if he had believed in gods.

When Beada was arming him before dawn, Hagena said, 'Bring me my old felt coat, that I wore when I came out of Hunland. Any my Hunnic sword-belt with the golden plates.'

Beada looked surprised.

'Waldere's in a strange land – to him. If he catches sight of an armed band on his track, he'll think we're hunting him as a raider. But he'll know this coat and belt even before he can see my face; I wore them often enough riding and fighting by his side.'

'I wish I could come with you, uncle. I want to see Attila's champion.'

'You'll see him later today, when he comes to the king's hall.'

'I'd like to see him first. Then, when the other boys are talking about him, I could say: *I know him. He's my uncle's sword-friend. I was there when they met again.*'

Hagena smiled. Such things mattered to boys. And that would be a golden moment, when his friend met his heir – the two he loved most in the world.

'Very well. Tell the stable-men to saddle your pony. Mind your manners in front of the king, don't push yourself forward.'

Waldere and Hildegyð were tired and hungry. They had travelled all last night and most of the day, with little food or rest. As soon as they were well into the hill country, they had dismounted to spare Lion. Now, their legs felt like boulders to move. They would have to sleep tonight, for the first time since they fled from Attila's camp.

Their way ahead seemed to be blocked by a cliff wall. A thread of a stream ran down from the rock face; they climbed beside it, looking for a level place where they could rest. Passing round an outcrop of rock, they saw that the stream was flowing out of the cliff through a gap about as wide as a hall door. It was not a cave-mouth; looking through, they could see grass and trees under open sky. They went in.

During some battle between the gods and the giants at the beginning of time, Thunor's hammer had struck the mountain, made a dent in its side and split the cliff. The travellers came through a narrow passage with sheer sides, into a little meadow sheltered under the mountain-crest. It was as safe as a fortress. They had fresh water, nuts and berries, grass for Lion. If an army waited outside, only one man at a time could come at them through that passage in the rocks. Waldere was yawning, he could hardly keep his eyelids open. Hildegyð, having splashed her face in the stream, swore she was as fresh as if she had slept all day long. She said she would take first watch. Waldere wrapped himself in his cloak and lay down by the fire. He was asleep almost as soon as his head touched the ground. Yet he was uneasy. Once or twice, as he tossed, he opened his eyes long enough to blink. He saw Hildegyð sitting at the other side of the fire, by the pile of fallen branches and twigs she had gathered to feed it. She was singing quietly to keep herself awake, the old tale of *The Battle of the Goths and the Huns*:

'From the south have I come
to speak these tidings:
fire in the marches
of Mirkwood is raging,
with the gore of men
all Gothland's sprinkled.'

When he fully woke, it was broad daylight. Hildegyð laughed at his protests. She told him he would not have slept so long if his body had not needed to and he would be all the better for it – which was true.

They ate their scanty breakfast and stamped out their fire. Waldere armed himself; Hildegyð strapped the chests to Lion's saddle. Then she went to the gap in the rock face and looked out. The gap opened towards the north. He saw her body tense. She stared at something for another moment or two, then turned to him.

'Armed men in the woods, coming this way'

He joined her at the gap and saw the glitter of spear-points among the leaves. Best stay in their stronghold. These horsemen might only be passing through the forest on business of their own.

But a rider came out into the open ground at the foot of the rocky slope leading up to the cliff. He was following tracks in the soft earth. He pointed with his spear at the cliff and shouted to the riders behind. There were twelve in the band: ten warriors, armed and helmeted, a young armour-bearer on a pony and a thick-set man in a Hunnic coat of dark felt, girded with a sword belt that glittered with golden plates.

Waldere gave a shout of joy.

'Look, it's Hagena! Our old friend's come to find us!'

He stepped out of the rocky jaws and waved to the newcomers.

When Guðhere reached the track that led down to the landing-stage, he sent his servants along the high-road to the south, to ask if the travellers had been seen on the way to Noviomagus. Meanwhile, Cymen and Wigheard, casting about like huntsmen west of the road, found tracks. A man, a youth or a girl, and a horse had stood for some while among the trees. Then the horse had set off southwards, away from the road, with the man running after it. Soon, the man's tracks vanished and there were only hoof-prints.

They followed the prints in the soft earth. Then, as the woodland track rose higher on the way to the mountains of Waskenstein there were three sets of prints again. The travellers were walking beside their horse; it would be easy to overtake them.

Æscrof shouted. They rode out into the open ground and saw their quarry standing high above them at the top of a rocky slope, in front of a gap in the cliff wall.

'Ride over and give him a shout, Æscrof. Tell him King Guðhere orders him to give up his treasure chests, his horse and the Frankish girl. If he does what he's told, he can take himself off to his own land with a whole skin.'

Æscrof had kicked his horse forward before Hagena got over his shock.

'Are you out of your mind? Is that the way for a king to speak to a harmless wayfarer? That man is my blood-brother and friend! Are you a king or leader of a pack of wolves' heads?'

'I don't need you to teach me how a king should speak, half-brother. I know how to guard my land and my folk. How can you be sure those two are harmless? They've come secretly with gold from Attila. Likely he's sent them to bribe the Romans to rise against me –' he sneered at Hagena '– or murder me by cunning and under-handedness, that's more the Roman way!'

Hagena looked at his half-brother; his Roman blood kept him from quarrelling like a barbarian in front of the warriors. Guðhere knew that his temper had carried him too far. They both turned to watch Æscrof.

Waldere was surprised that Hagena had not come first to greet him. However, he guessed that the man riding towards him was a hall-thane from Guðhere's household bringing a formal welcome from the king.

Æscrof drew rein where the slope became too steep to ride in comfort and yelled Guðhere's words just as the king had spoken them, with no effort to soften the insult.

Waldere was startled and angry but kept himself in check. In law, he was King Theodrid's son. He had ridden into Guðhere's land without leave or greeting; the king might have taken that as a challenge to his rule.

'That's a strange message from a king – but maybe your king doesn't like strangers wandering into his land. Let him know that I am Waldere of Aquitania. When I was a child, I was sent as a hostage to the Huns, like his kinsman Hagena. Now, I'm on my way home. Tell your king that I greet him, that I ask leave to cross his land in peace and that I offer him a hundred gold ingots and a sword of Weland's work –' as he touched Mimming's jewelled hilt, he heard Hildegyð hissing *'No!'* behind his back' – as a sign of my friendship and truth.'

Æscrof grunted and rode back with this answer. He could see that Guðhere and Hagena were both in a foul mood.

'Take the offer!' urged Hagena. 'It's noble, like himself. You can see by it that he's honest and means no harm.'

'I can see he's scared and trying to buy himself out of trouble. You talk like a Roman, Hagena, your folk have always liked gold better than blood. That's why you have to pay us Germans to do your fighting for you. *You'd* never lift a hand to put sword or shield between me and my foes. '

He glared at Hagena, whose face was like carved stone. He was seeing himself in Guðhere's eyes: the stranger, the outsider, the *Romwealh*. Fit enough to serve as a thorn-hedge but never taken into the circle of the kin.

'I'll never lift a hand against my sworn brother. I took an oath to be true to him. I drank his blood on it.'

'And what about our mother's blood? What about your oath to be true to me, your king? Æscrof here, my father's sword-friend, heard you swear it!'

'I swore to shield you from every danger. You're in no danger now, with nine champions to stand between you and a single way-worn man. If I ever do see you going into danger, I promise I'll shield you then, Roman though I am.'

Hagena turned his back on his half-brother and went away to a near-by hillock. He signed to Beada to tie their mounts at the edge of the wood, where they could graze in the shade. The boy had been waiting dutifully behind the cluster of warriors; he had not heard the dispute. He spread his cloak for his uncle to sit on, then sprawled comfortably on the warm turf beside him.

Hagena laid his shield flat, then drove the point of his spear into the ground beside it. He could neither fight beside his friend nor kill him. He sat brooding over his rage and pain.

Guðhere turned to Æscrof.

'Go and tell the Visigoth to do what I say, at once. If he stops to think about it, put your spear through him.'

Æscrof rode back up the slope, grinning. He gave Waldere his orders as if he were speaking to a beaten slave.

Waldere stood listening, leaning on his spear-shaft. He said slowly, 'I swear to all the gods, by my sword and my sword-hand, I'll never give your king one gold filing – no, not so much as would cover a grain of dust.'

Æscrof made as if to turn his horse, then whirled round and threw his spear with all his force, to catch Waldere unshielded and unawares.

The Huns had taught Waldere to move fast, for all his size. He had stepped aside, slipped his shield strap down his arm and caught hold of the hand-grip, met Æscrof's spear-point with the boss, so that it rebounded harmlessly, and hurled his own weapon – all before Æscrof could guard himself.

Waldere's spear went through the bottom of Æscrof's shield, just as he was drawing his sword to go in for the death-blow. The spear-head went through his right hand, skewered it to his thigh and went on into the horse's back. It screamed and reared. Æscrof let go of his shield-grip and tried to pull the spear out with his left hand. He would have fallen if he had not been pinned to his horse. While he struggled, Waldere ran down, grabbed him by the foot and drove his sword nearly to the hilt into the body. Horse and man fell together. Waldere jumped clear of the flailing hoofs, pulled his sword out of Æscrof, then tried to free his spear.

The watchers by the trees were still as carven images for a moment as Æscrof went down.

Then Cymen, his nephew, kicked his horse to a gallop and charged Waldere while he was wrestling with his spear. An arrow hissed; Hildegyð shot the horse in the breast. It crashed down. Cymen's neck broke as he hit the ground. Waldere got his spear free and went racing up the slope with it towards the gap in the cliff.

'Get after him!' shouted Guðhere. 'Strike him from all sides, keep at him, don't give him a breathing-space!'

Wigheard, Heaðuweard, Randwulf and Ecgfrið the Saxon set off in pursuit. They went on foot, behind their shields, for dread of the unseen archer. A horse is too big a target; if an arrow does not kill the rider, his wounded mount can.

Waldere stepped back between the cliff's jaws. Ecgfrið, with Wigheard a little behind and to his right, began to jeer at him as soon as he was within earshot, to goad him into the open.

'Scared of the sight of warriors, Hun? D'you bolt down your hole every time you see one coming? You're good for a gallop – did your father get you on his mare?' – and so on.

Hildegyð had meant to keep Waldere's back but inside the rock passage he was safe from any attack except to the front. Also, she could not use her arrows there for fear of hitting him. Further back, where the rocks opened into the meadow, she was able to find sufficient hand and footholds to pull herself up the cliff to a ledge, just wide enough for her to crawl forward, then kneel and draw her bow. Up there, she could see that while Waldere was listening to Ecgfrið and watching Wigheard, another man was edging round towards his unshielded side, hidden from him by the cliff.

Her arrow took Ecgfrið in the right side; it went through the byrnie and pierced his lung. He swung round vomiting blood and fell dead. Wigheard glanced up at the moment the bow twanged and threw his spear at Hildegyð. Waldere threw his almost at the same moment and hit Wigheard full in the chest while his spear-arm was still raised. Wigheard's spear struck the rock just under Hildegyð's knee; she nearly lost her balance and cried out as the spear fell with a scutter of loose stones.

Waldere thought that Hildegyð had been hit and had fallen from the cliff face. He stepped out of the gap just as Randwulf drove at him from the right. Hildegyð, clutching the ledge, could not use her bow but screamed a warning. Waldere just had time to jump aside, draw his sword and chop the spear-shaft close to the head.

He was now outside the rock wall, with Randwulf between him and the gap. He set his back against the cliff. Randwulf grinned, dropped the broken shaft and attacked him with his sword as Heaðuweard came up at a run on the left.

Waldere took Heaðuweard's spear with his shield-rim as he parried Randwulf's thrust. While Heaðuweard was off-balance, he swung the shield-boss into his face and sent him staggering back for a few paces. Randwulf kept up a hail of blows; Heaðuweard, firm on his feet again, came charging back into the fray with drawn sword. They hammered at him; he parried with sword and shield but they gave him no chance to strike back at them. They meant to beat down his guard, or drive him away from the cliff so that one of them could take him in the back. Waldere was a better swordsman than either of them but even his strength was bound to flag under such an attack.

Then suddenly, when he was almost spent, no more blows came from the right. Hildegyð had almost thrown herself down the cliff. Steadying herself as she slithered to the ground, she jumped at Randwulf's shoulders like a cat, gripping his back with her knees and catching him round the throat with her left arm. She drove her hand-seax into his throat and leaped clear as he fell. Then she circled around behind Heaðuweard, looking for a chance to slash his leg at the knee and hamstring him.

Now it was Heaðuweard's turn to draw back from Waldere and try to look two ways at once. He wanted to end Waldere quickly, before he had time to drawn breath. He half-turned, as if he meant to strike at Hildegyð, then suddenly sprang at Waldere with his sword raised for a mighty chop at his right shoulder.

But Waldere had not been battered stupid; he caught the blow with an upward stroke of his own blade. Heaðuweard's sword shot out of his grip, spun through the air and fell to the ground some yards away, where it glittered among the bushes under the noonday sun.

Heaðuweard's nerve broke; he tried to run. Waldere went after him. He picked up Heaðuweard's spear as he ran, brought him down with a blow in the back and then, as he tried to rise, pinned him to the ground and held him writhing for the last few heartbeats of his life.

Waldere did not know when the twitching and moaning stopped. He stood gripping the shaft, holding himself up with it like a drunkard, dazed with weariness. The three warriors left with Guðhere did not know Waldere was nearly spent; they thought he was gloating over Heaðuweard. They looked at each other uneasily, then at Guðhere who was staring white-faced at the bodies of his champions.

'They say Huns were spawned by trolls out of witches.'

'The Visigoth's learned their sorcery.'

'He made a good offer.' Helmstan glanced warily at his king. 'Wouldn't it be better –'

Guðhere turned on him, blazing with fury.

'Are you begging me to let him go now, after killing my hearth-companions? Did you only come to my hall for meat and mead? Will you feel proud when you're back on my ale-benches with their empty places beside you, listening to the scop singing about this fight? Gods, even the cats who haunt my kitchen serve me better than you – they kill their mice!'

They were stung with shame.

'We'll get him now,' said Torhtbrand, 'while he's out in the open.'

'If we could only get his shield away from him –'

Garulf suddenly chuckled.

'I know just how we can do it.'

Coiled at his saddle-bow was a long cord of plaited leather; it was thin and flexible but very strong. He told the others how they would use it.

At first, Hildegyð thought the Burgundian was dying hard under the spear. Then she supposed that Waldere was trying to free the spear for use, since his own had been broken. But he was as still as the corpse at his feet.

As she ran towards him, she was startled to see him unbuckle his helmet and take it off. When she was near enough to see his face she was too horrified to speak. His flesh was streaming with sweat; his head steamed like a cauldron; he was gasping like a landed fish. His eyes were fixed and staring; she was not sure he could see anything. Yet he knew she was beside him. When she gripped his arm he said 'Water . . . water . . .' between his gasps.

She glanced across to the Burgundians. They had their heads together, deep in talk. She decided she must risk leaving him, to bring him some water. She said, 'Be wary!'; then took his helmet and raced to the stream. She filled the helmet with

181

water and was just rising to her feet when a howl of triumph nearly made her spill it.

Garulf had hurled an angon at Waldere. He had blocked it with his shield; now the barbs on the spear-head held it fast. A rope had been tied to the neck; three men were tugging at the other end with all their might. Waldere could not reach them with his sword, or cut the rope; he must either drop his shield or risk having his left arm torn from the socket.

Waldere was struggling to keep his shield; he pulled back with all his strength. For one breath, he held all three straining against him. She screamed, 'Let it go – use Mimming – I'll keep your back!'

At that same moment, Waldere slipped his shield arm loose. The Burgundians were hurled back by their own force and fell sprawling in a heap. Waldere brought his sword down on the nearest head, smashing both helmet and skull, then ran the blade through the body of the next man who was lying underneath him. The third man scrambled to his feet. He looked round for the spears and shields that they had laid down to haul on the rope but Waldere charged at him before he could pick up a weapon. He turned and tried to run but he was shaken from his fall. Waldere had a longer stride and a longer reach; he put out the last of his strength and sliced the wretch through the back of his legs below the byrnie. He fell, his life pouring out with his blood.

Hagena heard his half-brother cursing. He himself had been watching the fights with interest and some bleak satisfaction, both at Guðhere's humiliation and his old friend's skill.

Even so, he thought, *I'm a match for him. I know all his best strokes. If he goes for Guðhere, I could kill him now he's spent, even with that little wælcyrie fighting at his side. But Waldere's not such a fool. He didn't come here looking for trouble. Guðhere will have to make terms. I'll see fair play between them. Pity Waldere can't join our war-band, he'd more than make up for the nine we've lost –*

'Beada, come back!'

Young Beadufrið's mind was full of his uncle's stories about German heroes and exploits among the Huns. He had seen the chance to perform a great feat of arms under the eyes of his king. He would kill the Visigoth, avenge the king's hearth-companions and win himself a deathless name. He took Hagena's spear, mounted his pony, kicked him to a gallop and was charging at Waldere before Hagena, deep in his own thoughts, saw what he was doing.

Hagena's shout brought death hurrying.

After the last chase, Waldere's legs had buckled under him. He was sitting on the ground beside the body of the last man he killed. Hildegyð had run to him, still clutching the helmet. He had swallowed some mouthfuls of water; she had splashed the rest over his head and face, telling him to put on his helmet while she fetched a shield for him from the pile of Burgundian weapons.

Hagena's shout made him look up. His eyes were still blurred with sweat. He saw a horseman galloping towards him, a small man on a small horse. The Huns had shown him that small men on small horses made the deadliest fighters.

A warrior's body will still act and fight for him when he is dead on his feet. Waldere waited till his attacker was almost on him before he stood up. Beada was leaning forward, intent on driving his spear down with all his force. The point of Waldere's longsword took him in the throat. Beada's eyes opened wide when he met death, with surprise not fear.

Waldere's sight cleared as he made his sword-stroke. He saw that his attacker was a very young boy, without body-armour, and caught him as he fell. Hildegyð hurried up, carrying a shield. Waldere was standing with the boy in his arms, staring at his face.

'He was hardly more than a child.'

He laid Beadufrið gently down on the turf, closed his eyes, straightened his limbs and put his spear by his right side. Hildegyð watched him, hard-faced.

'We were hardly more than children when our fathers sent us into the world to fend for ourselves. You could claim you've done this boy a favour sending him out of it so soon, away from false friends and cowards who fight ten to one.'

She shot her hatred out of her eyes towards Hagena and his king. Hagena had got to his feet; the two seemed to be arguing fiercely.

'Come back inside the cliff. Try to hold yourself upright and don't stumble. Likely they're afraid of you but if they guessed you're spent, they'd take horse and ride you down.'

When they reached the gap, Waldere's foot kicked against one of the broken spear-shafts lying there.

'Hel's curse! I'd meant to bring a spear with me. The boy put it out of my head.'

He paused as if he would go back for one.

'Never mind about a spear! You can trust to your sword in a place like this – so long as you don't let them tempt you out of your stronghold and take you in the back. And you've got Mimming! With Mimming in your left hand, you wouldn't need a shield either! Perhaps Prince Ðeodric foresaw your need when he gave it to you – he was trapped himself once in a fearsome place –'

She had meant to hearten Waldere with the thought that Ðeodric had escaped from that trap and won himself power and fame. But her words reminded Waldere of something very different.

'And then his best friend betrayed him.'

She looked at him curiously.

'*I'm* angry with Hagena – *you're* wounded.'

He shrugged.

'No use fretting over wounds.'

He threw himself down by the streamlet and drank.

'Rest now. I'll keep watch.'

She went back to the gap and stared at the distant figures of the Burgundians. She wished she could hear what they were saying.

'Your friend has killed your sister's son!'

Hagena was silent.

Guðhere moved to mount his horse.

'My brave companions are dead. I'm going to claim their blood-price from their slayer. Will you come and watch one of us die? I swear I'll never go back to my hall while that man lives unpunished. Or are you afraid to face death? You ran away from Attila.'

Hagena turned on him.

'Why should I be afraid to face death? I'll have to face my sister, when she asks me where I left her son. Why should I care if I never see your hall again? I'm going to kill Waldere.'

Guðhere beamed with satisfaction. He tried to put his arm across Hagena's shoulders.

'I knew it! That wretch made his own death sure when he put his sword into your brave lad. I knew you wouldn't fail your kin!'

'Don't ever speak to me about Beadufrið. He died for your greed, like your nine hearth-companions. But you're my king, you're in danger and I'm the only one left to shield you.'

He gathered up some of the cloaks that the dead men had laid aside when they went to fight.

'Help me to cover him from the wild creatures. Then we'll leave this cursed place.'

Guðhere began to protest; Hagena silenced him with a look.

'I'm going to fight my sworn friend and brother for your sake. I'll make sure I kill him.'

He pointed to the gap in the cliff.

'Six men died up there. We two have no hope of taking Waldere inside those rocks – and very little chance outside them, unless he's weary or badly wounded. So, we have to pretend to go away; then trail them when they come out, till we can take them at a disadvantage. Before sunset, while they're tired and hungry.'

'How can you be sure they'll come out?'

'They'll have to – before we come back with the war-host. Waldere will believe you've gone to summon it.' Hagena smiled unpleasantly. 'He'll hardly guess you've got a sense of honour.'

Guðhere followed him to Beadufrið's body. They saw that Waldere had laid him out decently. Hagena said nothing. They wrapped him in the cloaks, piled stones over him to make a small cairn, then took their horses and rode away north among the trees.

Hildegyð watched them go, then told Waldere.

'Then it's time we went too. We can't hold this place against a host. Attila wouldn't waste another man on us. He'd block that gap with rocks and camp outside till we starved – or send the country folk up to the heights to stone us.'

They led Lion out. After resting for a night and most of a day with plenty of grass and water, he was as fresh as the day he left Attila's camp.

Waldere paused among the dead outside the gap and found Ecgfrið's spear. It had dropped from his hand unbroken when Hildegyð shot him.

They followed the line of the cliff, then turned down into a wooded valley. The sun was well past noon and westering. They mounted Lion and went at a steady trot through the glades, bearing south and west as much as the ground would let them. Hildegyð was not at ease; she kept glancing back. After a while, she saw the gleam of armour on the crest of the hillside behind them. She told Waldere. As soon as a dip in the ground hid them from view, he dismounted. So did Hildegyð. He led Lion off the path, among the bushes, the bramble patches and the thickest groves. They had to go so much more slowly that she grew impatient.

'We won't shake them off like this. The ground's soft, they can follow our tracks. And they'll see the trampled ferns and broken twigs where we've pushed through.'

'Yes, but they can't ride us down with their big German horses among these thorn bushes. And they won't have room to use a spear.'

'Neither will you.'

'So I'll hand mine over to you to carry.'

Just then, they came out into a small clearing. Ahead, the forest grew thickly again but a narrow path led away to their right. A glitter among the trees showed that there was a tarn beyond them.

Waldere stopped, smiling at Hildegyð.

'You used to be handy with a spear when you were a boy – though you're much better with a bow.'

She laughed.

'I've only got six arrows left.'

'Never mind. The sight of a Hun bow is enough to scare off most folk without loosing a shaft.'

He pointed along the path towards the setting sun.

'My folk live to the south-west. You could reach them within a month, travelling from dusk to dawn, if you ride Lion. But the Romans hold the lands between. My advice is to make for a large Roman town. Ask for the governor. Say you've got a secret message from Attila to the Lord Aëtius and need a safe conduct. Aëtius has dealings with the Huns, so the Romans will believe you. Tell Aëtius who you are. King Chlodovech is his ally; they both mean to destroy my people. You'll be sent home with a guard of honour.'

Hildegyð was staring at him, stony-faced.

'Do you understand all that?'

'I understand you think you'll be killed in your next fight. I understand that I'm betrothed to you. I gather you believe I'll break my vow to you, but I can't understand why.'

'Dear Hildegyð, you're the truest sword-friend any man ever had. I don't believe you'll break your vow. I'm asking you – *begging* you to help me not to break mine. I swore I'd get you safe home. Don't let me die knowing I've failed. Keep my vow for me, love, and may the gods lead you back to your own land.'

'My land is wherever you are. If you live, we'll go to Aquitania together. If you die, Lion and I will soon catch you up on the road to Hel's kingdom.' She touched the handle of her knife. 'The Burgundians shan't have Lion either.'

She was shining with happiness.

'I'll wait among the trees by that lake. If you fall, I'll sink the treasure, then come riding after you on the Road of the Dead. Don't worry about me – I'll keep both our vows.'

She flung her arms round him. They kissed mouth to mouth; then he lifted her on to Lion's back and handed her the spear. She took the horse at a fast trot down the path towards the lake.

Waldere sat down, stretching his legs and resting his back against a tree-trunk, out of the glare of the sun. It was a while before he heard the sounds of crashing and cursing among the thorn bushes and brambles. He was on his feet, sword in hand, when Guðhere and Hagena, shoulders crouched and faces guarded with their shields, stumbled into the glade dragging their resentful horses.

Guðhere sneered when he saw Waldere.

'Caught slinking away from your bolt-hole – and without your spear, too! You've got careless.'

Waldere looked him up and down.

'You must be King Guðhere the Fearless. Have you come to prove how brave you can be against a man already worn out with fighting?'

'I've come to take payment for the loss of my men. You fool, you should have handed over your treasures before I wanted your blood as well.'

'You're wasting your breath and your time – and you haven't got much left of either. You'll not get a glimpse of my treasures, except the one I've got here in its treasure-chest.' He laid his hand on Mimming's sheath. 'I promise you, when I take it out you'll wish you'd never seen it.'

Guðhere blustered. 'I'll have your life and take your treasures!'

Waldere ignored him.

'I've a word or two to say to you, Hagena. You've changed since the time we swore blood-brotherhood. I believed if ever you saw me in danger, you'd be fighting at my side. Or if you had a grudge against me, you'd tell me frankly and settle it yourself. I never thought I'd see you sitting idly by to watch while ten other men tried to kill me. That boy, whoever he was, was braver than you.'

Hagena said nothing. Guðhere laughed.

'That boy was his sister's son.'

Waldere remembered the boy's face, bright and fearless, even when he saw the sword driving at his throat.

'Hagena, I'm sorry! I'd give all my treasure to the gods, to buy back that sword-stroke.'

'The time for giving gold is past, Waldere. I've nothing more to say to you.'

Hagena hurled his spear. If it had struck home, it would have gone through Waldere's shield, mail and body. He was not ashamed to leap aside. The spear went into a tree-trunk with such force that the head was buried to the nails. Guðhere threw his, hoping to catch Waldere off-guard. Waldere blocked it with his shield. The cast had nothing of Hagena's force behind it. The spear struck against the boss and fell harmlessly to the ground a few feet away.

The two set upon him with their swords, trying to wear him out, trusting that he would soon slow down or make a mistake from weariness. Waldere defended himself so cunningly, moved so nimbly and fought back so savagely, using his shield as well as his sword to strike with, that he gave his foes as hard knocks as he took. He put both of them in danger more than once.

There seemed no hope of getting in a death-blow past Waldere's longsword. Guðhere needed his spear, lying useless by Waldere's feet. He signalled to Hagena with his eyes to keep Waldere busy. Hagena redoubled his blows. Guðhere sheathed his sword, crouched, stretched out his hand, got hold of the butt-end and began to draw the spear away.

Waldere had been alerted by the fury of Hagena's attack. He made sure he could see from the corner of his eye what Guðhere was doing. He drove Hagena off with a mighty blow that hacked away part of his shield and caught him across the ribs, breaking the rings of his byrnie.

While Hagena was staggering, Waldere jumped back and set his foot on the spear-shaft. Guðhere, caught stooping and with his sword in its sheath, was disarmed and helpless. As he tried to stand up, Waldere slashed his leg and he fell, blood pouring from his wound.

Waldere raised his sword for the death-blow. Hagena, off-balance and wrongly placed for a sword-stroke, had only time to throw himself forward between his king and the blade. The blow came down on the boar-crest that guarded his helmet; the blade broke near the hilt.

Waldere threw the hilt away in order to draw Mimming. Hagena, still reeling from the blow to his head, his chin-straps broken and his helmet knocked askew, brought his shield-rim down on Waldere's outflung sword-arm, breaking his wrist.

Hagena pushed his helmet back from his eyes, shaking his head to clear the giddiness. The helmet fell off. He planted his feet firmly and readied his sword for the death-blow, smiling a little. While he savoured the moment, Waldere moved his shield-strap to his right arm and drew Mimming with his left hand, lashing out before Hagena could strike.

The seax struck Hagena's cheekbone, glanced up and smashed against his eyeball. Mimming's edge would have sliced his head in half. But Waldere had never fought left-handed with Mimming; he was clumsy with pain and haste. He had struck upwards as he drew; he hit Hagena with the broad, weighty back of the blade.

He took a better grip on Mimming and raised the edge for a chopping blow. Hagena struggled to fix his seeing eye on Waldere, to drive his longsword home through Waldere's guts, now he was no longer handy with his shield. They were moving in for their death-strokes, so intent on killing each other that they did not hear hoofs thudding on the turf. Lion ran past them; his rider jumped off his back and threw herself between them, nearly getting herself hacked down by their two blades.

Hildegyð held her spear-shaft to keep them apart. She shouted at them.

'Enough! You've done enough harm! Why destroy each other? For that?'

She pointed at Guðhere. He was sitting up, ripping the hem of his shirt to bind his leg, trying to stop the bleeding.

'Hagena's king ordered him to kill me,' said Waldere coldly. 'I've a right to kill any man who tries to take my life.'

'Waldere killed my sister's son. I claim death for death.'

'And don't you think you've already been the death of each other? Hagena may go blind. When the sight goes from one eye, the other often darkens as well. Waldere may never use his sword-hand again. Being blind and crippled is death to a warrior isn't it? I say, make an end of fighting. The one who strikes the other next must strike through my body!'

Guðhere pulled himself to his feet, propping himself by his spear. He was shaking with fury.

'*Make an end?* Do you think I'll go back to my city half-crippled, with ten men dead and nothing to show for it?'

Hildegyð sneered.

'You must have dwarf blood, you love gold so dearly. Will you take wergild?'

She turned to Lion, who had been quietly waiting for orders ever since she jumped off his back, and began to unbuckle one of the chests.

'No, Hildegyð! You heard me swear I'd never give him one piece of gold.'

'Of your gold. This is mine.' She pointed to the ᚼ rune. 'Hail for Hildegyð. My dowry.'

She looked at Guðhere.

'Will you trade? My dowry for a safe passage out of your land. You came across a band of Hun raiders hunting for Waldere and me. Though you were outnumbered and unready for war, you gave battle, drove them off and seized their loot, though you lost most of your men and were sorely wounded.'

She laughed. 'It's a good story, isn't it? Does you credit! I promise, you'll never hear a word out of Aquitania to gainsay it. Your scop can make a song about it – how you and Hagena fought on against Attila's horde after all your men were slain. Well, what do you say? Yes or no?'

Guðhere nodded. She drew her knife and they all took a peace-oath on the iron. The three hostages remembered another oath sworn long ago; it was bitter to think how their old friendship had ended in such a sordid pact. Hildegyð and Guðhere said the words of the oath for the two sides. Waldere and Hagena did not even look at each other; since their last fight began they had not spoken to each other. Hagena had been right: there was nothing more to say.

Hildegyð found some damp moss to make a pad for Hagena's eye and tied it on with a strip cut from her cloak. She helped him catch the horses, get Guðhere into his saddle and tie her treasure chest behind the other saddle. Hagena mounted; the Burgundians rode away north.

She hunted for a suitable piece of wood, shaved it into a splint and carefully bound Waldere's wrist to it, setting the bones in place.

'It's a clean break. You'll be able to use a sword again with your right hand.'

'And a fishing-line. Meanwhile, I'll have to teach you how to fish, or we'll starve before we reach home.'

'I wonder what your father will say when his heir brings him a dowerless daughter-in-law of enemy stock.'

'Hildegyð, I've never told you lies about myself but I've let you believe a lie. I wasn't born King Theodrid's son. I'm not his heir. My father was one of his nobles, killed fighting for him. We were left poor and in debt. The king said if I let him adopt me and send me to Attila, he'd provide for my family.'

He watched her anxiously. She smiled at him as if a burden had been lifted from her back.

'Well, a king's son who isn't a prince is a fit husband for a dowerless princess.'

'You're not dowerless!'

He pointed to the chest she had marked with his rune. 'All that gold rightly belongs to you. You're the one who took the risk of carrying it off. I never wanted you to give up your share – least of all to Guðhere, after I'd beaten him to the ground. I hate to think of him boasting over his ale how he won it by his skill and courage.'

Hildegyð burst out laughing. It was an eerie sound in the gathering dusk. She looked like a wælcyrie watching doomed warriors going into battle.

'He won't boast for long, once he's opened that chest! I took plain gold for you, Waldere – the coins and ingots the Romans send to Attila as tribute, or to hire his warriors to fight their wars. A coin with a Roman's head, or an ingot with a Roman stamp – they all look much the same. Gaul's full of them; who's to know where they came from? You could have won them anywhere.

'But I'm a woman, as Hagena kept throwing in my face, so I wanted to adorn myself for my wedding. I took jewelsmiths' work. The treasures in Guðhere's chest are famous among the Huns.

'I know Guðhere now as well as if we'd been nursed together. He's as vain as he's greedy. He's a man who likes to show off his wealth. He wants to hear the scops praising him as '*ring-giver*' and '*gold friend*'. Those diadems I gave him, the eastern necklets and arm-rings – he'll make them the talk of the Rhineland. If Attila wants his treasures back, he'll soon know where to find them – and he'll come himself to get them!'

Listening to her, watching her smile, Waldere felt cold.

'Hildegyð, it wasn't gold you gave Guðhere in that chest. You gave him death.'

Hildegyð took her spear in one hand, Lion's bridle rein with the other, ready to go.

'He asked for it,' she said.

'We þæt Mæðhilde mone gefrugnon
wurdon grundlease Geates frige
þæt hi seo sorglufu slæp ealle binom.'

Deor

(We have learned that the grief of Mæðhild, Geat's
lady, was boundless, so that the tragic love utterly
bereft her of sleep.)

VI The Harper and the River-Elf

When Beowulf was killed, the Swedes came south in force over the great lakes to take Geatland. His young kinsman Wiglaf fought his way to the coast with the last of his war-band. They shepherded as many of their women and children as they could rescue; they also carried the royal treasure. When they reached the sea they took ship and fled westwards.

It was late in the year; too late to set out on the whale-road unless there was no choice. The Geats had a grim voyage, driven by an icy north-east wind that turned rain into hail and scourged them. Wyrd stood their friend, though; she kept them from drowning. They made landfall at last among the Angelcynn who had settled in eastern Britain.

When the king's coastguards were sure they were not raiders, they were given shelter for the sake of Wiglaf's courage and high birth, his useful warriors and his treasure. The king was glad to have his house-troop strengthened by a group of battle-hardened fighters. As exiles, they would have to depend on his generosity. He took Wiglaf and the treasure into his own family by giving his sister in marriage to the Geatish prince.

Cyneburh did not fare so well, as she was a girl, an orphan, and had no close kinsmen to help her. Her brothers had been killed fighting the Swedes. Her father, already ill and weak from a chest-wound, had died during the voyage. His last few men took service with other lords, who were able to keep them. She was alone in a strange land, with nothing but her father's sword and a small whalebone box holding her trinkets.

Nobody wanted her. The young Geatish warriors were looking forward to fighting and raiding on the Anglian borders to earn gifts and land-right from the king. When they could settle, they wanted Anglian wives from noble families, who would help them take root in the new kingdom. The Anglian chiefs would only make marriages with other rich and powerful kindreds among their own people. Cyneburh was no use to them.

Yet though she was a forlorn exile, she was of very good birth. She had a trace of Geatish royal blood; her father's grandmother had been old King Hreðel's cousin. For his own honour, Wiglaf could not leave her for some Anglian chief to take her into service as a bower-woman or whore, likely both. So Wiglaf spoke for her to the king, who did his best.

One of his thanes had a well-to-do farmer living on his estate. This man, Brand, had fought bravely for his lord. Once he had saved the earl's life, standing over his body when he was brought down and fending off the attackers. He was free-born; rich enough to give Cyneburh a comfortable home and strong enough, backed by Lord Helm's goodwill, to keep her safe.

So Cyneburh got a kindly pleasant-looking husband – but he was not of noble rank. She was mistress of a warm roomy house, up near the springs of the Deben, with full barns, well-stocked byres and plenty good land for plough and pasture – but it was not a great hall with gilded carving and splendid tapestries. She had good food to eat, wore linen and dyed wool, had servants to work for her. But the lordly feasts, the hall-benches crowded with high-born warriors, the voices and harp-music of famous scops recalling the deeds of ancient heroes, the robes of brocaded silk gleaming with jewels, the shared talk and laughter over embroidery in a queen's bower – she would never enjoy those again except in memory or dreams.

She was not stupid or ill-natured. She had seen enough, during the last days in Geatland and on the sea, to know that she was lucky to get Brand. Her life could have been much worse. But it was not as good as it might have been.

She comforted herself as she went about her household tasks by making her lost world again in her mind and living there. She dreamed of the day when she would give her father's sword to a son who would win back the lost glories of his race.

Her first child was a boy, big and lusty. Brand, full of pride and joy, called him Leofsunu. While he was small, he was glad enough to listen to his mother's tales of king's halls and heroes, trolls and treasure. As soon as he was old enough to go about the farm with his father, he set her tales aside as childish. Once, he cut her to the heart by telling her that she would do better to give her gold-hilted sword and garnet brooches to Lord Helm in exchange for a useful bull.

The second son was lithe and wiry, with a sharp face and keen eyes like a hawk, so they called him Hafoc. He had a hawk's nature as well as name, wild and restless. He listened avidly when his mother talked about the kings and heroes of her race, their power and their gold-hoards. These tales made him proud and angry; he felt he had been robbed of his birthright. He would not settle to farm-work. Lord Helm spoke for him and got him a place in the royal household, under the chief huntsman.

It was a good start; Hafoc was a hunter by instinct, like a wolf or a bird of prey. He might have worked his way up to royal favour. But he was touchy and defiant. He thought of himself as a nobleman, equal to any warrior in the household troop. He took orders as insults.

One day, at the end of a long and disappointing chase, he gave a tongue-lashing to a young earl for letting the quarry escape. The earl gave him a blow on the mouth for his insolence. Hafoc stabbed him with his hunting-knife and was away, quick as a fox, before his companions could strike him down. He went north, towards the fens; he was never heard of again.

Luckily, the young earl did not die. However, his kin were furious that he had been struck and wounded by a churl's son. Hafoc was out of their reach, so they demanded a huge blood-price from Brand. It was far more than he could find, unless he and his family were sold as well as all his goods.

Cyneburh went weeping to Lord Helm with the gold-hilted sword and the best of her jewels, begging him to offer them to the earl's kin as wergild for her family. Helm took them; some time later he sent word that the matter had been settled. He never told them how much more he himself had given to the victim, to pay back the debt he owed Brand for saving his life. He warned Brand, though, against letting foolish lads get too puffed-up to fit their place in the world.

For a while, Brand had no more lads to worry about; Cyneburh gave him daughters. When at last she had her third son, she knew that her time for child-bearing had ended with him. She called him Geat, hoping that the name at least might keep some memory of her race alive for her grandchildren.

Geat was a healthy child, with his father's strong body, his mother's fine features and slender long-fingered hands. He seemed content with life. He loved sitting with his mother while she told him stories about her girlhood. Unlike his lost brother, he never muddled them with his daily life as Farmer Brand's son. Geatland, to him was another name for Elfland. It was another world, where the heroes and the gold-adorned queens of his mother's memory lived for ever, along with giants, elves and swan-brides. He loved that other world, because it was far more beautiful and exciting than the farm, but he only went there in his day-dreams.

His father put him to errands and light work about the farm as soon as possible. Remembering Hafoc, he kept a sharp look-out for truancy and sulks. Though Geat did not go seeking for jobs to be done, he carried out every task he was set cheerfully enough. His only outstanding gift was his quick ear for music. He could pick up any song at first hearing, tune and words; he could whistle an air as clear as a pipe. The farm-hands liked to hear him; it helped to get the work along.

The wheelwright made him a little harp out of left-over pieces of wood and strung it with horse-hair. Geat was soon able to pick out the notes of a well-known song. He took the harp indoors to show his mother what he could do. When she smiled and praised him, he told her in the pride of his heart that he was going to be gleeman, like Mul Harper.

Mul was a lordless Welshman. He had a hut out on the waste but spent most of his time going from one farm to another, getting a meal and a night's lodging as pay for his songs and stories. He played for bride-ales, shearing, harvestings and festivals. Geat thought he had the best life in the world – no drudgery, free to go where he chose, time to make music all day long, getting his living by his pastime –

He was happily explaining this to his mother when her hand smacked against his cheek. All the bitterness of her life was behind the blow. It took him off balance; he stumbled, hit his head against the wall and fell on his knees. The harp flew out of his hands and landed with a sharp crack on the floor. Cyneburh's rage broke over him like a hailstorm.

'Haven't I suffered enough even yet? Exiled. My kinsfolk dead. One son a clod of earth. The other a wolf's head, skulking in the fens with thieves and murderers if he's still alive. And now you say you want to shame me tramping from door to door like a beggarly outcast! Making a show of yourself to any pack of drunken churls for beer and a crust!'

'You're wrong. Mul isn't like that –'

'Be quiet! Don't you dare cut in when I'm speaking! If you ever talk about being a gleeman again, I'll have you whipped. I'll smash that harp and burn the pieces!'

She moved to seize the harp. Geat threw himself forward and lay over it, sobbing with rage.

'That's not fair! I hate you, I hate –'

'*That's enough.*'

Brand had hurried indoors to find out why Cyneburh was screaming. He heard their last words. Geat appealed to him.

'Tell her she's wrong! She says I mustn't –'

'Don't defy your mother, Geat. You must do as she tells you while you're under her roof.'

He turned to Cyneburh. 'And don't you be too hard on the lad, wife. He's only young yet. When I was his age I wanted to be an outlaw.'

He laughed at his young self. 'A few years in Lord Helm's war-band knocked that nonsense out of me. When Geat's a man, he'll be as glad of a plain steady life as we are.'

Cyneburh and Geat looked at each other. Neither replied to Brand's words. She put out her hand and touched her son's cheek.

'All's well, Geat. I know you'd never choose to shame me.'

Geat went out taking the harp with him. He followed his father's advice to the last word: he did as his mother told him – while he was under her roof. He never talked again about being a gleeman. He never let her see the harp in the house; he kept it in the stable loft. He never upset her by playing and singing within earshot of her. He made his music when he was away in the fields or visiting other folk's houses.

Other folk seemed to enjoy listening to him but he was never quite happy with the sounds he made, however much he practised. He thought his harp was too feeble and dull-voiced; his hands were too clumsy. He could not get within echoing distance of the music he could hear playing inside himself.

That music was sounding very sweetly on a morning at the beginning of summer, about two years after the clash with his mother. Brand had sent him with a message to his head shepherd and told him to bring back word how the flock was doing. Their sheepwalk was on the heath-land to the north.

Geat set off at a good pace, enjoying the strength and well-being of his body, the swing of his legs, the flow of sweet air in and out of his lungs, the thoughts that came and went: a day's freedom, time to play his harp as much as he liked, girls –

Girls had been coming into Geat's mind very often lately and staying longer each time they came. Ever since he was old enough to stand firm on his legs, he had been helping with the farm animals and listening to his elder brother swapping stories with the farm-hands. So he knew what to do with a girl but he had not done it yet. He was still shy; also he was afraid of failing and still more afraid that the girls would laugh about him with his brother and the other men. Yet he would dearly like to try.

Just then, girls' voices singing and laughing somewhere out of sight seemed to call on him to be man. He was a long way from home, they would not know him, it would be easier first time with a stranger. Herd-girls – so Leofsunu said, smacking his lips – were always grateful for a tumble to pass the time.

He was coming up to the crest of a low ridge. The slope around him was crowded with hawthorn bushes, white as snowdrifts with blossom. There was a fold in the ground just ahead, hardly deep enough to call a valley. To his left a thread of water ran out of it, one of the streams that met lower down to make the river Deben. He crawled on all fours to the top of the ridge and looked warily over the rim.

The dell beneath sheltered a grove of aspens. The stream flowed out from among them; its source must be at the foot of the hill. The girls were there. They were singing a dance-song; he caught glimpses of moving shapes among the trees.

> 'Maiden in the moor lay,
> In the moor lay:
> Sevennight full,
> Sevennight full –
> Maiden in the moor lay,
> Seven nights full and a day.'

He got up, went softly down the slope and trod like a cat between the aspens in case his foot cracked a twig to warn them.

There were four of them, come to dress the well. Garlands of leaves and flowers lay round it on the grass and hung over it from the aspen branches. Behind the spring, standing alone, was a young apple-tree, pink with buds. The girls were dancing round it. They had taken off their woollen mantles and trailing gowns to move more freely; they had nothing on but their smocks. Their linen was as light as morning mist, it floated round their legs, haunches and breasts rather than clothing them.

The costly stuff, and the whiteness of the limbs it hardly veiled, showed him that these were not weather-beaten herd-girls but noblewomen. They could only be Lord Helm's daughter and some of the high-born kinswomen who shared her mother's bower.

Geat would never dare try to romp or tumble with them; it would cost him his life. He sat down to enjoy the sight of their beauty as a gift from the gods. As an excuse for watching them, he took his harp from its bag and began to play the tune for them.

> 'Well was her drink.
> What was her drink?
> The chill water of the –
> The chill water of the –
> Well was her drink.
> What was her drink?
> The chill water of the well-spring.'

When the girls heard the harp, they looked over their shoulders, laughed, waved, blew kisses to him and went on dancing, stepping to each other in pairs, joining in a ring to circle the apple tree, breaking the ring to twirl singly, then giving hands in a chain till they paired off once more. Geat tried to pick out the one he would have if he dared.

One girl was lofty and slender, with silver-pale hair braided back and knotted like a warrior. She had a proud, clear-cut face; there was such fierce joy in her dancing that she made him think of a wælcyrie flying across a battlefield.

Her partner was not so tall and moved as shyly as a bride being led by her maidens to her marriage-bed. She was as fresh and delicate as the daisies and cuckoo-flowers she wore in a crown on her fair curls.

The third girl was darker and more full-bodied. Her hair was the colour of beech leaves after harvest-time, her lips were juicy-red like ripe berries, her breasts were round and firm as apples. For a moment Geat was sorry he had not found her alone.

Then the fourth dancer swung round to face him, coming down the chain towards him. He forgot about the other three.

She was a summer's day. The blue sky, the apple-buds, the sun itself seemed only reflections from her eyes, her cheeks, her hair. He wanted nothing now but to spend the rest of his life making music for her so that he could watch her dancing. He chose the songs he thought would please her, because their mood matched the summer and her looks – '*At a spring well under a thorn*' '*Up sun and merry weather*' '*The nightingale sings*' – changing the tune every time she changed partners, never taking his eyes off her.

He must have turned giddy and light-headed from staring at her whirling round the ring. Sometimes the other three – the wælcyrie, the flower-bride and the fruit-bearer – seemed to melt into body of the golden lady and she danced alone. Then, suddenly, there seemed to be as many as a dozen girls circling the apple-tree. Yet still, whatever tricks his eyes played on him, his fingers went on playing without a pause as if the dance would go on for ever.

He was taken aback when it stopped; his fingers lost their place, and the harp-strings jangled into silence.

The lady looked at her maids.

'All good things must have an end. Come Hreð, Eostre, Gyfu – it's time to be on our way.'

She turned to Geat.

'Thank you, gleeman. You made good pastime for us. What's your fee?'

'You've already paid me, lady. You let me play for your dancing.'

Hreð, Eostre and Gyfu clapped their hands, laughing. The lady raised her eyebrows.

'There's a flattering tongue, fit for a king's hall.'

As she spoke, her face changed; he was frightened to see how stern and grim she looked. Her voice sounded harsh as a bird of prey.

'So you're above taking pay from me? You despise my gold?'

He felt sick that she should think he had insulted her. He was too upset to pick his words carefully.

'The only true gold – the only gold I want is growing on your head. Yet I wouldn't rob you of one hair.'

She smiled. Suddenly she grew so tall that she towered over him. She was crowned with the sun, light streamed from her limbs. He knew she was The Lady, Freo, Mother of Earth, Queen of Heaven. He crouched on his knees, bowing his forehead to the ground in worship.

'So you won't take a fee? Then I'll make you a gift.'

He felt that she bent over him and that her hair brushed across his head and shoulders. The harp was drawn gently from under his hand.

'Hark what I am giving you.'

She played three tunes, each very short, with just enough notes in them to fit one phrase of a song. Yet there was enough music in them to fill the world with songs.

The first was rich with the joys of life, the fruitfulness of earth, the strength of beasts, the courage and pride of heroes.

The second was enticing with the promise of wonders to come, quests to follow, treasures and kingdoms to win.

The third was sharp as a spear-thrust with longing for past happiness and lost loves. Geat felt tears welling under his closed eyelids and pouring down his cheeks at the sweetness of it. Then there was silence. He opened his eyes.

She was gone. There was no one else to be seen in the wood, the valley or the sky above, except a hawk flying high and distant. The Goddess had put on her falcon cloak; she was soaring beyond the reach of his sight. Even as he caught a glimpse of her, she vanished.

He could not bear the valley without her. He looked round to take his harp and go. The sunlight dazzled his wet eyes. The harp seemed to be ablaze. He blinked and rubbed his sleeve across his face; he was young enough to be ashamed of crying. The harp still made a patch of glittering light on the turf. He put out his hand to touch it, hardly believing what he saw.

The wood was now corn-gold in colour, fine-grained and polished smooth. The arched yoke was clamped to the sound-box by two small plates of wrought gold, each plate crowned with falcons' heads. The bridge was amber and the strings were golden. They seemed to be made of gold wire but when he touched them, they felt warm and alive. His heart pounded like a smith's hammer at the thought that The Lady had strung the harp for him with her hair. As he stroked it, the harp began to sing under his fingers.

At last, his hands could make the music he heard inside him. He played every song he knew. Now he felt happy with the sounds he made - almost perfectly happy. One thing baffled him. He had prided himself on being able to catch and hold any tune at first hearing. Yet try as he would, he could not repeat The Lady's three strains just as she had played them, though he could hear them behind all the other music he made - the joy, the hope, the longing. He could get near enough to the joy and the hope but the sorrow-song escaped him. Again and again it slipped from his mind just when he thought his hands had caught it.

Time stood still while his fingers were searching for it. He was sure that if he played the three tunes right, he would meet The Lady again. Then he heard something else behind his music: the stamp, snort and shaken bridle of a restless horse.

He looked up, startled. A group of riders had paused at the mouth of the dell to listen to him. Lord Helm and some of his men.

'Well played, harper – Why, it's young Geat! Been up to the sheep-walks? That's a very fine harp you've got. One of your poor mother's heirlooms, eh? You shouldn't be loitering out on your own with a treasure like that, you're asking for a robber's knife in you. Better come back to the hall with us, you can have a bed for the night.'

Geat knew that this kindness was really a command: Lord Helm wanted to listen to more of his harp music that evening. He was happy to obey. It seemed fitting that he should end his day of wonders feasting as a guest in a lord's hall.

The day he met The Lady was the start of Geat's good luck. After listening to him that evening, Lord Helm swore that his harping was fit for a king's hall. Next day, when he set out for a meeting of the witan at Rendlesham, he took Geat with him.

Though Geat had never known his brother Hafoc, he knew his unhappy story. Leofsunu had been throwing it at him as a warning every time he showed signs of having a will of his own. He was determined not to make Hafoc's mistakes.

He had grown up watching his mother's manners and listening to her stories about King Beowulf's court, so he had some idea how to behave. He had his father's honesty and commonsense to steady him, so he did not let the company and notice of great folk go to his head. He got through the first days at Rendlesham without any serious blunders, even when he was bewildered, almost drunk on the splendours of the royal hall. He took his place under the eyes of the lords without cringing or swaggering. His music saved him from that. Whenever he played his harp, he was worshipping at The Lady's feet and cared for no one else.

One counsellor, a very rich man with a powerful following, gave him sour looks. He talked in a loud voice about churls, the need to keep them in their place, how disgusting it was when they got out of their sties and pig-runs and brought their stink into noble halls.

Geat was upset. As a churl's son, he did not know how he could either challenge the insults or take them meekly. Lord Helm told him not to hear them.

'Everyone knows why Herebeald's got a grudge against you. Your brother Hafoc sheathed a knife in him years ago. He's none the worse, except for a scar and the loss of a jugful or so of blood – the gods know he got enough wergild in exchange! Anyway, the matter was settled at the time in front of the king. So if Herebeald wants to question the king's judgement, he'd better do so to the king's face.'

Folk did not question King Wulf's judgement if they hoped to live and prosper. Likely, Helm said a word or two of warning; the insults stopped. The king was delighted with Geat's playing. The queen said he harped like one of the elves. Most of the nobles enjoyed listening to him and treated him kindly. Geat's best luck, in the long run, was that the royal scop took a liking to him.

Æschere was of noble birth. His warrior sons had not inherited his gift. They did not want or need to inherit his place as scop. He was glad to adopt the gifted boy as his pupil.

From him, Geat learned the precious words that were kept apart in the word-hoard for the scop's use and never heard in common talk. He learned to set them, like jewels in wrought gold, to make chains of linked sounds, interlacing many meanings in short spell-binding phrases. Now he could understand his mother's fury when he told her he meant to be a common gleeman like Mul Harper.

He grew very skilful at his craft. He never became such a wizard with words as Æschere. When he set his poems to his music, though, he played on his listeners as well as on his harp. He gave them the joys of life – the courage and pride of heroes, the splendour of kings and kingdoms, the enticement of quests to follow, monsters to kill and treasures to win. Even when he sang of last stands and loyalty held fast till death, he made them sound like victories.

He had given up trying to play the sorrow-song. At last, it faded from his mind.

He put his love for The Lady into every song he made. He sang of her power strengthening the heroes, her beauty reflected in king's daughters, her wisdom and bounty flowing from gracious queens. He was as welcome in the bower as in the hall.

Geat learned another use of word-craft during his years with Æschere. Scops were honoured in every tribe. They could pass freely from one kingdom to another even in war-time. So kings often sent them as envoys, to confirm friendships, arrange marriages, settle feuds. Geat made many such journeys with his master, first as his servant, then as his partner. At last, the old man grew tired and chose to live quietly on the estate the king had granted him. Geat took his place as the royal scop.

So the years passed, bringing him fame and rich gifts. Many of the gifts went to enrich his father's farm and fill his mother with happy pride.

A time came when the king himself took ship and went in state to visit King Iurmenric of Kent. The chief aim of both kings was war against the East Saxons. Also, each king wanted to impress the other with his greater power and splendour.

The Anglians found that they had Franks to impress as well. There were envoys, stiff with pride and jewellery, come from King Charibert of Paris about a marriage between his daughter and Iurmenric's son. Even these Franks admitted that they had never heard harping to equal Geat's.

King Wulf was gratified, then alarmed. Iurmenric often remarked when Geat could hear him, that if he had a harper like that, he would know how to reward him. The Franks said courteously that no doubt such a great scop would soon be setting out on his travels. He could be sure of a welcome whenever he came to King Charibert's palace.

Wulf knew that he might lose the wonderful harping – and the fame it brought to his court – unless the harper was firmly tethered there by loyalty and gratitude.

As they were being rowed back up the Deben, the king talked to Geat about how good it was to come home, how glad he would be to see his hall and his queen again.

'It's time you were settled too, Geat, with lands and a hall of your own. If ever any man deserved land-right, you do. You'll need a wife to oversee your household. I know the very one to suit you – my young kinswoman Maeðhild, the queen's fosterling. She loves the girl like a daughter; she doesn't want to part with her. But you'll spend so much time at court, she won't have to suffer much loss when the girl's a wife.'

He paused, smiling, watching Geat's face.

Geat said the right words about his joy, his thankfulness, his undying loyalty to the king. He was telling the truth; he wanted an estate and meant to repay the king with honest service. While he spoke he was trying to remember what Maeðhild looked like. He knew who she was, of course, it was a scop's business to know everyone in the royal household. She was young, an orphan, daughter of one of the king's cousins, the queen's darling. He tried to see her in his mind's eye. He could only recall a patch of silence that the queen liked to have at her side rather than any of the talkative giggling girls who waited on her in her bower.

Geat shared the queen's taste. He hated folk chattering near him, most of all when he was working on a song. A silent wife with royal blood, sure of the queen's goodwill, would be a useful gain. Anyway, whatever Maeðhild was like, he would have to take her. Also, his mother would be pleased about the marriage.

Cyneburh was more than pleased. When he came to her with the news, her worn face glowed. For a moment she looked like a girl.

'Oh my dear son, I'm so proud of you! Though it's not more than you deserve. I hope your bride knows you have royal blood too. I want you to take her a gift from me, to show her what family you come from.'

She hurried to her chest, unlocked it, rummaged and took out a little box of whalebone, carved with scenes of Sigemund fighting the dragon.

'I brought these treasures from Geatland. The last time I wore them, I was welcoming King Beowulf in my father's hall. I could never wear them here. I didn't even want to show them to churls who only thought of exchanging them for cattle – But now your lady will wear them for me at Rendlesham.'

She lifted the lid and held the box towards Geat. He looked inside; his heart sank.

His mother had given her best jewels to pay for Hafoc's crime. All she had left were a few small brooches, a couple of finger rings, one set with a Roman coin, and a little chain of linked pins in wrought gold. Memory had turned them into priceless treasures in Cyneburh's eyes but they would look poor at Rendlesham.

He took the box, told his mother that Maeðhild would be overjoyed, kissed her and left her happy. All the way back to the king's hall, he was asking himself what to do with the gift. Hide it and give Maeðhild something costly in his mother's name? Or fill the box with some of his own jewels to make a better show?

Then he felt angry for his mother's sake. She had given up her last treasures for Maeðhild. He would make Maeðhild take them, in front of the queen and all her bower-maidens. And if Maeðhild showed the least sign of disappointment or scorn, then for all her royal blood he would despise her for ever.

He looked so grim when he came into the queen's bower and offered the box to Maeðhild, he might have been giving her gold stolen from a dragon's mound with a curse on it. The bower-maidens crowded round, eager to see treasures from Geatland, craning over her shoulders to look into the box as she lifted the lid.

There was a moment's silence. Then Lord Herebeald's daughter sniggered aloud. None of that family had ever forgiven the stabbing. They would be glad to see Geat look small.

The queen frowned a warning; the other girls tried to stifle their giggles. They stared at Maeðhild greedily, waiting to hear what she would say.

Maeðhild touched the little brooches with her fingertips.

'To think your mother wore these when she gave the mead-cup to King Beowulf! That's treasure upon treasure.'

She glanced shyly at Geat. 'Your mother has done me a great honour. You must lend me some of your scop's words to send to her, so that my thanks can match her gift.'

Geat felt grateful to his bride. Though he had seen her often, he looked at her for the first time with some interest. She was small and sturdily-built, though her waist was slender and she moved gracefully. She had smooth braids of light-brown hair, greyish-blue eyes, a round childish face with pink cheeks. She had none of the radiant beauty of a goddess, yet there was something about her that recalled the day he had seen The Lady. Then he remembered the young apple-tree that grew by the holy well.

He heard the other girls muttering among themselves.

'Some folk are easily pleased!'

'I should have thought he was rich enough to give her –'

Herebeald's daughter leaned her head towards them, pretending to whisper: 'I suppose those things look very wonderful to churls.'

Geat took as little heed of them as if they were buzzing flies. He smiled at Maeðhild.

'You don't need a scop to lend you golden words, my lady, any more than you need jewels to set off your beauty.'

Geat was pleased with his bride. He looked forward to having her in his bed. He did not see her again, though, till his wedding feast. He had to go north into Lindsey on the king's business, then to ride round his new estate, meet his steward and order his hall to be new furnished. Cyneburh came to see that all was ready and to welcome her daughter-in-law when Geat brought her home.

He came back to Rendlesham at the end of harvest. The weather was as sunny as his spirits.

The queen herself had decked Maeðhild for the bride-ale. The girl was so covered with embroidered robes, golden ornaments and garlands that she looked like a temple image on a holy day. She gazed at the ground when she was led to meet him, as a modest maiden should. When they were sitting side by side at the feast, he was able to whisper to her and try to coax a smile out of her. He leaned against her shoulder and looked closely at her downcast face. He was shocked, alarmed, angry.

If he had been making a poem out of some old story, he might have said that a young apple-tree in bloom had been changed by evil spells into a fading windflower. Her cheeks were pale, there were dark shadows under her eyes, her face was thinner. She was only making a show of eating and drinking.

Of course, well-bred maidens did not stuff themselves like pigs or get helplessly drunk at their bride-ales. They had to pretend not to understand most of the jokes. But they were not forbidden to look happy or to smile at their bridegrooms from time to time. Maeðhild's face might have been carved out of whalebone; it showed no glimmer of joy or even interest.

If she had been taken sick, surely the queen would have sent him word and put off the bride-ale till she was well again.

Perhaps she was scared of bedding with him. She was very young; the other girls might have frightened her with their talk. Girls liked to boast of their knowledge and tell tall stories just as much as men; he'd heard them on the farm. Herebeald's bitch would take delight in turning his bride against him, telling her that he'd come into her like a bull – like a *churl*.

He winced, feeling his mother's blow on his face, hearing the cold scorn in her voice – '*Haven't I suffered enough even yet?*' – seeing her bending over the jewels she had worn as a girl in her father's hall – '*I could never wear them here. I didn't even want to show them to churls who only thought of exchanging them for cattle –*'.

His mother was pitiable and he had always pitied her. For the first time he pitied his father, an honest good-natured man living for years with the knowledge of his wife's scorn.

He made up his mind that he would settle his married life that night, once and for all. If Maeðhild was only scared, he would be very gentle with her. If she thought she had been lowered by getting an honest churl's son as her husband, he would teach her to think better.

In his years as a scop and a king's spokesman, he had learned to master his voice and his face. He could brood, resent, plan, all the while he was talking, laughing and drinking with the wedding-guests. After the queen and the other women took Maeðhild away to undress her and put her to bed, the drinking got deeper and the jokes lewder. At last, he set out by torchlight in a rowdy procession to join her. A small bower had been made ready for the couple. The queen was waiting in the porch to give him the key. She went away with her maidens. There was a bout of cheerful insults between Geat and his companions, offers to undress him, to come in with him and show him what to do. Then he told them to go and drink good luck to him, slammed the door in their grinning faces, locked it and went to take his bride.

He meant to begin kindly; he put his arms round her and kissed her. Her flesh was cold in spite of the blankets. He felt her shudder at his touch, then stiffen. Her cheek was wet and salt to his lips. He drew away from her.

'Why are you crying? Isn't my estate big enough for your pride to live on? Isn't my father's name noble enough for you? Do you feel shamed marrying a churl's son?'

She came alive at that, turned to him wide-eyed, reached for his hand and clutched it.

'No, that's not true! The gods know how glad I was at first – how proud to be chosen bride of the greatest harper on Middle Earth. I'm crying because I'll never be your wife.'

They had just shared their wedding feast; they were naked in bed together. She could see the look on his face by the firelight. She shook her head.

'I'm not mad. I wish I were. Then the cunning-women could give me herbs and charms to cure me.'

'You're talking madness. You are my wife, that's why you're lying with me. I've a right to know what ails you.'

She nodded.

'A week ago, I went out to gather garlands for the queen's bower. She says I make them better than the other girls. That's because I go just before sunrise, when the plants are fresh with the morning dew. I was so happy, thinking of the garland I'd wear on my wedding day –'

She sighed.

'I went down to the water-meadows. I've always loved Deben River, it flows near my father's hall. There was a grassy bank close by the water's edge, where my nurse used to sit and spin on sunny days. The water-flowers grew thicker and brighter there than anywhere else. I used to pick them to make myself necklaces and bracelets. I wove crowns of rushes and played I was a queen. When I was very young, I thought the sound of the water was the river talking and singing to me. I'd sing and talk back to it, I felt it was my friend – though once it tried to drown me when I fell in and got caught among the weeds. But even after that, I wouldn't – I couldn't keep away from the river bank. And then, when my father was killed and the queen took me to live here in her bower, I always liked to walk in the water-meadows. I felt I was still at home because I was still beside the Deben.'

Geat let her go on talking about her childhood as long as she liked. It did not seem much to the purpose. He thought she was just talking to steady herself, till she felt ready to put her fear into words.

'When I went out last week, there were still patches of mist like women's veils lying on the grass and hanging on the bushes down by the river till the sun came up to dry them. I saw that the mist was thickest near a willow that leaned out from the bank. I made up my mind not to go too close in case I lost my footing. I thought – I hadn't remembered it for years – how I had tumbled in and how the weeds had clutched me. I knew there was nobody within call to help me and suddenly I was afraid. Yet I couldn't stop my feet from walking towards the tree – or turn my eyes away from the mist that was rising beside it – even when I saw –'

Geat felt her beginning to tremble. He put his arm round her shoulders. Her eyes were fixed and staring, as if she could still see what she had seen down by the Deben.

'- I saw the mist taking shape - like a man - a king in flowing robes of green - or blue - or sword grey - they changed every moment and they were glittering with jewels, so that my eyes were dazzled and my head seemed to be full of swirling water. I could see a face in the mist, very beautiful but cold and white with eyes like glass. Then, even as I looked, the face melted and there was nothing but mist in drops on my eyelids and cheeks and lips - and always the sound of the river swirling in my head - and it - he - was saying that I had belonged to him ever since I had taken his betrothal gifts to wear - that I had exchanged vows with him - he had desired me ever since he held me in his arms - and now I was a woman he had come to take me to his hall and his bed -'

She was shaking so much that she could hardly gasp out her words.

'The mist reached out to fold round me. The face came again and kissed me, its mouth was corpse-cold. The waters seemed to rush over my head and I knew I was drowning. I was struggling but I could feel my strength washed out of me - then the sun rose and hurled her golden spears through the mist. It drew back, so I could pull myself free and run back to the stronghold.'

She clutched at Geat as if she had just reached the guardhouse at the gate.

'Did you tell anyone - the queen, the priest?'

'No, I didn't dare. I was afraid if they knew the river-lord had claimed me, they'd give me to him, for the luck of the king and the land. A year ago, I'd have been proud to be chosen. I'd have woven my garlands with a glad heart, I'd have taken my place on the wicker bier and let them carry me down to the water - but since I knew you wanted me for your wife, I couldn't bear to leave the earth and the sunlight, to drown -'

'You won't. I'll not let you go. You belong to me.'

'He says I've been his since I was a child. He's been waiting for me.'

'You must never go near the river bank.'

'He comes here. He comes up from the river with the evening mists.'

'Never go outside after sunset. Wait for the sunrise.'

'He keeps calling me. Whenever it's quiet I can hear the river singing.'

'Don't listen. I'll play sweeter music for you. You must sing and be merry, darling. If you lose heart, you'll give him power over you.'

'I haven't told you the worst. I can keep him away while I'm wide awake. But whenever my mind slackens guard over my body, he can reach me.'

She began to sob.

'As soon as I close my eyes, I can feel his cold arms clasping me and the river runs over my head. If he ever finds me fast asleep, he'll come into me and take me. I can't rest because of his terrible love. I haven't slept for a week.'

Geat hugged her.

'That's because you were lying alone. It's my arms you can feel clasping you now. I'll never let him take you, I give you my word. I have you and I'll hold you. Hold me close too, sweetheart – we won't leave him any room to come in!'

He handled her gently, as if he were tuning a harp that had been roughly misused. She answered to his touch; soon they were playing sweetly together. When she fell asleep in his arms, he lay as still as he could for fear of disturbing her rest.

But then she began to stir and moan. She struggled to tear herself out of his arms and woke herself, screaming. Her eyes were blank with terror.

'Hush now, love. You were only dreaming. I've been awake all the time. Nothing came near you, I swear it. Lie still. I'll light the candles and make up the fire. Then we'll drink mead together, you hardly touched a drop during our wedding feast.'

He kissed her. She was cold; her flesh was damp with sweat. As he stroked her hair away from her face, something slimy coiled round his fingers and gripped them. He was thankful that she was resting her forehead against his shoulder and did not see that his right hand was bound with a trail of waterweed.

He got out of bed and, under cover of making up the fire, pulled off the weed and threw it into the flames. He enjoyed watching it writhe and shrivel as it scorched to ash.

After that, they passed every night of the wedding celebrations with candles burning and the hearth ablaze. When they were not love-making, they talked and drank. He played the harp or told stories to help them stay awake. They only let themselves sleep after sunrise. Nobody was surprised that they stayed late abed and looked drowsy when they joined the company. There were more jokes and congratulations.

Nothing else happened to frighten Maeðhild. Geat was sure she would be safe once he had got her away from the Deben. His estate was away on the uplands to the north-west. The hall was nowhere near a river; it had a well. There was good pasture-land but the streams that watered it flowed north into the Dove.

The sun was high before the bridal procession set out with Maeðhild to her new home. She had four maid-servants from the queen's household. A band of young warriors came to guard her on her way and to drink with Geat in his fine hall. They brought their grooms; some of them had their best hawks perched on their wrists and their favourite hounds trotting beside them, ready for any sport that might offer during Geat's house-warming.

They had not gone far, riding at an easy pace, talking and laughing as they went. Suddenly one of the hounds, that had gone nosing into a thicket, gave tongue. The leading horse reared and plunged when a great hart sprang out of cover almost under its nose. The beast's hide was pale and drenched with dew. In the sunlight it seemed glistening white and its horns shone like silver. It fled with the hound at its heels.

The leading rider, who owned the hound, gave a whoop of joy and went after them. All his companions hallooed to their own hounds and hurtled off in a wild chase. Geat left Maeðhild's side at a reckless gallop to catch and pass the others. He was lusting to kill the hart himself and set those magnificent silver horns as a trophy on the gable of his hall.

After a moment's bewilderment, the girls shrieked with excitement and set off in pursuit of the men.

The hunt took them far out into the waste land. Sometimes the hounds were snapping at the quarry's heels. Then it would outstrip them with a sudden burst of speed. At last it flagged and the hunters closed in, yelling.

Just then, under the noonday sun shining from a cloudless sky, they were wrapped in a blanketing swirl of mist. It melted almost as soon as it rose. When it vanished, so had the hart. There was no cover within sight. There were no tracks. The hounds were running back and forth, baffled by lack of scent.

Several of the hunters made the sign of Thunor's Hammer. Someone muttered, 'Sorcery!'

Geat screamed, '*Maeðhild!*'

He swung his weary horse round and forced it as fast as it could go back the way they had come. The other hunters called their hounds and followed him.

It was some time before they met the girls, who had dropped out of the chase when the going got too rough. They were pacing slowly along, breathless and dishevelled. Four of them.

Geat rode up calling, 'Where is Maeðhild?'

They looked startled.

'Isn't she with you?'

'She rode after you like the wind!'

'She went so fast we could hardly see her!'

Geat groaned.

'You didn't see her riding after me. We've all been spellbound.'

They rode back with growing uneasiness. They came to the thicket where the hart had appeared. Ahead of them was the track to Rendlesham. Near the thicket the ground had been badly cut up when the riders started to jostle for a place in the hunt.

One rider had turned aside. One horse had gone straight towards the Deben.

They followed the hoof-prints to the bank. They saw none returning. Yet there was no ford on that reach of the river. No one in her senses would have tried to cross at that place.

The girls cried out in horror.

'Her horse must have bolted when we followed the hunt!'

'We scared it with our noise!'

'And none of us stopped to help her!'

They burst out crying and wailing for the dead.

One man said hopefully, 'Maybe the horse swam downstream and clambered out. If she kept her seat, she'll have gone back to Rendlesham.'

'They'd have sent someone to tell us.'

'No. They'd know we'd be coming back to look for her.'

'Best go on to Rendlesham anyway. We'll send the fishermen out with poles and nets –'

They turned their horses. Geat was staring at the river; he did not move. When they asked him gently if he was coming with them, he shook his head without looking round.

'I'll ride along the bank as far as the bend and wait for you there.'

Hoof beats and the clink of bridle-reins told him they were going away. There was no talking or laughing as the wedding procession went back to Rendlesham.

Geat was not sure why he stayed beside the Deben – to be silent, to avoid his friends' pity, to get out of earshot of the girls' snivelling. Most of all, he felt he would be deserting Maeðhild if he left her in the river. Yet he had no hope of saving her or even of finding her body without the help of the fishermen's poles. The water was flowing smoothly, without a ripple. It looked as hard as a silver mirror. He could not see through it; nothing showed but the banks reflected on its face.

The brightness dazzled him; he shut his eyes. When he opened them he could see down through the water. Maeðhild was sitting on a silver throne, in a hall that seemed to be made of green glass, like the king's wonderful Frankish goblets. She was crowned with a wreath of pearls and dressed in a jewelled robe that shimmered like water-drops. She was as still as a carved image. Her face looked frozen with despair.

He only saw her for a moment. Then there was nothing but the dazzle blinding him again. Yet her image was under his eyelids whenever he closed his eyes.

If Maeðhild was being held captive in the river-elf's hall, he would have to go there and get her out. He remembered his mother telling him how King Beowulf in his young days had tracked a water-troll to its lair at the bottom of a lake and killed it. What man has done man can do.

But he was a scop, not a hero-king with a bear's strength in his arms. Perhaps craft and skill would help him in place of might. He could give rich gifts to the gods to get them on his side, get the priest to offer sacrifices, hire a sorcerer to fight magic with magic –

It would all take time. His heart ached to think of Maeðhild's despair meanwhile, shut up in the glass hall under the water, clasped in the water-elf's cold arms.

Perhaps he had not really seen her. The elf might have cast a spell in his eyes, to lure him into the river and drown him. Perhaps he himself had made a wish-dream out of his grief and longing to see her again. He might have said that Maeðhild had been dreaming her terrors if he had not found the water-weed in her hair. He might even have believed he had dreamed his meeting with The Lady, if he had not got his harp –

The Lady's harp, strung with her hair, touched by her hands. Her power was in it. Its voice could dive through the water, quick as a thought, pierce the elvish hall, comfort Maeðhild and give her hope. It would tell her that he was coming to bring her back to the world of humankind.

His took the harp from its bag of beaver's fur, sat down on the bank and began to play the music that Freo had taught him. He sang of the joy of life under the sun, the warmth and fruitfulness of the earth.

His horse stopped grazing to listen. The herds in the pasture turned their heads, then began to move towards him. A wolf came out of the woods like a grey shadow and stretched on the grass beside the herdsman's dog. Linnets and reed-buntings fluttered round his head; they showed no fear of the man nor of the hawks, kites and ravens that now crowded every branch of the nearest trees.

Geat sang of hope – of quests to follow, treasures to win, lovers' meetings. On turf where he sat, plants that had ended their blossoming for the year suddenly swelled with next year's spring buds and burst into flower. In the fisherman's hut downstream, the goodwife clutched her belly and called out to her younger sister, 'Run and fetch the cunning-woman! The child's coming before its time!'

But Geat was growing aware that something was badly amiss. For the first time since he became a harper, he was having a struggle to play. He meant to send Maeðhild a message of hope and joy. He could no longer make his hands obey his will. The strings he touched sounded more and more sadly, till the harp seemed crying out with the pain of loss and longing.

Against his will, he was playing the third melody The Lady had given him, the sorrow-song that for a while he had tried in vain to remember, then cheerfully forgotten during the years when luck was with him. Now, he could play nothing else.

In her bower at Rendlesham, busy with her embroidery, the queen thought of her only daughter, whom she had loved more than all her sons, who had died of marsh-fever just as she was growing into womanhood. Her eyes filled; she looked up, blinking, from her stitches. Eadgyð was coming in, her fair head bright in the sunlight, bringing flowers for her mother as always. The queen stretched out her arms; Eadgyð smiled at her and vanished. There was nothing in the doorway but a shaft of afternoon sunlight. Eadgyð was lying in her mound in the grave-field. The queen bowed her head and wept. Her women stared at her in alarm. The bride's maids, coming in fearfully to break the news about Maeðhild, wondered how she could have heard so soon.

Geat was in despair. The sun had been hidden by a cloud; he felt chilled to his heart. The river was troubled; its waters were tossing restlessly, dark with churned mud.

Then the sun broke free. The waves sparkled like splinters of broken glass. A streak of white foam came whirling past – then he saw it was a woman's veil. Maeðhild's body floated to the surface. It was being carried downstream towards the sea.

He jumped into the water, calling on Freo for help, and fought the river for possession of her. It nearly drowned him, for he would not let her go even to save himself. He was washed towards the bank at the bend and managed to drag her out. At least he could lay her in the earth, under the light of the sun and the moon.

Maeðhild stirred, coughed, gasped, blinked at him.

'Whatever made my horse bolt and throw me like that? If you hadn't been close by to pull me out, I'd have drowned!'

Geat was too busy for the next few moments, pulling off her wet clothes, drying her with his shirt, dressing her in his woollen tunic and cloak, to wonder at what she said or even feel glad she was alive.

Maeðhild wrung some of the water out of her hair and shook the tresses loose. She held out her arms towards the sun.

'The air's so warm. I'll soon be dry.'

He mounted his horse and pulled her up in front of him, holding her in the crook of his left arm. The feel of her body made him at last believe that he had got her back. She was The Lady's gift to him. Freo had foreknown this moment, when she gave him the harp that had called Maeðhild back to him.

As they rode back to Rendlesham, his spirits were as sunny as the weather. Yet he could hear someone sobbing. The voice came from the Deben. The river-elf was mourning for his lost love.

Geat looked anxiously at Maeðhild. He could see that she did not hear the sobbing. She did not know how long she had been under the water. Her mind held no picture of the elvish hall where she had been throned and crowned as queen of the Deben. She seemed to have forgotten the unearthly love that had robbed her of her sleep. Just now, she was laughing to think of the figure she would make at Rendlesham in her man's tunic and cloak.

'I'll say I've come to join the king's war-band!'

Geat was glad for her sake. Still, he could not get the sound of that desolate sobbing out of his ears. In his mind, it blended with the sorrow-song, the world's grief for lost beauty, dead love, longing that could never die.

He knew that he would have to listen to that song as long as he lived, that he would hear it behind every joy that life brought him, that its notes would sound in every song he made.

This also was The Lady's gift.

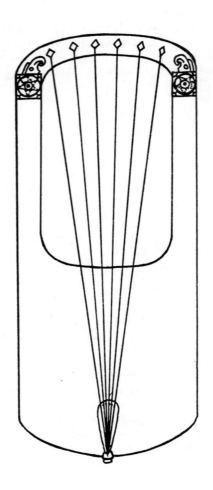

Spellcraft

A 'spell' in Old English was an announcement or an account of something that had happened. So originally a spell was offered to its hearers as a true story. Time, and the workings of human nature, gave the word another meaning fairly soon: 'Ealdra cwena spell' – old woman's tale, fable, false or foolish story.

Any story, or other creative work, crafted in the 20th century, runs the risk of being 'false and foolish' if it is set in a distant age. We should speak about what we know and create our art from and for our own time. Yet to be forced to stay mentally and imaginatively in one time is as great a loss of liberty as to be forced to stay physically in one place. We learn more about our own country by travelling, including time-travelling.

If 'the past is another country', we need to learn its language and customs before we write about it, always remembering that no visitor, however curious, conscientious and sensitive to the atmosphere of a period, will ever know it or experience it like a native.

The best way to learn a language, with its own modes of thinking and feeling, is to listen to the natives talking. The best way, indeed the only way, to write stories and poems (or operas, film-scripts, plays for stage and television) about the early English, is to listen first while they are telling their own stories, expressing their own ideas and feelings, until you begin to catch the tone of their voices, follow the movement of their minds. Working with Old English themes begins with reading Old English literature.

Ideally, that means reading it in Old English to experience its full flavour. Luckily, story-tellers and story-hunters who want to enjoy the literature first, then tackle the language later, have been well-served by translators. I can recommend the two Penguin Classics: *The Earliest English Poems* and *Beowulf*, both by Michael Alexander, because they can be read and enjoyed as poetry in their own right, have stimulating introductions and useful notes, and are easy to carry around. Kevin Crossley-Holland and Richard Hamer have also made expressive and moving verse translations. The Everyman Classic: *Anglo-Saxon Poetry* by S A J Bradley, is in prose which stays as close to the original wording as is possible in Modern

English. It is the largest available collection of translations in one easily-portable book. The headnotes, which deal with the manuscripts as well as the poems, are very illuminating. For sheer beauty of presentation, Julian Glover's version of *Beowulf* for an evening's dramatic recital, with Sheila Mackies' superb glowing designs, is unequalled: it gives a sense both of the excitement of a scop's performance in hall and of the magnificence of early English illuminated books.

However, the Old English language is not difficult for English people to learn. Readers who find that hard to credit, try this short text as an experiment (and appetiser), seeing how many words you find you already know. It is Riddle 74 in the Exeter Book numbering:

> 'Ic wæs fæmne geong, feaxhar cwene,
> ond ænlic rinc on ane tid;
> fleah mid fuglum ond on flod swom,
> deaf under yþe dead mid fiscum,
> ond on foldan stop, hæfde ferð cwicu.'

Taking it apart word by word we have:

ic	*wæs*	*fæmne*	*geong*	*feaxhar*	*cwene*
I	was	woman	young	'hair-hoary'	queen
		maiden		grey-haired	quean (whore)
		virgin			

ond	*ænlic*	*rinc*	*on*	*ane*	*tid*
and	'one-like'	man	on	one	time
	unique	warrior	in		
	matchless		at		

fleah	*mid*	*fuglum*	*ond*	*on*	*flode*	*swom*
(I) flew	'amid'	'fowls'	and	on	'flood'	swam
	with	birds			tide, sea	
	among				flowing	
					stream	

deaf	*under*	*yþe*	*dead*	*mid*	*fiscum*
(I) dived	under	wave	dead	among	fishes

ond	*on*	*foldan*	*stop*	*hæfde*	*ferð*	*cwicu*
and	on	earth	'stepped'	(I) had	spirit	'quick'
		dry land	advanced		soul	alive
			went			living

'I was a young maiden, a grey-haired queen (or, I was a virgin, a grey-haired whore – or both; Old English poetry used words with double or multiple meanings). I flew with birds, swam on the flowing tide, dived under the wave dead among fishes, I walked on dry land, I had a living soul.'

Or, in Michael Alexander's freer, but much more beautiful translation, composed in a modern version of Old English verse-form:

> 'I was in one hour an ashen crone,
> a fair-faced man, a fresh girl,
> floated on foam, flew with birds
> under wave dived, dead among fish,
> and walked upon land a living soul.'
>
> (*The Earliest English Poems* p.101)

Faced with a creature that is both old and young, male and female, virgin, queen and whore, that flies with birds, swims on the tide, dives to the sea-bed and lies dead among the fishes yet walks on dry land with a living soul, editors and translators have suggested: a cuttlefish, a swan, water, rain, a ship's figure-head, a siren – or have frankly given up.

There are some very old poems in other languages, in which the poet or shaman recounts his incarnations and shape-shiftings. Keats said that a poet had to have 'negative capability': he must stop being John Keats (or Geoffrey Chaucer or William Shakespeare, Joseph Turner or William Blake) and *become* whatever he is creating.

I believe the answer to Riddle 74 is 'Scop' (poet, maker); the riddle enacts both the workings of the creative imagination and the 'spell' (in the Old and Modern English senses of the word) that it brings to its listeners, who are *absorbed* in what they hear.

So this enchanting riddle offers very good advice to anyone meaning to practise spellcraft. Old English stories were created from as well as for early English society. When using early English material, the story-teller has to re-create that society and the world in which it existed, as well as follow the traditional story-line. This does not mean that a fight, a love-scene, an ambush or a feast has to be interrupted after every other paragraph for a historical or archaeological essay; only that a story-teller must be at home in that world before the listeners or readers can be taken into it as well.

The physical relics of the society can be found in local museums – the jewellery, the weapons, the tools, the pottery, the runic inscriptions. Some collections and sites are richer, more rewarding, or just more evocative than others: Jarrow, the City Museum in Liverpool, West Stow, the grave-field at Sutton Hoo are a few examples. Some centres may from time to time offer a chance to handle the material, or work with replicas to find out how the originals were made– to throw a pot, weave, feel what it was like to put on the clothes and armour, forge and carry the weapons, cook and eat the food. As Old English food and drink were 'organic', this is a tasty and nourishing as well as instructive experience.

The Early Medieval Room in the British Museum is exciting: it has the Sutton Hoo treasure and much more English material; it also sets the early English among their contemporaries – Franks, Goths, Scandinavians, Slavs, Finns. Once upon a time, the English were a Baltic people, much more at the centre of this world than they were after they moved to Britain. The list of kings, heroes and tribes in *Widsið* shows that they brought stories and memories of their old home with them when they came, so modern story-tellers and artists need to be aware of it if they are working with the material.

Ideally, the European settings should be visited, especially the fine sites and collections in Scandinavia. Early material in Denmark is early Jutish and early English as well as Danish. We share a common past: this is the country where Amleth got the better of his wicked uncle, who had killed his father and married his mother; where Offa marked out the English border with his sword along the River Eider.

Even if it is not immediately possible to cruise around the Baltic or down the Rhine, or visit what remains of the Hungarian puszta and try to visualize Attila's headquarters, a story-teller should at least read about the lands where the heroes and heroines lived. Although they might, at any time or place, cross the frontiers of other worlds, or be accosted by beings who had come from one of those other worlds, they were living in Europe, not in an 'Arthurian' fantasy land. Their movements can be plotted on a map– or rather, on two maps. A good modern atlas will give the physical features of the territory; a historical atlas will place the settlements, cities and trade routes that existed in the Migration Age. The Cornell and Matthews *Atlas of the Roman World*, for example, gives a clear idea of the Roman frontier zones along the Rhine and the Danube.

When the research has been done, and the story-teller feels imaginatively at home in Germanic royal halls, Roman cities and Attila's camp; making last stands, feasting, or crossing the sea in the Nydam or Sutton Hoo ship, there will still be some problems to deal with.

In this early time, there was no clearly-marked frontier between everyday life – 'real' life, as it is called in the 20th century – and the supernatural. Particularly in the legends, the gods walk on Middle Earth. Beings of different worlds meet and mate. Matter can be changed by magic. The makers of the legends believed this; the characters in the legends believe it and experience it; the modern story-teller or script-writer using this material must write as if he or she believed it. But – believed what?

When imagining the gods and religious practices of heathen Germany, people of the modern world tend to think first in terms of Scandinavian mythology, vivid, sophisticated – and recorded much later than the German Heroic Age. In fact, it is impossible not to think of Scandinavian mythology; it is the only one we have.

However, the gods of Asgard and 9th century Viking practices should not be taken wholesale into stories of the Migration Age or earlier, without considering the evidence from Roman writers such as Tacitus, from the native 'histories' of the Goths and Lombards and from the scanty traces of early English, Danish and German folk-customs.

Tacitus said that the only noteworthy peculiarity that marked off the English and their neighbours from the other Germanic tribes was that they were goddess-worshippers. I think that Old English heathenism was much less Woden-(Odin) – centred than genealogies and place-names seem to suggest; that The Lady was more important; and that early English rituals had more in common with the fertility cults. Therefore, I think it is allowable for a story-teller to make imaginative use both of older material such as the Bronze Age art of Denmark (since there is no evidence of invasion or large-scale immigration after this period to the time of Tacitus and beyond, these images existed in Anglian and Jutish minds) and of later folk-customs *when they seem to be giving a similar message.* Customs that clearly originated in post-Christian times – or have clearly been invented as tourist attractions – should, of course, be ignored. If a particular custom or tradition is tested against what is known about early English or continental Germanic beliefs and practices, it will either fit in or show up as incongruous. Let me emphasise that I am writing about the use of these details, with all due care and thought, in creative work, not presenting them as proven historical or archaeological facts.

Another problem is the choice of names and name-forms for the characters. Perfect accuracy and consistency could only be reached by an expert in philology, who knew all the Germanic and Scandinavian languages from Gothic to Frankish.

All the stories in this collection are based on legends that were known in early English society. They are referred to in Old English literature. Most of the references are allusive; the poet expected his listeners or readers to supply the linked story from their own memories, as soon as they recognized a name. (Similarly, Shakespeare relied on his audience's knowing that all the classical heroes and heroines mentioned at the beginning of Act V of *The Merchant of Venice* figured in stories of tragic love. He would not risk having his audience bewildered or bored for six speeches at the opening of his last scene.)

Since the chief characters' names are recorded in Old English, I have used the English forms: Hroðulf rather than Hrolf, Hagena for Hogni, Hildegyð instead of Hildegunde or Hiltgunt. So the names of the minor characters – kinsfolk, maids, warriors, churls – are also given in Old English, except when it is needed to stress that they are alien – Romans or Huns. There is a wide choice of names to be found in easily accessible sources: the Chronicle, the Durham *Liber Vitae* (Sweet's *A Second Anglo-Saxon Reader*), collections of wills and charters, early forms of place-names.

Where there is no name recorded in Old English, or where the Old English name would not be immediately recognizable, I have used a generally accepted form, for example, Merovech for a Frankish prince.

The English knew Attila as Ætla ('Ætla weold Hunum' – Attila ruled the Huns) but 'Ætla' lacks the impact and associations of 'Attila'. This means 'Little Father' in *Gothic;* his real name would have been Turkic and probably sounded something like 'Avitokhol' – but modern readers would not react to that either.

There are other difficulties caused by using names from old texts. The main problem is that the sounds of some old names suggest the wrong associations to readers' minds. For example, tradition says that the Burgundian kingdom of the Rhine was centred on Worms. This name has developed from the Latin

Borbetomagus. The city of Worms has the same associations in the *Nibelungenlied* as Camelot has in the Arthurian legend. But, in an English story, one cannot have the villain referred to as 'the king of Worms' without risking a laugh in the wrong place. The medieval Latin 'Wormetaria' is not much better, so I kept the Roman name. In the early 5th century, the Roman government still existed in Gaul, so however the Burgundians may have mispronounced Borbetomagus, that was still its name.

The English king who gave his name to the East Anglian dynasty is entered in the king-lists as Wuffa. That was probably the hypocoristic (shortened) form of a name with the first element 'wulf', just as Cutha is the short form of Cuthbert. However, it might sound incongruously like baby-talk. A modern writer on Suffolk wondered if the king's war-band were known as 'Wuffians'. This is intensely annoying to anyone who is sensitive to language, but a story-teller is not writing only for etymologists. One hopes that people will come to know better; meanwhile one has to avoid striking wrong notes.

There is also a danger of confusion, if more than one character has the same name. Theodoric was a very popular name among Gothic royalty and nobility. In legend, the great Ostrogothic king of that name was brought forward in time and made a contemporary and friend of Attila. That made him also a contemporary of the Visigoth, Theodoric I, the gallant old king who died leading his warriors in a charge against Attila's Huns at the Battle of Chalons. So I called Theodoric the Ostrogoth by the English form of the name, Ðeodric, as in the poem *Deor*. I used the form Theodrid for the Visigothic king, as this is how his name appears in Jordanes' *Getica*, the 'native' Gothic history.

The greatest problem is the naming of the Goddess herself. Writers on Old English religion usually spell her name 'Frig' or 'Frigg', the Scandinavian form. English readers probably think immediately of 'frigging' and snigger. Kemp Malone has given strong reasons for taking the noun 'freo' – a free-born woman, a lady – as also her name and title. I have used it (or called her The Lady which is what Freo means) in all the stories.

A story-teller or artist who is working with old legends has to keep faith with the past and be true to the legend. Being true to the legend includes trying to make sure that the legend has its true effect in the mind of the reader. There is a gap to be crossed before a modern reader can live in the Heroic Age and before the legends can come alive in the 20th and 21st centuries. Like the speaker of Riddle 74, the modern scop has to live in several worlds at once.

The booklist that follows is not intended to be a bibliography of Old English literature or of the history and archaeology of the Dark Ages. The books will be helpful to anyone who wants to work with this material. Each book has its own bibliography, so story-hunters can follow their own chosen trails.

Translations

The Earliest English Poems: Michael Alexander, Penguin Classics 1977.
Beowulf: Michael Alexander, Penguin Classics 1973.
Anglo-Saxon Poetry: S A J Bradley, Everyman Classics/Dent 1982.
A Choice of Anglo-Saxon Verse: Richard Hamer, Faber pbk 1970 (with parallel OE text).
Beowulf (based on the M Alexander translation): Julian Glover, Magnus Magnusson, Sheila Mackie, Alan Sutton 1987.
The Exeter Riddle Book: Kevin Crossley-Holland, The Folio Society 1978.
The Anglo-Saxon World: Kevin Crossley-Holland, World's Classics, OUP 1984.

The material background:

A Guide to the Dark Age Remains in Britain: Lloyd & Jennifer Laing, Constable 1979.
The Making of England: ed. Leslie Webster & Janet Backhouse, British Museum Press 1991.
(This contains photographs, many in colour, of the superb exhibits.)
The Sutton Hoo Ship Burial: Angela Care Evans British Museum Publications 1986.
Dawn of the Middle Ages: Michael Grant, Weidenfeld & Nicolson 1981.
The Northern World: ed. David Wilson, Thames & Hudson 1980

(These two books have fine colour illustrations and they set the English among their contemporaries.)

Myths and rituals:

The Lost Gods of England: Brian Branston, Thames & Hudson 1974, pbk 1957.

Rites and Religions of the Anglo-Saxons: Gale R Owen, David & Charles 1983.

The Way of Wyrd: Brian Bates, Century Publishing 1983.

Gods and Myths of Northern Europe: H R Ellis Davidson, Pelican/Penguin 1964.

The Norse Myths: Kevin Crossley-Holland, Andre Deutsch 1980; Penguin 1982.

Edda (the prose Edda): Snorri Sturluson, trans. Anthony Faulkes, Everyman/Dent pbk 1987.

The Poetic Edda: trans. Lee M Hollander, Univ. of Texas Press 1962.

Runes:

Runes, an Introduction: Ralph W V Elliott, Manchester UP 1959.

An Introduction to English Runes: R I Page, Methuen 1973.

Runes (Reading the Past series): R I Page, British Museum Publications 1987.

Tacitus' account of the early Germans, including the Anglii (Engle, English):

On Britain and Germany: trans. H. Mattingly, Penguin Classics 1948.

Tacitus I (*Agricola, Germania, Dialogus*) Loeb Classical Library no 35 Heinemann 1970.
(This has parallel Latin and English versions, with good notes.)

De Origine et Situ Germanorum: J G C Anderson, OUP 1938 reprint 1961. (This is the Latin text without translation, but the notes are so full and excellent that the book is worth consulting by non-Latinists. The best method is to use it with the Loeb and read the Penguin for ease and enjoyment.)

'Native' historians:

The Gothic History of Jordanes: (Getica) trans. C C Mierow 1915 reprint. Cambridge 1966.

History of the Lombards: (De Gestis Langobardorum) Paul the
    Deacon trans. William Dudley Foulke Univ. of Philadelphia
    1974.
The History of the Franks: Gregory of Tours trans. Lewis
    Thorpe Penguin Classics 1974.

Maps:

Atlas of the Roman World: Tim Cornell & John Matthews,
    Phaidon Press & Book Club Associates 1982.
The Times Atlas of World History: ed. Geoffrey Barraclough (3rd
    ed) Norman Stone Times Books & Book Club Associates
    1989.

I The Story Of Heoden And Hild

'Hagena Holmrygum ond Heoden Glommum'
(Hagena [ruled] the Holmrygas and Heoden the Glomman)

Widsið,1.21.

This story of a doomed relationship was very popular; it was told across the Germanic world from Iceland to Bavaria. It is fascinating to see how the tale changes with the teller, in its plot-line and in the motives and personalities of its characters. Yet, however many times the story changes, it always shares at least one element with at least one other version.

The tribes named in the Old English poem *Widsið* lived on the southern coast of the Baltic. By the time the surviving versions of the story were written down in Norse, Latin and High German, they had been long forgotten. The Roman Tacitus, writing at the end of the 1st century AD, places the Rugians west of the lower Vistula. Jordanes, the Gothic historian, writing in the 6th century, mentions the Ulmerugi (Island-Rugians) as living at the mouth of the Vistula.

The next tribe to the west, according to Tacitus, was the Lemovii, whose territory stretched to the mouth of the Oder. Hiddensee, a small island just west of Rugen, is 'Heoden's Isle' where according to the Danish version of the story the fight to the death and the conjuring of the dead warriors took place. Kemp Malone says that the Lemovii of Tacitus are the Glomman of *Widsið* and that the root syllable is the same in both names. He identifies the tribe with the Wulfings, taking this as the name of the dynasty, which became the tribal name by extension. I used this name, rather than Glomman or Gloms, to avoid an unsuitable echo of *The Glums*.

Saxo Grammaticus tells Heoden's story rather scrappily in Book V of his *Historia Danica*. His version is a romance that would have ended happily if it had not been wrecked by scandal-mongers:

Hithin (Heoden), a Norwegian kinglet, and Hogin (Hagena), a Jutish prince, were both subject-allies of the great Danish king Frothi III. They took to each other when they met and went sea-raiding together. *Heoden* and *Hagena's* daughter Hild had already fallen in love with each other before they met, from listening to each other's praises which were widely spoken.

When they met, they could not stop gazing at each other. *Hagena* betrothed Hild to *Heoden*: the two men swore that if one of them was killed, the other would avenge him.

Then, while *Heoden* was away collecting King Frothi's taxes from the Slavs, mischief-makers came to *Hagena*. They told him, falsely, that *Heoden* had seduced Hild and bedded her before the betrothal (and had presumably been careless or boastful about it, so that the affair had become common talk.) The rumour not only disgraced Hild but her father as well. *Hagena* believed the tale-bearers, put to sea and attacked *Heoden*. He was defeated and fled back to Jutland.

Their overlord, King Frothi, tried to make up the quarrel but as *Hagena* was insisting on breaking the marriage contract and taking Hild back, he allowed them to settle the matter with a sword-fight. *Hagena* disabled *Heoden* who was bleeding profusely and unable to ward off the death-blow. However, *Hagena* was moved by his courage, youth and outstanding beauty. Instead of killing him, he let *Heoden*'s friends carry him to his ships. *Heoden* lived and recovered his strength.

Then, seven years later, the two met and fought again on the island that now bears *Heoden*'s name. This time they hacked each other to death. Saxo does not say whether this was a chance meeting, or if they had a new cause for quarrelling or had spent the seven years brooding and seething over the old grievance. He adds, as a folk belief, the story that Hild yearned so passionately for her husband 'that she conjured up the spirits of the dead men at night so that they could renew their fighting.'

As there is nothing of the wælcyrie in Saxo's Hild, this seems an odd way for her to enjoy some extra time with the ghost of her beloved.

The wælcyrie strain in Hild's nature comes out very strongly in the version told by Snorri Sturluson in his *Prose Edda* and also in the quotations he gives from the 9th century poem *Ragnarsdrapa*, by Bragi the Old. Since Hild is the name of one of Woden's maidens, sent by the god to every battle, who 'allot death to men and govern victory', possibly her nature and some of her powers have been attributed to Hagena's daughter.

Snorri tells his story to explain two kennings: *battle* is called the Hiadnings' (Heodenings') weather or storm; *weapons* are called the *Heodenings'* fires or rods.

While King Hogni (Hagena) was away at a meeting with other kings, Hedin Hiarrandason (Heoden Heorrenda's son) raided his land and carried off his daughter Hild. When *Hagena* learned of this, he set out with his troops to hunt the raiders. He learned that *Heoden* had sailed north and tracked him to Norway. There, he learned that *Heoden* had sailed west. *Hagena* went in pursuit and caught up with him in Orkney, on the island of Hoy. At that point, Hild went to her father and offered him a neck-ring, as from *Heoden*, to make peace – but she followed this up by saying that *Heoden* was ready to fight and there was no chance of his yielding or making any concessions. *Hagena* was short with her; she went back and told *Heoden* that her father had no idea of coming to terms, so he had better get ready for battle.

When the two kings came face to face, *Heoden* once more suggested that they might come to terms. He offered more gold but *Hagena* said the offer came too late: he had drawn his sword Dainsleif. This weapon had been made by dwarfs and had to kill someone every time it was drawn. *Heoden* defied him, pointing out that victories are won by swordsmen not swords. The battle began. Every night, Hild went to the dead men and woke them up by magic. At last, all the warriors on both sides were 'undead'; they turned to stone with all their weapons and shields until Hild called them up again. It is said that the *Heodenings* must fight over and over again until the end of the world, when the gods go out to the last battle.

Snorri quotes verses from Bragi's poem which suggest that Hild was indeed a wælcyrie and that she deliberately wrecked the peace-negotiations between her father and her ravisher:

'And the Ran who wishes too great drying of veins (Hild) planned to bring this bow-storm against her father with hostile intention'

'She always pretended to be against battle, though she was inciting the princes to join the company of the quite monstrous wolf's sister (Hel)'

' – the victory-preventing witch of a woman –'

One can see why a woman carried off by force and raped would want her captor to meet an unpleasant and long-drawn-out death but not why she would want her father (and would-be rescuer) to be included in the doom – unless she was angry and resentful that he could even for a moment think of taking gold as a payment to *him* for *her* wrong.

In the *Sorla þattr*, which is much later (14th century), the sex-war has been raised to a higher and more frightening plane. Odin was angry with Freya (The Lady) because she had paid for her wonderful necklace, the Brisingamen, by giving herself for a night each to the four dwarfs who had made it for her.

The neck-ring of a fertility goddess carries the same sexual symbolism as the rings that Portia and Nerissa give to their lovers in *The Merchant of Venice*. Gratiano says:

'Well, while I live, I'll fear no other thing
So sore, as keeping safe Nerissa's ring.'

He is not worried about the trinket but his exclusive right to her body.

Odin got Loki to steal Freya's neck-ring while she was asleep and refused to return it unless she brought about a war between two mighty kings, each of whom had twenty kings as his subjects.

This introductory myth shows male resentment of unrestricted female sexuality; also that bullying or domineering imposed on sexuality lead to acts of violence and murder.

The two kings of the story are Hogni (Hagena), who in this version is the son of Halfdan (Healfdene) King of Denmark, and Heðinn (Heoden) son of Hjarrandi (Heorrenda) King of Serkland (North Africa).

Once day, going through a forest, *Heoden* met a big handsome women who said her name was Gondul. This is a wælcyrie name but the rest of the story shows that if the woman was not The Lady, the Goddess herself, she was acting as an agent of The Lady's will. She incited *Heoden*'s jealousy and assertiveness by telling him that *Hagena* of Denmark was the only king in the world who could equal him. *Heoden* set out at once for Denmark with a war-band of three hundred warriors. Their voyage lasted a year.

This first attempt at inciting war failed because of *Hagena*'s courtesy and the liking that the two kings took to each other when they met. *Heoden* was received as an honoured guest. The kings competed in various trials of strength but neither could outmatch the other, so they swore oaths of lifelong brotherhood. When *Hagena* had to make an expedition away from his kingdom, he left *Heoden* in charge of his land, his queen and his daughter Hild.

One day, *Heoden* was again walking in the woods alone. He found Gondul sitting in a glade. She gave him a magic potion, a drug that made him forget the past. Then she told him that it was a disgrace to his honour that he had no wife, while *Hagena* had a queen of noble birth. He must take Hild by force and kill the queen by crushing her on the rollers when he launched his ships. *Heoden* rushed off to follow these suggestions.

When he seized Hild, she begged him to wait for her father to come home, as he would gladly let them marry. But in his drugged madness, *Heoden* forced her aboard his ship and launched it over the queen's body.

Before he set sail, Gondul appeared to him for the third time and by her magic potion made him sleep with her. When he woke up, his mind was clear and his memory had come back; he knew the evil he had done. He left Denmark, taking Hild with him.

When *Hagena* learned of the outrage he set off in pursuit and caught up with *Heoden* at Hoy in Orkney. *Heoden* came to *Hagena* and told him that he had been under a spell of evil enchantment when he killed the queen and took Hild. He offered to give her back to her father, pay wergild and leave the north for ever. *Hagena* said that as far as the abduction was concerned, he had always meant to give Hild to him as a wife so there was no quarrel between them over that (I wonder what Hild felt!) but he would not forgive the murder of his queen.

When the fighting started, the dead rose up as soon as they were killed and the battle went on, unceasing.

Later, this story was joined to the legends about King Olaf Tryggvasson (reigned 995 – 1000) and given a Christian slant. When Odin made his terms for returning the Brisingamen, he had foretold that the battle would go on until some Christian man should have the courage to go in among the undead and strike up their weapons. This was done by one of Olaf's Christian warriors.

Helgakviða Hjorvarþssonar (The Lay of Helgi Hjorvarth's son), one of the Eddic poems, shows how a powerful legend can pull other stories, once unconnected, into its orbit. (As, for example, the Arthurian legend 'captured' the stories of Tristan and of Owain ap Urien). In this case, the legend is the one of the thrice-born Helgi and his tragic love for the wælcyrie Svava-Sigrun-Kara.

In his first incarnation, Helgi was the son of King Hjorvarth (Heoroweard) of Norway and Hethin (Heoden) was his half-brother. They were children of two of the king's collection of beautiful women. From his childhood, Helgi had been befriended and guarded by the princess Svava, King Eylimi's daughter, a wælcyrie. When he grew up to be a great warrior, Helgi asked her father for Svava's hand. The two lovers confirmed their betrothal by taking oaths of faithfulness to each other.

On Yule Eve, *Heoden* was coming home alone through the forest. He met a troll-woman riding on a wolf, with live snakes for reins. She invited him to lie with her but he refused. She told him that he was going to regret the refusal when he was making his vows over the mead-cup.

That evening, the boar that was to be sacrificed to Frey (Frea, the Lord) was led into the hall. In turn, the warriors laid their hands on the animal and made their binding vows for the coming year, confirming their words by drinking ceremonially. When it was *Heoden's* turn, he was impelled to swear that he would have Svava, his brother's lover and promised bride. As soon as he had made the vow, his mind cleared and he bitterly regretted what he had done, but the words could not be unsaid. So he set out at once, in the depths of winter, and travelled alone along wild ways till he found Helgi in the south. He confessed what he had done, expecting his brother to kill him.

Helgi had been challenged to single combat in three days' time, by a man whose father he had killed in the course of a family blood-feud. He had foreknowledge of his death in this fight. He was gentle with *Heoden* and told him that he need not blame himself. The vow would come true without any breach of faith – when he was dead, *Heoden* must take his place.

When Helgi was dying of his wounds, he sent for Svava and told her not to grieve for him once he was dead. She must marry *Heoden* and give him her love. Svava said that she had vowed if she could not lie with Helgi, she would never give herself to any man who was not a proved hero. *Heoden* asked her for one kiss – he swore he would never see her again till he had avenged Helgi, 'the best of all heroes under heaven.'

In this story, Helgi takes it for granted that the wolf-rider who accosted *Heoden* was his own *fylgia* – his guardian spirit who had come to him at birth but had now left him because he was doomed to die. She had chosen *Heoden* to take his place. We might guess that if *Heoden* had received her graciously and lain with her at her request (as in the English ballad of *King Henry*) she could have become lovely for him: that is, he might have inherited his brother's rights without the terrible burden of betrayal and bitter remorse.

The south German epic *Kudrun* (composed about 1240 in Bavaria or Austria) was strongly influenced both in content and style by medieval romance but has some interesting traces of much older material. Its central section is a version of the Heoden and Hild story. One of its characters, Horant (Heorrenda) links it to the Old English poem *Deor*. Another, Wate (Wada) connects it with a very long-lasting English oral tradition.

King Hagen (Hagena) had a daughter called Hilde (Hild). King Hetel (Heoden) heard of her beauty and wanted her as his wife but he knew that *Hagena* was a cruel, fierce king who would kill any man he suspected of wanting his daughter.

Heoden gathered a band of chosen warriors. Their leaders were Wate the Old of Sturmland (Wada; the Wade of medieval English tradition), Fruote of Denmark (King Frothi) a skilled diplomat, and Horant (Heorrenda), his kinsman, a gifted minstrel. He provided ships for them but did not go himself. The adventurers pretended to be traders and carried a cargo of treasures provided by *Heoden*.

When they arrived in *Hagena*'s land, they said they had been outlawed by *Heoden*. There is an interesting detail here. In *Kudrun* the heroine is said to be the daughter of the king of Eyerlanndt, and this is taken to be a memory of one of the Viking kingdoms in Ireland. Yet at one point, the poet says indignantly that those story-tellers who say that *Hagena* ruled in Poland are quite wrong; they do not know the story. So there were other versions to be heard in 13th century Germany. More than one story-teller put *Hagena*'s kingdom where Old English tradition had said it was: the Holmrygas had lived around the mouth of the Vistula.

Heoden's men set up their booths on the sands, offering their wares at give-away prices. They also sent rich presents to the king and were invited to his court. Here, *Heorrenda* entertained the company with singing so sweet that the birds fell silent to hear him, the woodland creatures stopped feeding and the fish stayed motionless in the water. For his human listeners, time stood still while he was singing; they were drawn to him by great longing. The princess was enchanted; she invited him to her bower to sing for her every day. *Heorrenda* pleaded his master's cause so well that she willingly agreed to run away with the 'merchants' and marry *Heoden.* Under the pretence of seeing the remaining merchandise before the visitors set sail, she went with her parents to the harbour, gave them the slip, and was out at sea before her infuriated father realised what was happening. As soon as his own ships were ready, he set off after them.

Heoden was celebrating the arrival of his bride when *Hagena*'s fleet was sighted. Battle was joined on the shore and the bridegroom came face to face with his father-in-law. *Heoden* was wounded but his comrades rallied round him and *Wada* took up the combat. A terrible duel followed but at last *Wada* struck *Hagena* a blow that could have finished him. *Hild* begged *Heoden* to stop the fight and he bravely threw himself between the duellists. *Hagena* was impressed, forgave his daughter, satisfied himself that his son-in-law was very rich and gave his consent to the marriage before he set off home.

Possibly the German version of the story did not always end so happily. An earlier poem, the 12th century *Alexanderlied* has an allusion to the death of Hagen 'at the hands of Wate.'

The adventures of Heoden were known in pre-Norman England – so well known that an allusion to two names was enough to recall his story to the listeners' or readers' minds. But which story? Was it like any of the much later versions that have been summarised here, or something quite different?

> 'þæt ic bi me sylfum secgan wille:
> þæt ic hwile wæs *Heodeninga* scop,
> dryhtne dyre. Me wæs Deor noma.
> Ahte ic fela wintra folgað tilne,
> holdne hlaford, oþþæt *Heorrenda* nu
> leoðcræftig monn, londryht geþah
> þæt me eorla hleo ær gesealde.'

Deor 1.35 – 41.

(I want to say this about myself: that for a time I was the poet of Heoden's court, dear to the prince. Deor was my name. For many years I held a high position, had a gracious lord, until now Heorrenda, a man skilled in song-making, received the grant of land that the protector of nobles formerly gave me.)

The reference to Heorrenda as a 'leoðcræftig monn' suggests that, like *Kudrun*, the Old English story included a poet who could perform services for King Heoden (such as composing and singing irresistible love-charms) that were beyond the power of his official scop. However, the context in the poem *Deor* indicates that the events of the English story (whatever they were) must have been more terrifying than those in *Kudrun*: an elopement, followed by a scene with an angry father that ended in 'Bless you, my children!' The ordeals of the other legendary heroes and heroines mentioned in *Deor* were grimmer than that.

Another character in *Kudrun*, Wate of Sturmland is mentioned in the *Þidrekssaga* as the father of Weland. According to this story, he was a giant, son of a king and a sea-woman. Wada, or Wade, was long remembered in England, at least in oral tradition. One of the last men who could have recorded that tradition, Thomas Speght, the 16th century editor of Chaucer's works, refused to do so, clearly thinking that such stories were unworthy of a scholar's notice:

'Concerning Wade and his bote called Guingelot, as also his strange exploits in the same, because the matter is long and fabulous, I passe it over.'

Chaucer refers twice to Wade. In *Troilus and Criseyde*, Pandarus is trying to get his niece Criseyde into bed with his friend Troilus. He has asked her to a supper-party at his house (where the hopeful lover is hidden in a closet near the guest-bedroom) choosing a night at dark of the moon, when heavy rain is threatened. After supper, to spin out the time until it is too late, dark and wet for Criseyde to go home, Pandarus gets various members of the party to entertain her:

'He song, she pleyde, he told tale of Wade . . .'

Book III 1.614

That is, the tale of Wade was used to help trick the heroine into the arms of her lover.

In *The Merchant's Tale* an elderly lecher decides to get married at last, for safe sex and an unpaid nurse. He explains to his friends why he will not marry an old woman (anyone over twenty):

'And bet than old boef is the tendre veel . . .
And eek thise olde wydwes, God it woot,
They konne so muchel craft on Wades boot,

237

So muchel broken harm, whan that hem leste,
That with hem sholde I nevere lyve in reste . . .'

1.209-14

(Tender veal is better than old beef . . .and also these old
widows, God knows they're able to play so many clever tricks
abroad Wade's boat, get up to so much mischief when it suits
them, that I'd never have a moment's peace with them . . .)

Widows know too much; they have too much skill in playing
the game; they can deceive their next husbands how and
whenever they choose.

It seems from these allusions that Wade and a boat and
love-trickery were linked in the medieval English mind – as
they were in *Kudrun*. There is no proof that they already were
linked in the Old English period. Taking the reference to him as
a giant and his sea-ancestry from *Þidrekssaga*, and the verb
'waden' – 'to go, to advance, to proceed' from Old English, I
made Wada the personification of the ocean currents and also
(because I have always loved Sir Walter Raleigh's poetic by-
name 'The Shepherd of the Ocean') an immortal fish-herd and
game-warden of the sea-creatures.

Beyond including Heorrenda as a singer of love-charms, to
keep the link with *Deor*, anyone re-making this story in English
has a free hand and a wide choice of material to pick from. I
chose Snorri's version for my main plot-line, as I thought it
was clearer, faster-moving and gave a more interesting part to
Hild than the other stories. I gave Heoden the father he has in
Helgakviða Hjorvarþssonar, so that he could inherit his
father's temperament and attitude to women as beautiful
collectibles. I also took the meeting with the wolf-rider from
that lay, but took a hint from *Sorla Þattr* that the ill-will of Freo
was directed against Heoden.

There are at least four other, totally different story-lines in
this legend, each with innumerable variations according to the
story-teller's mood and choice.

Wiðsith: A Study in Old English Heroic Legend ed. R W
Chambers, CUP 1912.

Wiðsith: ed. Kemp Malone, Rosenkilde & Bagger 1963.

Deor: ed. Kemp Malone, Exeter Medieval Tests, Univ. of Exeter
1977.

The History of the Danes: (Historia Danica) Saxo Grammaticus I
& II trans. P Fisher; ed. with commentary H E Davidson D S
Brewer 1980.

Edda: Snorri Sturluson trans. A Faulkes, Everyman/Dent 1987.

Three Northern Love Stories: (for Sorla Þattr) trans. W Morris & E Magnusson, Longmans Green 1895.

The Poetic Edda: (for The Lay of Helgi Hjorvarth's Son) trans. Lee M Hollander, Univ. of Texas 1962.

Kudrun: trans. B Murdoch, Everyman/Dent 1987 with introduction and notes.

Sidelights on Teutonic History in the Migration Period: M G Clarke, CUP 1911.

II *Beowulf* and the Scylding Family Tree

'Hroðulf ond Hroðgar heoldon lengest
sibbe ætsomne suhtorfædran.'   *Widsið*, l.45-6

(Hroðulf and Hroðgar, nephew and uncle, kept peace together
for a very long time.)

Heoden has at least five different stories to his name; his
character and motives change from one to the next. Heremod
is a powerful haunting presence in *Beowulf*. His memory falls
like a shadow on the hero's two great moments of triumph. His
story, however, is only given in tantalizing hints and allusions.

He is first mentioned in lines 901-15 of the poem. Beowulf
had carried out his promise to rid the Danish royal hall of the
monster Grendel. The night before, he had wrestled with
Grendel, tearing off one of his arms, and the monster had fled
to his lair, mortally wounded. In the morning a band of
warriors followed his tracks through the fens to the haunted
mere, where the water was turbid and red with blood. Sure now
that the monster was dead, the warriors turned back to Heorot
in high spirits. Sometimes, when the track allowed, they raced
their horses. During quieter moments one of the royal
household, who was a gifted scop, began to set Beowulf's feat
into highly-wrought alliterative verse. He compared Beowulf to
the hero Sigemund Dragonslayer and this was the highest
praise, for of all wandering adventurers, Sigemund was the
most widely-famed throughout the inhabited world for his
deeds of valour:

'Se wæs wreccena wide mærost
ofer wer-þeode . . .
ellen-dædum'   l.898-900

But Sigemund was only ranked as the world's most glorious
hero after Heremod was no longer worthy to hold that title,
because his warlike spirit, his might and his courage had
failed:

'siððan Heremodes hild sweðrode
eafod ond ellen'   l.901-2

These words might make us think that success had made Heremod lazy and self-satisfied, that he had let himself go slack, that his strength and courage had failed with easy living and old age. According *Beowulf,* what happened to Heremod was much worse than that. He became a cause of deadly grief to his nobles and his people:

'he to his leodum wearð
eallum æpellingum to aldor-ceare'   1.905-6

Later in the poem (lines 1709-23) King Hroðgar gives some details of what Heremod had done to his nobles and to the Danish people.

Beowulf had performed his second great feat, killing Grendel's mother in her underwater lair, so freeing the Danish court of the death that had stalked it by night. The old king praised the hero but, out of his long experience and his warm affection for the young man, warned him that great power for good can turn into great power for evil. Beowulf must be a long-lasting comfort and support to his people – unlike Heremod.

Heremod did not grow up to fulfil the Danish people's hopes of him. Instead he brought them bloodshed and violent death. He even killed his own hearth-companions, men who had feasted beside him in hall and stood shoulder to shoulder with him in the battle-line: his 'beod-geneatas, eaxl-gesteallan'. The words used by King Hroðgar to describe these murders suggest fits of homicidal mania: he is 'bolgen-mod, (belgan means to swell with anger); the heart in his breast grew blood-thirsty (literally 'blood-savage').

This was all the more dreadful to the Danes because they had looked forward to his reign with such very high hopes that he would be the remedy to make good all the miseries they had suffered and would take care of his people, the gold-hoard and the royal stronghold. It seems that before he became king, Heremod had been forced to go into exile, to the grief of the more responsible Danish folk, and that they had looked forward to his return as the saviour of the nation:

'Swylce oft bemearn ærran mælum
swið-ferhþes sið snotor ceorl monig.'   1.907-8

This would be the period of exile when Heremod was a 'wrecca' and did the great deeds that made him more famous than Sigemund.

Heremod is not the only king whose reign began like the return of the Golden Age but who ended as a bloody-minded tyrant. The Roman Emperor Gaius 'Caligula' and King Henry VIII are historical examples. What makes Heremod so interesting is the stress that is laid on his own grief at what had happened to him, at the hatred that his people felt for him and the horror of his lonely end:

> 'Hine sorh-wylmas
> lemede to lange.'   1.904-5

(The surgings of sorrow oppressed him too long.)

> 'Dreamleas gebad
> þæt he þæs gewinnes weorc þrowade
> leod-bealo longsum.'   1.1720-22

(He lived joyless, suffering the agony of that hostility, the people's long-lasting tribulation.)

Usually when a Germanic king did not hand out jewelled collars and bracelets to his nobles and killed his hearth-companions in fits of rage, either the hearth-troop murdered him themselves or one of his kinsmen organized his murder and took the kingdom. But Heremod went away from human joys, alone. ('He ana hwearf . . . mondreamum from' 1.1714-5.)

Either 'among the monsters, he was decoyed into the power of demons' or 'among the Jutes he was betrayed into the power of his enemies'. The second interpretation of his fate entails taking 'mid eotenum' (among the giants or monsters) in 1.902 as a scribal mistake for 'mid Eotum'. This is possible; also, Jutland makes political and geographical sense as a refuge for a king of Scedenig on the run from an infuriated war-band and tribe. However, the whole atmosphere of Heremod's story, as hinted in *Beowulf* suggests that he was possessed, so I think the MS reading should stand.

The old texts give no details of Heremod's crimes, nor what happened to turn a splendid young adventurer into a psychopath, so the storyteller can give a free rein to imagination.

Heremod was king of the Danes; he is nowhere described as a usurper. The Danes expected him to protect the native land of the Scyldings, 'eðel Scyldinga', having inherited his father's excellent qualities and noble rank, 'fæder-æþelum'. Yet his father's name is never mentioned in *Beowulf* and he does not fit into the Scylding line of descent as given in the poem. Nor is there any Heremod in the much longer Danish king-list provided by the *Historia Danica*.

In the first 63 lines of Beowulf, King Hroðgar's ancestors are named in order:

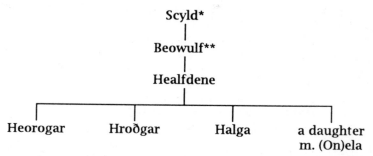

Scyld*
|
Beowulf**
|
Healfdene

Heorogar   Hroðgar   Halga   a daughter
m. (On)ela

*from whom the dynasty and, by extension, the war-band and the people were named.
**not the Geatish hero of the poem.

As there is no room here for Heremod, most editors of *Beowulf* put him before the time of Scyld's arrival. His mental collapse and disappearance caused the period of kingless misery from which Scyld delivered the Danes when he grew up.

Scyld is an uncanny child who came to the Danes from beyond the sea in a ship that, according to lines 43-46, was laden with treasure. Therefore the word 'fea-sceaft' (destitute) in line 7 must refer to the child's exile from his own people with no nurse or guardian to care for him and comfort his loneliness, at the mercy of whoever found him and his wealth. The arrival of Scyld as a helpless child from – *elsewhere* – and the departure of his crewless ship carrying his corpse and his treasures make a wonderful opening to the poem, both splendid and mysterious. There is a suggestion in the wording that the child was sent by magic; also, that the ship carrying the corpse knew where it was going, that it went back to those who had sent it, making landfall somewhere beyond human ken.

The great Danish scholar Axel Olrik wrote; 'The basic element in the legend is Scyld's role as the progenitor of the Danish royal house of the Scyldings, hence his warlike character.' He points out that in Old English poetry, proper names ending in –ing are 'on the division line between designating the royal race and the host of the warriors, with the meaning of the chieftain somewhat preponderating.'

He continues: 'We have, therefore, good reason to cling to the view, toward which our oldest sources point, that the term 'skioldungar, scyldingas' designates the troop of the Danish king, or the warriors of the Danes. In itself this name fits excellently, meaning precisely 'shieldmen' . . . The name Scyld has thus found its explanation. He is the eponymous founder of the race of the Scyldings. As we know, it is frequently the case that *the name of the people antecedes that of its supposed progenitor invented to explain the name.* (My italics). There is no reason to suppose Scyld to be an historic personage . . . He was created as a reflection of the nature of the Scylding kings . . .' (*Heroic Legends of Denmark*, pp 436-41).

In the English version of the story, Scyld as a mysterious, possibly otherworld foundling cannot have a known family. Yet there is an epithet attached to his name: Scefing, which can mean 'Son of Sheaf'. In *Widsið*, Sceafa is named as king of the Lombards, though he does not appear in their own king-list. The word 'scefing' could also mean 'with a sheaf' or 'of the sheaf'.

In some 9th and 10th century English genealogies of the West Saxon dynasty, the royal line was extended beyond Woden, who was no longer considered to be a god. This was done by adding the names of famous Germanic heroes as forebears of Woden, to bring the number of generations up to Noah, whose sons were the ancestors of the races of Europe, Asia and Africa. From Noah, the line went straight back to Adam, which made the West Saxon genealogy complete in Christian eyes.

In one version, Scef is the father of Scyld, who is the father of Beo (not Beowulf). In others, Beaw is the son of Scyldwa, who is the son of *Heremod*, with Scef coming several generations higher up!

These genealogies have nothing to do with either early history or early legends; they were constructed by Christian antiquarians. Their implications have been discussed at length by R W Chambers in *Beowulf, an Introduction to the study of the poem*. The relevant texts have been translated by G N Garmonsway and J Simpson in *Beowulf and its Analogues*. There is general agreement that the original name in the

Scylding family tree was not Beowulf but Beow, meaning 'grain, barleycorn', and that the first three 'ancestors' Sheaf, Shield and Barley are not human beings.

However, in *Historia Danica*, Skiold (Scyld) does not come at the head of the Danish royal line. The first king is Dan son of Humbli; he has a brother called Angul. Like Scyld, Dan and Angul are examples of Olrik's statement that 'the name of the people antecedes that of its supposed progenitor invented to explain the name.' They are the progenitors of the Danes and the Angles.

Dan had two sons, Humbli and Lother, who each became king: Skiold was Lother's son:

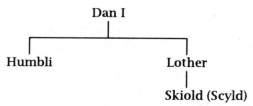

Humbli succeeded his father but was weak and easy-going; he was deposed by his brother. Lother was a murderous tyrant; the Danes rebelled and killed him. Skiold had his father's energy and military skill but none of his vices. He ruled with justice and set a high moral tone.

R W Chambers mentions a theory that in his career Saxo's Lother corresponds to the Old English Heremod. Their two names have a common element: Hloð*here*, *Here*mod, and they both stand accused of cruelty and tyranny. For what it is worth, Scyld is the son, or successor, of Heremod in the later West Saxon genealogies. New dynasties often justify themselves by claiming descent or rightful inheritance from the line they have replaced. But if Scef, Scyld and Beow are mythical personages, then the first mortal successor to Heremod – and founder of the 'new' Scylding line – would be Healfdene.

For the purposes of my story, I took Scyld to be, as Olrik said, the legendary ancestor of an ancient royal house in southern Scandinavia. Heremod was its last legitimate descendant. I linked Saxo's history with the *Beowulfian* version of the family tree by making Hloðhere his original name and Heremod a by-name that he used in exile and came to prefer. I have taken 'Barley' and 'Sheaf' to be names of the primeval fertility god of the common people, worshipped in his two aspects as seed-corn and ripe corn-stalks.

As there are no surviving texts describing Neolithic or Bronze Age religious ceremonies in Scandinavia or recording their liturgies, any modern reconstruction of an ancient Danish festival will have to be made up from folk customs, reports of pagan Germanic rituals by classical or medieval writers (often misunderstanding or disapproving of what they heard and saw), archaeology and (mostly) imagination.

In *The Chariot of the Sun*, there is a detailed description and analysis of the Scandinavian rock-engravings, considering what might be deduced from them about early religious beliefs and rituals. *Land of the Tollund Man* deals with the prehistory and archaeology of Denmark, giving an account of the finds and relating them to the nature of the land, the climate and the life of the people:

'The size and splendour of the lurs (Bronze Age ceremonial trumpets) suggest great cultic assemblies, which may have met both by the barrows of the great and the elongated flat and graveless mounds which have been ascribed to the Bronze Age and are often still called 'dance-hills'. Here, girls in corded skirts may have turned backward somersaults in the magic ecstasy of cult dances. The celebrations will almost certainly have centred on fertility and the rock engravings show that in this respect there was no resorting to remote symbols. In their fertility images they were extremely frank, the procreative powers of bull and man being plainly manifested. The same idea was undoubtedly the object of the spring and midsummer rites: a young, confident age and its people were celebrating spring and summer in unrestrained optimistic cult dances and lustful festivity. The custom of 'riding summer in', of choosing a 'May king' and 'May queen' and driving them round the village, is a form of cultic nuptials that has been observed down to our own time.' (*Land of the Tollund Man*, p90).

Most of the work on Scandinavian and Baltic stone labyrinths – the 'Citadels of Troy' and 'Maiden Dances' that are found throughout the region – is in the Scandinavian languages. The best source of information in English is the *Caerdroia Project*, the international centre for information and research into mazes of all kinds. The *Caerdroia* publications have many articles on the northern stone labyrinths: their history, traditional games and superstitions, the location of the Trojeborg names.

The second city of Troy (2,500 BC) imported amber from the Baltic; Palle Lauring says that the amber trade was the source of the great wealth of Bronze Age Denmark. Of course, most traders did not go the whole way to the Aegean and back. Goods passed from hand to hand, from trading post to trading post. However, some human beings have always had the urge to explore beyond the horizons of their birthplace. Maybe some adventurous Myceneans made their way north and brought back stories about the Land beyond the North Wind, where the folk enjoyed a simple carefree life in their fields and sacred groves – the climate of Bronze Age Denmark was much milder and sunnier than it was in the Migration period. Maybe some 'Hyperboreans' went south down the Amber Road and saw the walls of Troy and the high citadel.

The climate changed for the worse; the savage, iron-weaponed Celts cut the trade-routes. Yet it is just possible that some memories of what Palle Lauring calls 'the Eden of the Northern Bronze Age' did survive, in the legend of Glasisvellir (the Glittering Plains) – and in the Trojeborgar.

It has often been remarked that 'half-Dane' would be a very strange name for a king of the Danes to give to his legitimate heir. Since many Dark Age kings and chiefs married princesses from neighbouring tribes, to confirm an alliance or end a war, any son of a Danish king and his foreign queen would be a 'half-Dane', so there would be no reason to pick out one of them for special comment.

There are many ways in which a story-teller could account for Healfdene's claim to the Danish kingship and the Scylding name; also for the fact that Heremod has no place in the Scylding line. Germanic history, legends and folk tales all offer material. For example, Bede states that the 7th century keepers of the Northumbrian king-list decided that the name and memory of both Eanfrið of Bernicia and Osric of Deira should be blotted out; also that their disastrous year, 632-3, when Cadwallon and Penda ravaged Northumbria, should be given to King Oswald, who turned disaster into triumph. (Hist. Ecc. Book III, chs. 1 & 9). But though after that the two wretched kings officially had never existed, their stories were still used as warnings and examples of what not to do.

J R R Tolkien suggested that the Scylding dynasty rose to power when the Danes seized control of Sjælland (Old English Sillende) and the other islands, then took the Cimbric peninsula. The Jutish kingdom was breaking up, the English were moving away to Britain, so there would be a good chance for a forceful and capable man to take over and enlarge a territory. He calculated that this was happening in the first half of the 5th century.

The account of Healfdene in *Beowulf* contains another puzzle about the Scylding family. After stating that Healfdene's people were happy and glorious during his reign and that, though he lived to be old, he never lost his warlike strength and energy, the poem continues:

> 'Ðæm feower bearn forð-gerimed
> in woruld wocun weoroda ræswan:
> Heorogar ond Hroðgar ond Halga til;
> hyrde ic Þ elan cwen
> Heaðo-Scilfingas heals-gebedda'   1.59-63

(To him, the leader of war-hosts, four children were born into the world, one after the other: Heorogar and Hroðgar and Halga the good; *I heard that elan queen*, the beloved bed-fellow of the warlike Scylfing.)

The fragmentary state of line 62 was probably caused by the scribe's eye moving ahead of his text after he had written the abbreviation for 'þæt'. It is possible to supply the missing parts. According to line 63, Healfdene's daughter was married to a member of the Swedish royal family, the Scylfings. It is unlikely that she was 'Queen Elan', as that is not a Germanic name-form. '-elan' is the ending of her husband's name in the possessive form: '-ela's queen'. The only Swedish king of the dynasty and period whose name fits is Onela. 'I heard that (?) was Onela's queen'. The need for correct alliteration in the verse line means that the missing name must begin with a vowel.

Even if line 62 had been complete in the manuscript, there would be something odd about the account of Healfdene's children. The statement begins confidently. The poet is giving established facts; four children were born to the king: Heorogar and Hroðgar and Halga the good. The metre and wording of line 61 indicate the end of the statement. Yet only three of the four children have been listed. Line 62 begins less confidently: 'I heard that . . .' as if the poet were not quite so sure of his facts – or was reluctant to mention them.

Scandinavian sources do mention a marriage between a Swedish king and a member of Healfdene's family circle. Yrse, the mother of his grandson (Halga's son Hrolf Kraki, the great Danish hero-king) married King Aðils. Hrolf is the Hroðulf of

Beowulf, Hroðgar's nephew; Aðils is Eadgils, who rebelled against his uncle Onela and, with Beowulf's help, killed him and took the Swedish kingdom. If he took the widowed queen as well, as Kemp Malone argues, he would only have been following ancient Germanic practice, also shown in the Anglo-Jutish Hamlet story. Yrse is said to have loathed Aðils and to have fled from his court with her son Hrolf's help.

Her name fits line 62, which can then be completed by adding the verb 'wæs':

'hyrde ic þæt Yrse wæs Onelan cwen'.

However, as critics have pointed out, whether Yrse married Onela before Eadgils or not, if she was the mother of Halga's son Hroðulf, she was Healfdene's *daughter-in-law,* not his daughter. The dreadful truth, according to the Old English tradition, seems to have been that she was both.

The stories about Yrse's birth and her mating with Halga before either of them knew of their relationship, are given in *Beowulf and its Analogues,* section II F. Like the stories about Heoden, they offer a story-teller a wide choice of plots, motives and characterisation. As I wanted to keep to the English traditions, as far as they survive, I have made Yrse Healfdene's daughter rather than Halga's. This avoids trying to make credible the tedious and improbable episode of a man returning to the same place to commit another rape without having his memory jogged, though the girl he rapes is the daughter of the woman he raped there before. Apart from that change, I made most use of *Hrolfs saga kraka* for the story of Yrse's begetting, with Healfdene in Halga's place. It is a good story, told with robust humour. Chaucer's Miller and Reeve would have loved it.

Olrik points out that Oluf, the name given to the Saxon queen in the Scandinavian versions, is not a Saxon name, so I have given her one. Yrse, on the other hand, is not a Scandinavian name but a northern form of Ursa. Olrik collected all the Germanic names he could find beginning with the stem 'Urs-'. He has shown that they are derived from the Latin 'ursus' (bear), that they are found among tribes which had a long and close connection with the Romans along the Rhine frontier and that they are particularly common among the Franks.

So I made Yrse's mother ruler of one of those groups of Saxons who moved west into Frisia and Frankish Gaul before crossing to Britain. I settled them on and around the ruins of the former Roman frontier from the mouth of the Old Rhine near Lugdunum Batavorum (Leiden) inland to beyond Traiectum (Utrecht) and along the coasts of the Schelde and Maas estuaries. There was a great temple of the goddess Nehalennia on the island of Walcheren; she was also worshipped along the neighbouring coastlands. Her altars and sculptures are in a handsome Roman-provincial style; they show that though she was associated with the sea, and travellers prayed to her for safe voyages, she was a type of the Holy Mother.

That Queen Irminburg's people became the South Saxons and that her sister's son was Ælle the first bretwalda (or brytenwealda) are inventions of my own.

Beowulf: An Introduction to the study of the poem. R W Chambers with supplement by C L Wrenn, CUP 1963.

Beowulf and its Analogues: G N Garmonsway, J Simpson, H E Davidson, Dent/Everyman pbk 1980.

The Heroic Legends of Denmark: Axel Olrik, trans. Lee M Hollander, OUP 1919.
    ch 5 The Race of Halfdan,   ch 8 Scyld

Land of the Tollund Man: Palle Lauring, trans. R Spink, Lutterworth Press 1957.

The Chariot of the Sun: P Gelling, H E Davidson, Hamlyn 1982.

The Caerdroia Project (for northern labyrinths): J & D Saward, 53 Thundersley Grove, Thundersley, Benfleet, Essex SS7 3EB.

Finn and Hengest: J R Tolkien, ed. A Bliss, Allen and Unwin 1982

Studies in Heroic Legend and Current Speech: (for Healfdene's daughter), Kemp Malone, Rosenkilde & Bagger 1959.

The Literary History of Hamlet: vol I The Early Tradition (for Onela), Kemp Malone, Anglistische Forschungen LIX, Heidelberg 1923.

III Offa Of Angeln

'Offa weold Ongle, Alewih Denum;
se wæs þara manna modgast ealra,
no hwæþre he ofer Offa eorlscype fremede
ac Offa geslog ærest monna,
cnihtwesende, cynerica mæst.
Nænig efeneald him eorlscipe maran
on orette. Ane sweorde
merce gemærde wið Myrgingum
bi Fifeldore; heoldon forð siþþan
Engle ond Swæfe swa hit Offa geslog'

Widsið 1.35-44

(Offa ruled over Angeln, Alewih over the Danes – he was the bravest of all these men – that is, the thirty-three kings already listed by Widsið, including Alexander the Great, Attila and Eormanric! – yet he did not surpass Offa in heroic feats. For Offa, earlier than any of these, while he was still a boy, conquered the greatest of kingdoms. No one of like age has ever achieved a greater heroic feat in battle. With his own sword alone, he fixed the border against the Myrgings at Fifeldor. Ever since, the English and the Swabians have kept it as Offa won it.)

Offa of Angeln lived in the eighth generation before King Penda of Mercia, in the twelfth generation before his namesake Offa Rex Totius Anglorum Patriae (king of the whole fatherland of the English). Taking the notional number of thirty years to a generation, Offa of Angeln would have lived some time after the middle of the 4th century.

The story of his great feat of arms by the River Eider (bi Fifeldore) is very old. In *Widsið*, the account of it ends with the statement that from the time of Offa's single combat, the border between the English and Swæfe stayed where he had set it.

Bede finished his history of the English church in 731. When he was working on the first section, he wrote of: 'illa patria quae Angulus dicitur et ab eo tempore usque hodie manere desertus inter provincias Iutarum et Saxonum perhibetur' (I ch.15) – that country which is called Angeln, and which from that time (i.e. the coming of the English to Britain) is said to be uninhabited to this day, between the provinces of the Jutes and the Saxons.

The border between the Engle and the Swæfe ceased to exist when the English moved out, so the tradition about its establishment (not the poem *Wīdsīð*) must have existed before the emigration.

Penda and Offa of Mercia both claimed descent from Offa of Angeln. The determination of both those proud and dynamic men to be overlords in England was perhaps not just an expression of personal drive. They probably believed that the achievements of the first Offa gave them a hereditary claim on the loyalty of the English.

In tradition, it is a very interesting family. Offa I's grandfather killed Amleth (Amloði, Hamlet) of Jutland and married his widow, Hermenthrud (Eormenþryþ, Ermintrude). She was a determined and formidable lady, a reigning queen who killed every man who came to court her. However, she took a fancy to Amleth. He had been sent to woo her by his father-in-law, who wanted him killed but preferred it done by someone else. So she saved Amleth from the penalties of proposing to her by asking him to marry her – never mind that he was already married; his wife was not worthy of him, unlike herself. (*Historia Danica*, Bk 4).

By her second marriage to King Wihtlæg of Angeln, she became Offa's grandmother and must have brought a forceful strain into the future royal family of Mercia.

The English brought the stories of Offa I and his family to Britain and passed them on, to the 13th century at least. The Danes, who took over the Cimbric peninsula, also took over any good stories they found in their new territory and fitted them into their own traditions.

('This is I, Hamlet the Dane!' – By the way, *Hamlet* is an outstanding example of what a later English writer can do when reworking old Anglo-Jutish stories.)

By coincidence, the two chief Danish versions of the story were written down almost at the same time as the last, and only surviving, full length English version.

The English remembered that Offa was an Englishman but re-set his story in 'the kingdom of the Western Angles', that is, in English Mercia, the part that kept free of Danish occupation and fought for the re-conquest of England under the Lady Æðelflæd. King Wærmund's capital was said to be Warwick, interpreted as 'Wærmundes wic'. In this version, Offa's duel has become a battle against the forces of a rebellious noble. This rebel was encouraged in his bid for the kingship by the fact that Wærmund's only son had been dumb from birth and also blind till the age of seven. Offa was cured, just in time to lead the royalist forces, by a miracle granted when he silently prayed to the Holy Trinity.

Some memory of his single combat against two opponents, while cut off by water from English help, does remain in this very late and garbled story. When the royalist and rebel forces faced each other across a river, Offa dashed through alone to get at the enemy. Later, during a pause in the main action, he was set upon by the two sons of one of the rebel leaders; he killed both.

The Danish chroniclers, Sven Aageson and Saxo Grammaticus, came across the tradition on its home ground. They tell a story that is not only excellent in itself but is much more in line with the episode mentioned in *Widsið*. The texts of both the English and Danish versions are given in the original Latin in *Beowulf, an Introduction . . .* and translated in *Beowulf and its Analogues*. A translation of Saxo's version, with a full commentary, is in Book IV of the Fisher/Davidson edition of *Historia Danica*.

I suppose it might be possible to concoct a romantic novel, set in pre-Norman England, or more vaguely in 'the olden days', from the material in the *Lives of the Two Offas*. However, as material for any work set in the 4th century, the Danish versions are much better and far closer to the spirit of *Widsið*, though they need modifying in some details.

The Danish chroniclers saw Wærmund and his son as Danes defending Denmark against the might of Germany. For them, the enemy south of the Eider were the (Old) Saxons and, from the 10th century, the forces of the Holy Roman Empire as revived by the Ottonians of Saxony. They had no memory of the Myrgings or the Swæfe.

The account of the border dispute in *Widsið* has the Myrgings as the immediate enemies on the other side of the Eider, with the Swæfe as the greater and more permanent power in the background. They would come face to face with the English once the Myrgings were defeated.

According to Tacitus, writing at the end of the 1st century, the Suebi (Swæfe) were not one tribe but a great confederation of tribes, each with its own separate name but all calling themselves 'Suebi'. He says that at the time of writing they occupied the greater part of Germany. We may assume, if we like, that the Myrgings were one of the tribes that claimed to be Suebi.

The chiefs and free-born warriors of this people did their hair in a distinctive style, sweeping it back off the face and diagonally across the crown, then twisting it into a knot above or behind the right ear. Young men of other tribes often imitated this fashion, but the Suebi wore it to old age. Their chieftains wore a more elaborate style, building their hair up on the crown of their heads to make themselves taller and more terrifying to look at.(*Germania*, ch.38)

In Schleswig, the old Anglian land, a head was found in a peat cutting in 1948. There is a description of it, with a photograph, in *The Bog People*. The man's hair was knotted up at one side of his head in the way Tacitus described. He had been between fifty and sixty years old when he died; his hair had been fair, sprinkled with grey. ('apud Suebos usque ad canitiem horrentes capilli retorquentur' – among the Suebi, even till the hair is grey the shaggy locks are twisted back.) The head had been struck off with a sharp blade and wrapped in a cape of roe-deer skin.

It seems as if one of the Engle had brought a souvenir back from the border with the Swæfe and made a votive offering of it.

The border was along the River Eider: 'fifeldor' in place of Egidora, Ægisdyr (Old English Egordor). 'Fifel' means a giant or monster, particularly a sea-monster, a cause of dread and terror; 'fifel-stream' and 'fifel-wæg' both refer to the ocean in its terrifying aspect; 'fifel-dor' is 'monster-gate'. From this, one might imagine that Offa's duel was fought near the river-mouth but, according to H.M. Chadwick in *The Origin of the English Nation*, it took place at Rendsburg:

"Even the exact spot on which Uffo (Offa) fought his single combat was clearly known to Saxo, although he does not give its name; for in a later passage, Book XIII, he states that Bjorn (Bero) the brother of King Eric Eiegod (1095-1103) fortified 'the island where Uffo the son of Wærmundus fought two chosen champions of the Saxon nation.' This fortress is said to have been built on the island on which the old part of Rendsburg stands."

As the Danes had forgotten about the Myrgings and their king Eadgils, they assumed that the king treacherously killed by Offa's two fellow-countrymen was Aðils of Sweden (the

Eadgils who was Beowulf's protégé). This confusion causes some loss of emotional logic and narrative tightness in the Danish version. Offa's crazily chivalrous decision to fight two champions at once is explained by Saxo as an attempt to expiate the shame of his country for the killing of Aðils. Expiating the killing of a Swedish king by tempting death at the hands of Germans is not so satisfying as expiating the death of a Myrging king at the hands of his kinsmen or nobles.

In the *Widsið* 'framing-narrative', Eadgils is king of the Myrgings, a generous lord to the wandering scop when he is at home, clearly an admirable king.(1.88-96) In the king-list, however, 'Meaca ruled the Myrgings'.(1.23) Both kings can be brought into Offa's story by making Eadgils the king whose death loaded Offa with such a heavy burden of guilt; Meaca can be his successor. If the story-teller chooses, he can be given some of the unpleasant characteristics of the Scandinavian Aðils, so that Offa need feel no regrets in killing him. On the other hand, Meaca – or whoever comes to fight Offa (one of the champions *must* be of royal blood) – can be wholly sympathetic, so that Offa's triumph is shadowed by grief.

The Danish versions also create difficulties over Offa's age, therefore about his dumbness and when and why it started. They agree with the medieval English story in making Offa a man of thirty, well on into middle age. It seems, if not impossible, highly unlikely that a man could deliberately keep unbroken silence during such a long time. Also, if the refusal to speak came from shock and disgust at the killing of Eadgils, when did he know about it and how was he behaving before? According to Saxo, he was a married man, brother-in-law to Eadgils' killers. That, of course, would make him feel even more deeply tainted by their dishonour and more responsible for paying the penalty – but it is hard to imagine his married life.

It has been suggested that some lost English version of the story might have used the phrase 'pritig missera' – thirty half-years – to fix Offa's age when he fought; that is, he was fifteen years old. Hroðgar, giving advice to young Beowulf from his accumulated experience, says: "Swa ic Hring-Dena hund missera/weold . . ." (So I ruled the Ring-Danes for a hundred missera – for fifty years. 1.1769-70)

But when the word 'missera' did not follow a precise number, it was used in a general way meaning 'a period of time' and so came to have a sense of 'years': 'fela missera – many years'; 'misserum frod – wise with the passage of time, *well on in years*. So 'þritig missera' might gradually come to be mistaken as thirty *years*.

The Old English *Widsið* emphasises that it was his extreme youth, as well as his courage and success, that set Offa's achievement high above those of all the other kings, even Alewih. After all, his feat was not just a reckless boyish 'dare'; it was a political action that would decide his people's future safety and self-respect. At fifteen, a young man would have been liable for military service but he would not have reached his full strength, or have had time to learn from fighting experience and get weapon-wise.

On this point, the Old English tradition is both more moving and makes more sense. Offa's feeling of personal involvement in Eadgils' death can be kept by making the killers his foster-brothers rather than his brothers-in-law. In the Old English tradition, according to *Beowulf* (l.1931-62), Offa was not married to Freawine's daughter. He wooed and won the heart of a proud and beautiful princess, who had been used to order the execution of any man who dared to raise his eyes to her . . . But that is another story.

In addition to works already cited, the following are useful:

Germania: Tacitus trans. M Hutton Loeb Classical Library; rev. E H Warmington, No 35 1970.

also translated as:

On Britain and Germany: (with the Agricola), H Mattingly Penguin Classics 1948.

The Bog People: P V Glob trans. R Bruce-Mitford Faber pbk. 1977.

The Origin of the English Nation: H M Chadwick CUP 1907 repr. 1924.

IV *The Husband's Message*

'Ytum Gefwulf,
Fin Folcwalding Fresna cynne
Sigehere lengest Sædenum weold,
Hnæf Hocingum.'

Widsið 1.26-29

(Gefwulf ruled the Jutes, Fin Folcwalding the Frisian race. Sigehere ruled the Sea-Danes for a very long time, Hnæf the Hocings . . .)

Most of *Widsið* is made up of names that have lost their stories. *The Husband's Message* suggests a story that has lost its names, if it ever had any. Surviving Old English literature shows that the early English relished allusions. Poets could rely on their listeners' ability to recognise a story and recall it to mind at the mention of a name, with perhaps a brief reference to some event or well-known detail. It may be that they also used the opposite device and left their listeners to supply names to a well-known story. Even today, when someone mentions 'burning the cakes', 'finishing the game of bowls', 'turning the blind eye', most people can supply the name of the original hero. Perhaps the story of the exile who carved out a kingdom for himself in a southern land beyond the sea, and the gallant lady who set out to join him when she read his secret message, was as well-known then as the plot of *Romeo and Juliet* is today.

The Husband's Message is an intriguing poem for several reasons. The one surviving text is in the Exeter Book. This was owned by Leofric, Bishop of Exeter and left to the cathedral when he died in 1072. The date of the manuscript has been placed around 1000, so the poem cannot have been composed later than that. As the Exeter book is a large collection of poems in different styles on widely differing subjects, any item in it could be older than the end of the 10th century, though it would not be easy to guess, still less prove, how much older.

Whenever *The Husband's Message* was composed, it was written down in its surviving form at least half a century before the Norman invasion. At least another century passed before the supposedly novel concept of 'courtly love', with the stories and poems that expressed it, was introduced from France to help civilise the supposedly uncouth English.

In courtly love, the meaning and value of a knightly warrior's life are given by the existence of a high-born woman whom he adores. Her smiles and praise are the greatest prizes he can win; her presence is heaven; her anger, coldness or absence are desolation, death, hell.

Long before the Normans came to wreck English civilisation for a while, an English poet imagined an exile sending a message to his absent lover:

'Nu se mon hafað
wean oferwunnen; nis him wilna gad –
ne meara ne maðma ne meododreama
ænges ofer eorþan eorlgestreona,
þeodnes dohtor, *gif he þin beneah.*'

The Husband's Message 1.43-47

(Now the man has overcome his troubles; he lacks nothing he wants – horses, precious jewels, the joys of the hall, or any noble treasure in the world, king's daughter – *if he may have you.*)

His lady is the one treasure that will give value to all that he has won by his own efforts. Yet he cannot win *her* by his own efforts; she must come to him – if she remembers and still feels herself bound by the promises they made to each other in happier times. He cannot demand that she carries out her side of the bargain, he only *begs* her, in his message, to remember.

The rune-stave, carved with the message, is supposed to be speaking to her:

'Hwæt, þec þonne biddan het se þisne beam agrof
þæt þu, sinchroden, sylf gemunde
on gewitlocan wordbeotunga
þe git on ærdagum oft gespræcon,'   1.13-16

(Listen! He who carved this wood ordered me then to *beseech* you, jewel-bedecked [lady] that you yourself should remember in your secret heart the vows you two often spoke in former times.)

If she does hold to her former vows, it will not be because he has a right to her but, as the later medieval poets would say, because she granted it 'of her grace'.

Yet there are two great differences between the Old English poem and the later 'courtly love' poetry. First, it was a dictum of the courtly love code that a wife could not be her husband's 'lady' in the courtly sense because she was legally his chattel and he had a right to her services. Chaucer's married lovers Dorigen and Arveragus get round this by making a pact to behave to each other *as if they were not married*, though in public she treats him as her master, so that he can retain the respect of their social circle.

The couple in the Old English poem have exchanged vows that make them either troth-plight or husband and wife – the difference between the two states would be whether they have already bedded. In English law, such vows were valid until the Marriage Act of 1753; the plots of *Measure for Measure* and several Restoration comedies depend on this fact. The life that the exile in the poem wants to share with his lady is marriage as it is defined in the Old English *Maxims* I, 1.81-92: 'boldagendum bæm ætsomne' – joint master and mistress of the house together – dealing out the treasures to deserving thanes, presiding graciously over the rituals of the hall. 'Freondscype' with all its implications of comradeship and respect, was the Old English word for both love-affairs and marriage.

The other difference between *The Husband's Message* and the courtly love romances is that the later medieval 'heroine' sat in her castle while her knight went off to follow quests or joust at tournaments. If she was besieged, he arrived to save her; if she was carried off, she waited for him to rescue her. The lover in the Old English poem expects his lady to take ship and come to find him, wherever in Dark Age Europe he may be and whatever dangers on sea and land a high-born, wealthy (and presumably beautiful) woman might meet on the way. Yet the whole tone of the poem shows that he is not whistling her to him as if she were a faithful dog. He shows some doubt, or polite hesitation, whether she still wants him. He has no doubt whatever that she has the energy, initiative and courage to make the journey successfully if she decides to set out.

How would she go about it? He had to leave in a hurry because of a feud which is still raging; he can't come back for her in spite of his wealth and loyal house-troop. She is of royal blood. As she is neither poverty-stricken nor under duress as a result of his flight, we may assume she is one of the royal family, that his feud was with them, and they either do not know about the exchange of vows or believe that she had finished with him. In which case, they are hardly likely to let her set out publicly with an escort to join him. How would she get away secretly? Would she risk taking her servants and luggage? If she went alone, how would she escape robbery, rape, slavery or murder? Would she disguise herself as a boy, like Shakespeare's Rosalind, Julia or Imogen? Had she any idea exactly where she was going; had they kept in touch? Where was she going – and did she get there?

There is not the slightest evidence that *The Husband's Message* was inspired by, much less connected with, the story of Hengest. It can be made to fit, using only details based on the Finnesburh texts and the many studies and reconstructions that they have provoked. The Finnesburh fragment, with the episode in *Beowulf* 1.1063-1159, is to Old English what *The Mystery of Edwin Drood* is to modern English literature; working out the missing story from the clues is a fascinating game and anyone can play.

I have followed the suggested story-line given by R W Chambers in sections X-XII, Part III of *Beowulf, an Introduction*, using the refinements of detail provided in *Finn and Hengest*. This is a commentary on the Finnesburh texts compiled and edited by Alan Bliss from the lecture notes of J R R Tolkien.

Tolkien had been working on the Finnesburh poetry and thinking about it for most of his professional life; his knowledge of the Old English language was only matched by his love for it. The core of *Finn and Hengest* is an examination of the grammar and implications of nearly every word in both texts. Tolkien was lecturing to students who were reading Old English for a degree; he could assume that they had a knowledge of grammatical and other technical terms and that they had edited texts, Old English grammars and dictionaries to hand. Also, in notes meant for his own use, he had no need to translate Old Norse passages; he could do that in the lecture room when he quoted them.

The published result is not an easy read for the non-specialist, though a fascinating one. There are many rewards in the book even for those who do not know Old English, let alone Old Norse, and prefer to skip the grammar: for example, the Introduction and the Glossary of Names. Above all, when Tolkien is commenting on the action and the motives of the characters, rather than on points of language and grammar, he makes the story as gripping as anything in *The Lord of the Rings*.

Tolkien sets the Finnesburh tragedy in the period when the old Jutish kingdom had broken up or was breaking up, after King Amleth had been killed by Offa's grandfather Wihtlæg. Perhaps a civil war followed between rival Jutish claimants; perhaps there was an Anglian overlordship, with all the resentments and revolts that would follow – as happened in Mercia after Oswiu defeated and killed Penda. At the same time, the Danes were moving out from their original home in what is now southern Sweden, Skane (Old English Scedeland, Scedenig) into the islands and Jutland. Some Jutes threw in their lot with the Danes; others may have gone to seek their fortunes by taking service in foreign kingdoms, Frisia for one.

The young warrior Garulf, who was the first to die as he attacked the hall door and was cut down by Sigeferð, may have been a descendant of Gefwulf, king of the Jutes according to *Widsið*. One of his companions tried to hold him back, urging that such a precious life should not be risked in the first charge. As this is such unusual, not to say shameful advice to give to a young warrior, Tolkien deduced that Garulf might be the last of the old Jutish line, that would die with him. As Chambers and Tolkien see it, the meeting between the Jutes in Finn's household and those in Hnæf's following (supporting the new Danish line) turned what was meant to be a pleasant Yule-tide visit into a bloodbath and led to the sacking of Finnesburh the following spring.

No one knows where Finnesburh stood. The chief and most famous settlement in Frisia was 'Dorostates of the Frisians' (mentioned in the Ravenna Cosmography c.700) that is, Wijk bii Duurstede near Utrecht, not far from Rhinemouth. There is no evidence that there was a 'wic' there in the 5th century, though the increasing proofs of a brisk trade between the Empire and the Germans beyond the Rhine show that there might have been. However, I have imagined that Finnesburh was in the north of Frisia, perhaps built by Finn as a stronghold to keep the north of the country and the mouth of the Ems. In the province of Groningen there are still the remains of a number of *terpen*, some with villages on top. Biessum, immediately west of Delfzyl – now the largest port on the north coast of Holland – was a terp. I have put Finnesburh on Biessum terp and supposed that the haven where ships came in was at the nearest suitable place in the Ems estuary.

There is no absolute proof that the Hengest of the Finnesburh tragedy and the Hengest who took power in Kent were the same man. So far as the scanty evidence of traditional dating goes, those two events were not far apart in time. In the *Historia Brittonum*, a Welsh compilation of ancient traditions, Hengest is said to have been an exile from Germany. The Hengest of Finnesburh had good reasons for not going back to Frisia if he had exchanged vows with a woman of Finn's family. Both Hengests were involved with Jutes. Also, if Hengest had set out 'suð heonan ofer merelade' – south from hence over the sea-way (*The Husband's Message* 1.27-8) – and then followed the sun's path .ᚻ· ᚱ· bearing westwards, he would quite likely have made landfall in Thanet, or at Regulbium or Rutupiae.

I have taken R W V Elliott's second interpretation (he gives two, both probable) of the lover's rune-message, in his book *Runes, an Introduction*.

The text of *The Husband's Message* is in:

The Exeter Book: vol III Anglo-Saxon Poetic Records ed. G P Krapp & E V K Dobbie, Columbia U P/Routledge & Kegan Paul 1966.
Three Old English Elegies: ed. R F Leslie, Manchester UP 1961.
A Choice of Anglo-Saxon verse: ed. & trans. R Hamer, Faber pbk 1970 (with a parallel translation).

Finnsburh: Fragment and Episode ed. D K Fry, Methuen 1974. Most editions of *Beowulf* include the 'Finnesburh Fragment' as well, with a discussion of its relation to *Beowulf* 1.1063-1159 e.g. A J Wyatt, revised with introduction and notes by R W Chambers, CUP 1943.
F Klaeber, D Heath & C O Lexington Massachusetts 1956.
C L Wrenn revised by W F Bolton Harrap 1973.

Reconstructions of the Finnesburh story can be found in:

Beowulf, an Introduction: R W Chambers, Part III especially pp 266-288.
Finn and Hengest: J R R Tolkien, ed. A Bliss, Allen & Unwin 1982 (this also contains both texts, edited and with parallel translation pp 146-155).

For the rune message see:

Runes: R W V Elliott, Manchester UP 1971. (Chapter VI, The Uses of Runes, includes an interpretation of both possible readings of 1.49-50, which contain the runes.)

V *Waldere* & the Fate of the Burgundians

Ætla weold Hunum . . .
. . .Burgendum Gifica . . .
. . .ond mid Burgendum, þær ic beag geþah
me þær Guðhere forgeaf glædlicne maþþum
songes to leane. Næs þæt sæne cyning.

Widsið, 1.18, 19, 65-67

(Attila ruled the Huns . . . Gifica the Burgundians . . . and [I
have been] among the Burgundians where I received a ring –
probably an arm or neck ring i.e. a bracelet or a collar – there
Guðhere granted me the gleaming treasure as the reward for a
song. That king was not dully irresponsive!)

The two surviving leaves of the poem *Waldere* are tantalizing.
They are dramatic; people are speaking under stress of
emotion, in a dangerous situation:

A man is in a tight corner; he has already had to fight off a
number of attackers, though he seems to have put paid to
them. He has a friend to keep his back, a chest of treasure and
a sword called Mimming, Weland's work.

Any weapon made by Weland was a valuable object, to be
treasured as an heirloom; this sword was particularly famous.
In Germanic story, it had belonged to Ðeodric – Theodoric the
Great, who ruled Italy from 493 to 526. Ðeodric had meant to
give it to his friend Widia (Vidigoia) Weland's son, along with a
great treasure. This was no ordinary act of generosity from an
open-handed prince; he intended to show his gratitude to
Widia for saving him when he was trapped by giants.

This reference in *Waldere* shows how heroic legend, folk-
tale and history share easily-crossed frontiers in Old English
poetry. In 448/9, a Greek scholar called Priscus visited Attila in
what is now Hungary. He went at the invitation of his friend
Maximinus, who was heading an embassy, and he seems to
have taken detailed notes of what he saw and heard. The party
was ferried across the Danube, then crossed the Tisza and
other rivers and 'we came to the place where long ago Vidigoia,
the bravest of the Goths, perished by the treachery of the
Sarmatians.' C D Gordon, who translated this passage in *The
Age of Attila* puts the death of Vidigoia, the Gothic warrior, in

331/2 or 334, during the reign of Constantine, when the two tribes were at war. Theodoric was not born until about five or six years after the embassy of Maximinus, when Attila was already dead. Medieval German poems show Theodoric as the nephew and younger contemporary of Eormanric, who died in 375. Hounded by Eormanric, who had a murderous suspicion of all his kin, he took refuge with Attila. Widia, a famous champion in Eormanric's hearth-troop, supported and turned against both uncle and nephew – possibly torn (like Hagena in the *Waldere* stories) between two impossible loyalties.

By saying of the sword Mimming: 'hit *ðohte* Ðeodric Widian selfum onsendan' – Theodoric thought about, considered, intended sending it to Widia himself – the Old English poet indicates that the story has changed; the sword is in other hands.

In *Waldere*, the present owner of Mimming, when his assailants first confronted him, had offered some of his treasure and one of his two swords – probably Mimming, which he does not seem to have used in the first stage of the fighting – in an attempt to keep the peace. This is not because he is a coward or a poor swordsman. He is called, without irony, a strong and daring fighter 'wiga ellenrof'. He has already killed a number of his enemies against the odds:

'ðeah þe laðra fela

ðinne byrnhomon billum heowun'   Fragment I, 1.16-17

(though many foes hewed at your byrnie with their swords)

In fact, he went for them so savagely that his friend was afraid he would go too far outside his defensive position and let himself be surrounded. So his peace-offering must have been made because, for all his reckless courage, he was a reasonable man, not a killer. Or he might have had some special reason for not wanting to fight at that time. He was not looking for trouble, but if trouble came he would give more than he got.

One of his enemies is mentioned by name: Guðhere (Scand: Gunnar; Ger: Gunther). The hero's friend says that Guðhere came looking for the fight with no just cause. He was the one who refused the peace-offering (so he must be the leader of the other side); the friend adds with grim pleasure that Guðhere is going to regret doing that.

The beleaguered hero is not named in Fragment I but is referred to as 'Ætlan ordwiga' 1.6 – Attila's warrior-who-fights-in-the-front–line. He is one of Attila's champions.

In Fragment II, the warrior himself speaks to the enemy leader, calling him 'wine Burgenda' – King of the Burgundians – taunting him with having expected Hagena to have finished the dirty work for him, sneering at him for attacking a man already weary with fighting and daring him to come over and try to take his gilded byrnie off him as spoils of war.

The Burgundians, Guðhere and Hagena (Gunther and Hagen in the *Nibelungenlied* and in Wagner's *Götterdämmerung*, the last opera of the 'Ring' cycle) are a well-known pair in Germanic legend. In the poem and the opera, they are concerned with greed for treasure and the treacherous murder of a young hero. Later in the poem, as also in the Eddic lays and the Volsunga saga, they die at the hands of Attila's forces, fighting heroically against great odds until they are overcome, then facing their deaths without flinching.

But the hero of this Old English poetic fragment about treasure and an ambush set by Guðhere and Hagena, is not the son of Sigemund. He is named as Waldere, Ælfhere's son. His name gives us the name of the friend who is keeping his back. She is his lover and betrothed wife, Hildegyð.

Their story was very popular, especially in Germany, though there were also versions of it in Scandinavia and Poland. These have been summarized in F Norman's excellent edition of *Waldere* and translated in F P Magoun and H M Smyser's *Walter of Aquitaine: Materials for a Study of his Legend.*

Of all these other versions, *Waltharius,* an early 10th century epic composed in southern Germany, is the nearest in time to the Old English poem and the closest in spirit to Old English poetry – which does not mean very close, only that the other versions are much further away. The monk who wrote it had a good story to tell and told it well. Lines 559-1061 deal with the first attack of Guðhere's men on Waldere, which has just ended before Hildegyð speaks in Fragment I. It is something of a *tour de force*: eight single combats, all different, fought mostly with spears; then a final three-against-one assault.

The second Old English fragment deals with the same stage of the story as *Waltharius* 1.1228-84. Guðhere had brought twelve men against Waldere; eleven of them have been killed. Now the king himself is confronting Waldere. Hagena, who has refused to fight his friend up to this moment, is about to come into the fray.

However, though at this stage of the action the English and Latin poems were following a very similar story-line, they are not identical in detail or in mood. *Waltharius* translated into English verse, even into Old English verse, would not give us *Waldere*.

In *Waltharius*, most of the hero's fighting is done with a spear. The English poem lays great stress on the fact that he has two fine swords, one of which is Mimming. Of the surviving 63 lines, 13 are about Mimming, its excellence and its history; clearly it was going to play a decisive part at one stage (probably the last) of the fighting.

In *Waltharius*, Hagena advises Guðhere to pretend to go away, so that Waldere and Hildegyð will leave their strong position among the rocks and try to escape. It will be easier to attack them when they are in the open country. The plan works but Waldere eats his supper and takes a night's rest before moving out. In Fragment II, however, he taunts Guðhere for gathering enough courage to attack a man who is already weary with fighting; so this confrontation must come fairly soon after he has killed the eleven champions, not next morning. Any Germanic warrior who complained about being 'heaðuwearig' after a meal and a sleep would not rank as a hero but a wimp.

The Latin poem is suitably decked out with Latin rhetoric and classical allusions: Phoebus inclines towards the western parts; Lucifer as Herald of Day is climbing Olympus. One of Guðhere's warriors, taunting Waldere with being non-human, calls him 'Faunus, familiar to the forests'. Hagena is 'descended from the stock of Troy'.

The greatest difference between *Waltharius* and *Waldere* is in the character of the heroine. In *Waltharius*, she is well on the way to being an 'Arthurian' heroine; she is not unlike Geraint's Enid; she holds the horses, she watches the fighting from a distance, she 'trembles at every murmur of the breeze', when a spear lands near her she screams and it is some time before she has the courage to peep out of her hiding-place to see if her lover is still alive.

Hildegyð, by contrast, is taking a keen expert's interest in the fighting and urges Waldere to carve up his enemies with Mimming. According to *Waltharius*, the passage between the rocks where the hero is making his stand is too narrow for two to fight side by side; Hildegyð is guarding his back. It is not hard to imagine her taking a hand in the fighting if need be.

Roberta Frank accuses Hildegyð of talking: 'out of both sides of her mouth ('Fight, don't be a coward' and 'Be careful, you impetuous fool!') which must have annoyed Waldere if he were listening. After playing the valkyrie to perfection and inciting him to battle, she starts to worry . . .' *Germanic Legend in Old English Literature*

I think this is unjust; to me, Hildegyð sounds like a sensible 'second' or trainer, giving advice between rounds: Get in there, boy, and hit him with all you've got – you've got the punch to finish him – mind now, don't get carried away and leave yourself wide open – had me worried once or twice – etc.

The loss of the complete *Waldere* from the body of Old English poetry is particularly galling. It had a story in which the heroine went literally every step of the way with the hero and was an intelligent partner in all his dangers. Also, as far as one can judge from 63 lines, it could have been an epic poem rather than a lay. It suggests a large scale and ample time for its story. Swords have names and pasts; a hero can pause, even while facing an attempt on his life, to give a history of his. Behind the characters in the main story are other great heroes of legend: Waldere thinks of Ðeodric and Widia after his great feat of killing eleven champions, just as the Danish scop thinks of Sigemund and the dragon after Beowulf's feat of killing the ogre.

If *Waldere* were an epic, it could have made a satisfying complement to *Beowulf*. *Beowulf* is the epic of northern and western Germania; it is not just about the exploits of its Geatish hero but about the fate of the Geatish, Danish, Swedish and Frisian dynasties. *Waldere* could have been the epic of the south and east: the fate of the Goths, Franks and Burgundians, their strange love-hate of Rome and Constantinople, how they met the onslaughts of the Huns.

When history turns into legend, one of the results is that time gets telescoped, so that famous characters can meet and have dramatic scenes together that would have been impossible during their earthly lives.

If Waldere's story ever happened, it must have been before the year 437, when the Huns (instigated by Aëtius, the Roman commander in Gaul) attacked the Burgundians, who were defeated in an appalling disaster. Their losses are given as 20,000; their king, Gundahari, (Guðhere) was among the dead. This was the end of the Burgundian kingdom of the Rhine, traditionally based on Worms (Borbetomagus).

'The destruction of their nation caught the imagination of contemporaries. Alone among the events of this period of Burgundian history it is mentioned by no less than four of the chroniclers, and it provided the historical basis for the epic of the Nibelungen. It was indeed a *bellum memorabile:* yet the reason for it is, to us, an utter mystery.' E A Thompson, *A History of Attila and the Huns.*

Aëtius was also using Huns against the Visigoths of Toulouse, who destroyed them in 439. They were ruled at this time by Theodoric I (Theodrid in Jordanes) who died heroically at the battle of Chalons in 451, fighting with Aëtius against Attila. Jordanes' description of the old king's death and the raging grief of the Visigoths may have helped to inspire Tolkien's description of King Theoden's death at the battle of the Pelennor Fields. Theodrid was succeeded by his son Thorismund; there is no mention of an Ælfhere or a Waldere (or their Gothic equivalents) in the Visigothic king-list at this period of their history.

The early history of the Frankish Merovingian dynasty is very obscure; even Gregory of Tours is frankly unsure about it (*History of the Franks* Book II, ch 9) He mentions a Clodio, otherwise spelled Cloio and Chlogio – probably Gallo-Roman garblings of the shortened form of Chlodovech. He *might* have been the father of Merovech (who gave his name to the dynasty) who *might* have been the father of Childeric, the first Frankish king whose existence we can be sure about. He died in 481 and was sumptuously buried with much treasure in Tournai (Turnacum).

The Franks seem to have been on reasonably good terms with the Romans at this time, probably because they did not seem to be so powerful or so much of a threat as the Visigoths and the Burgundians. When the Burgundians tried to move into Belgica, where Franks were settling, Aëtius threw them out in 435, two years before he used the Huns to destroy them.

So a story-teller wanting to 'date' the action of *Waldere* would have to put it in the earlier 430's. But at this time, the Huns were ruled by Attila's uncle Rua, or Rugila. He was the Hunnic lord who supplied troops to Aëtius. He died in 434 and was succeeded by his nephews, Bleda and Attila, who had been campaigning in Scythia. Attila did not murder his brother until 445, eleven years later. It was only after 445, until his death in 453, that Attila attained supreme power. The embassy of Maximinus to Attila's extraordinary 'capital', somewhere on the puszta north of the Körös, took place in 448/9. In the 'legendary time' of the story, the period of Attila's supremacy has been moved forward about fifteen years.

Attila's three hostages represent the three chief Germanic races in Gaul. Waldere, who lives in Aquitaine but has a Germanic name and is supposed to be a member of the royal family, must be a Visigoth. The author of *Waltharius* makes Gifica and his son Guðhere Frankish. This is probably because by the time *Waltharius* was written, Worms was in Frankish territory and the Burgundians were living further south by the Rhone. So the heroine had to be Burgundian. As history, the rest of Germanic legend and Old English poetry are unanimous that Gifica and Guðhere were Burgundians, Hildegyð must be Frankish in the story.

Waltharius does not say much about the early lives of the hostages, the growth of their friendship (historically, their three peoples were bitter enemies most of the time) and the betrothal of Waldere and Hildegyð. This leaves an open field where the story-teller's imagination can range freely. However, the Latin poem does give one interesting detail: Hagena is not a member of the royal family.

In later legend, Hagena is a grim figure, very close to the royal family, having great influence over its members, yet somehow always an outsider. In some versions, he is not fully human: an 'incubus' lay with the queen when she was drunk, asleep or bespelled and so begot him. In Wagner's opera, he is the son of a vengeful dwarf, deliberately begotten to retrieve the Ring. A Hagena of this kind, half-troll or half-etin, with his human feelings of friendship and loyalty struggling against cold destructive impulses, could be a very powerful character – possibly too powerful for the story. *Waldere* does not seem to demand a supernatural element, as *Beowulf* does, or the stories of Heoden or the Wælsings. Most versions end 'happily', in that none of the principal characters gets killed and the hero and heroine marry. A demonic Hagena would be out of place.

In *Waltharius*, Hagena is described as 'descended from the stock of Troy'. The time came in medieval Europe when most of the western races, even the Norse gods, were said to be 'descended from the stock of Troy'. However, I think that to a Latin-schooled monk of the early 10th century. 'the stock of Troy' would mean the Romans, the people of Aeneas. So I have made Hagena a Gallo-Roman, in the Burgundian world but not of it, though he would like to be and tries to be more 'German', in Tacitus' sense, than the Germans themselves.

Romans did quite often idealise the very people they called 'barbarians'. When the Hun mercenaries under their Roman general Litorius (one of Aëtius's men and acting under his orders) were besieging Toulouse, the Visigoths, who were Arian Christians, offered up prayers and intercessions. Finally, they wiped out the Huns and executed Litorius. A Gallo-Roman, Salvianus, wrote bitterly:

'praesumeremus nos in Chunis spem ponere, illi in deo' – while we laid our hopes in Huns, they (the Visigoths) laid theirs in God.

In an epic, every chief character has a pedigree and a family history, so I have made Hagena a descendant of Quintinus, a late 4th century general, who saved the city of Trier from Frankish raiders. He believed in stopping invasions at the source, so he led his troops across the Rhine, was decoyed into a trap in the wild country and wiped out with most of his men. (Hist. Franc. Bk II ch9)

The substitution of Hagena for Guðhere gave me the idea of making the other hostages substitutes as well. The fact that each had a guilty secret would bind them together and force them to keep faith with each other in spite of racial hostility, before they had learned to like each other: the step-son, the son by adoption and the daughter who felt she should have been a son. Many commentators on *Waldere* have remarked on the 'wælcyrie' strain in Hildegyð's character. Even in *Waltharius*, the heroine has to walk most of the way from Hungary to the Vosges (they spare Lion as much as possible because he is carrying the luggage) travelling by night and sleeping rough. Timid as she is in the Latin poem, she would have to be bodily tough. The life she was leading in the house of Attila's women would not have toughened her. Huns respected their chief wives (Priscus met the widow of Attila's murdered brother governing a settlement) but their girls did not fight as shield-maidens.

In the later German epics. Attila's 'permanent camp' has become a medieval city with a minster and a royal palace. There is nothing much to distinguish Huns from Germans. I think it is far more effective to present the Huns as they were seen in the 4th and 5th centuries. The first horrified comments, starting from the time when Eormanric's Gothic kingdom went down under their attacks, make them subhuman or of demon stock. The Huns sound just like Tolkien's orcs – broad-shouldered, bow-legged, devilishly effective fighters, moving fast, talking a language that sounds like no human speech (probably Turkic) and practising ghastly tortures with great relish.

It is startling to turn from these horror stories to the account given by Priscus of his visit to 'Hunland' and his meetings with Attila. This has been translated by C D Gordon in *The Age of Attila*, a collection of contemporary documents with a linking commentary. There is a freer and briefer translation in chapter 9 of Bury's *History of the Later Roman Empire* and an analysis of the episode in E A Thompson's *A History of Attila and the Huns*. The section of my story set in Attila's household has been based on Priscus – Attila's behaviour, his family relationships, the buildings of his 'capital', the etiquette and entertainments at his feasts. The details of Hunnic dress, jewellery and ornament, weapons, horses and names – and much more – are to be found in J O Maenchen-Helfen's great compilation *The World of the Huns*. Truth is far more vivid and interesting than any fiction could be where the Huns are concerned.

The account of the embassy is given a richer flavour from the knowledge that the ambassador, Maximinus, and his scholarly friend Priscus, were the innocent front-men for an attempt by the Constantinople government to buy the murder of Attila by one of his most trusted officers, Edecon. The go-between was the official interpreter, Bigilas (or Vigilas). In fact, the embassy had only been arranged for Bigilas to get a footing in the Hunnic headquarters, so that he could come back later with the price of Attila's death – 50lbs weight of gold. Edecon pretended to be won over, so that he would know what was planned, and promptly reported everything to Attila, who knew all about it before the embassy arrived.

One might have expected that he would put them all in chains; most rulers would take a poor view of using an embassy as a cover for assassination – King Edwin of Northumbria did. When the ambassador gave the conventional greeting: that the Emperor prayed for the safety of Attila and all who were his, Attila merely answered gravely that he wished the Romans all that they wished him. Apart from some understandable moodiness, with what seemed to Priscus at the time some inexplicable outbursts of temper against Bigilas, Attila was a good host.

When the embassy had gone home and Bigilas returned with the 50lbs of gold to pay for the murder, the Huns arrested him. On their record, it might be taken for granted that he would be torn apart, flayed, impaled or roasted over a slow fire. Attila said that he would be held prisoner unless and until the Eastern Emperor (Theodosius II) ransomed him for another 50lbs of gold.

Attila's method of demanding the ransom is significant of his character. His envoy was instructed to wear round his neck the bag in which Bigilas had brought the gold and to ask the emperor and his chief minister if they recognised it. As ambassadors were received publicly, this must have made an interesting moment. Then the envoy was to recite a speech composed and taught him by Attila to the effect that:

Theodosius is the son of a noble father. Attila also is the son of a noble father, Mundzuk, and *he* has preserved his father's honour. Theodosius has thrown away his own ancestral nobility, since he pays tribute to Attila, which makes him his slave. He has not acted rightly towards his master, since he has made a furtive attack like a wretched house-slave. Attila will not exonerate those who have sinned against him unless Theodosius should hand over the minister (the eunuch Chrysaphius) for punishment.

That was meant to be scathing; it must have caused some embarrassment in the imperial audience chamber, though I doubt whether it wounded the cynical Byzantine politicians. It could only have been composed to scathe by a man with a sense of dignity, who believed that people would and should be ashamed if they disgraced themselves.

To its credit, the Constantinople government bought back its wretched tool. Attila behaved with lordly generosity: he not only freed Bigilas, in one piece, but he also set free many other prisoners of war without ransom.

Attila was a terrifying and destructive war-lord, but after reading Priscus, one can see why so many of his Gothic allies and subjects were willing to fight to the death for him.

The varieties of culture, the range of experiences open to the Germanic mind at this period almost defeat modern imagination. To the east were the Huns; to the west, the 'country-house' life of wealthy Romans and Gallo-Romans like Cassiodorus and Sidonius Apollinaris. In the middle was 'Mirkwood'.

What the complete *Waldere* was like, we can only guess. It is a great pity that we have lost it.

Waldere: ed. F Norman, Methuen's Old English Library 1933.

Waltharius: translated in:

Walter of Aquitaine: Materials for the study of his legend, F P Magoun & H M Smyser, Connecticut College Monograph 4 1950.

Sidelights on Teutonic History in the Migration Period: M G Clarke, CUP 1911.

The Gothic History of Jordanes: trans. and ed. C C Mierow, Princeton 1915.

The History of the Franks: Gregory of Tours trans. L Thorpe, Penguin Classics 1974.

The Age of Attila: C D Gordon, Univ. of Michigan Press 1960 (for the translation of Priscus).

The World of the Huns: J O Maenchen-Helfen, Univ. of California Press 1973.

A History of Attila and the Huns: E A Thompson, Oxford Clarendon Press 1948.

Barbarians and Romans: J D Randers-Pehrson (Book Club Associates 1983) Croom Helm Ltd.

The Barbarians: Goths, Franks and Vandals, M Todd, Batsford 1972.

The Franks: E James, The Peoples of Europe, Blackwell 1988.

Sidonius Apollinarius and his Age: C E Stevens, OUP 1933.

VI The Story of Geat and Maeðhild

'We þæt Mæðhilde monge* gefrugnon
wurdon grundlease Geates frige,
þæt hi seo sorglufu slæp ealle binom'

Deor 1.14-16

(We learned that: Mæðhild's moans, [they] became numberless,
[the moans] of Geat's lady, so that distressing love robbed her
of all sleep.

Kemp Malone

(*'monge' is often amended to 'mone' – moans, lamentations –
as the word 'mong' is not found in Old English. The scribe was
thinking ahead to the 'ge' of 'gefrugnon' and duplicated it. The
same mistake is found not much further on in the Exeter Book
manuscript, in Judgement Day, 1.74, where 'mongegum' was
written for 'monegum': 'geond middangeard mongegum
gecyþeð')

'All have heard of Hild's ravishing:
the Geat's lust was ungovernable,
their bitter love banished sleep.'

M Alexander, The Earliest English Poems.

'About Mæðhild many of us have heard tell that the affections
of the Geat grew fathomless, so that this tragic love reft them
of all sleep.

S A J Bradley, Anglo-Saxon Poetry

'We know that Mæðhild the sad wife of Geat
Had endless cause for tears and lamentation.
Unhappy love deprived her of sleep.'

R Hamer, A Choice of Anglo-Saxon Verse.

'Who *are* Mæðhild and Geat?'

S B Greenfield
A New Critical History of Old English Literature

You have to know people's names before you can be sure
who they are. Every other section of *Deor* (except lines 28-34
which are about any member of the human race coping with
grief and ill-luck) refers to characters well-known in history or
legend – Weland, Beadohild, Ðeodric, Eormanric, Heoden – so it
is natural to assume that the pair in lines 14-16 were equally
well-known to the poet's readers and listeners.

A Geat is a member of the Geatish tribe, either by birth, marriage or adoption. There are a number of them mentioned or active in *Beowulf:* the hero himself; his father Ecgþeow, who was involved in a Wulfing feud, went into exile, married a Geatish princess; Hygelac, his father and his brothers; Eofor, who killed a Swedish king and won the hand of a Geatish princess; his brother and battle-comrade Wulf. They all led exciting lives that deserve a story; in surviving tradition, none of them takes part in a passionate and tragic love-affair or is linked with a woman called Mæðhild or Hild. This is no reason why a story-teller should not make one up but it would be a fiction with no legendary base.

The name Geat appears at the head of the list of ancestors of Ida of Northumbria (Parker Chronicle under the year 547) in the 5th generation above Woden. Geat also comes as one of the ancestors of the West Saxon kings, ancestors of Æðelwulf, listed under the year 855. Here he is in the 7th generation above Woden; the line has been extended beyond him to bring it up to Noah and so to Adam. These extensions of the royal pedigrees beyond Woden were made by Christian antiquarians who did not believe he was a god. The names they added would be chosen to add dignity to the line.

The related Scandinavian form of the name –Gaut – is listed as one of the names of Odin, probably as the divine ancestor of the Geats and the Goths. There is a story that before his death, the god Balder was troubled by evil dreams. In the Eddic poem *Baldrs Draumar* (Balder's Dreams), his father Odin rides to the eastern gate of Hel's kingdom and calls up a dead seeress from her mound. He asks her to explain what the dreams forebode. She tells him that Balder will be killed and that his slayer will be killed in turn by Vali, a son of Odin as yet unbegotten. He will be born to Rind. (Her name suggests a mountain giantess, though Snorri lists her among the goddesses.) Odin gets her with child; he is said to have won her by spells.

Saxo Grammaticus did not believe that Odin and his family were gods, merely sinister tricksters who practised necromancy and persuaded gullible folk that they had divine powers. In Saxo's version of the story (Hist. Dan. Bk III), Balder is killed by a human rival for the love of Nanna (who infinitely prefers the rival and marries him!) and Odin is ready to do anything to get revenge. He consults a Lappland shaman and learns that the avenger must be born to Rinda, a human girl, daughter of the king of the Ruthenians. Odin takes a place in

the king's household with the intention of seducing her. Like
Lovelace hunting down Clarissa, he uses various disguises and
tricks, but the girl will have nothing to do with him. Finally he
disguises himself as a woman to get access to her bower and
bed, and so manages to rape her, getting her pregnant.

On the human level, this is as nasty a story of sexual
harassment as one could imagine. However, if the 'lover' were
totally non-human, a being from some other world, the story
could be given a dark, eerie power, like the old ballad *The
Demon Lover*. The desire of such a being could well be defined
as 'sorglufu' – love that brings sorrow. To the unwilling human
victim it would be a terrible misfortune, fit to be ranked in
Deor with the fates of Weland, Beadohild and the subjects of
Eormanric. Doubtless, if 'Geat' were Woden, his lust would be
'grundleas' – bottomless like the pit of hell, limitless,
insatiable.

However, when a story like this is applied to the lines in
Deor, it sounds wrong, apart from the woman's name. There is
no 'Mæðhild' in any story about Woden. This, by itself, would
not be a difficulty for a story-teller; Woden had many loves.
The trouble comes from the wording of the lines.

Usually, the phrase 'Geates frige' is translated politely as
'Geat's *embraces*'; or 'frige' is treated as an emotion: lust,
desire, affection. In fact, the word means' sexual intercourse',
though older dictionaries are needlessly coy about their
definitions. In the first poem of the Exeter Book, *Christ*, the
word is used, precisely and reverently, in an account of the
Incarnation:

'Wæs seo fæmne geong,
mægð manes leas þe him to meder geceas
þæt wæs geworden *butan weres frigum.*'   1.35-37

(The virgin was young, a maiden free from sin, whom he chose
as his mother. That was accomplished *without her knowing a
man.*)

In this context, the language of the King James Bible has to
be used, because the word is 'frigging'. Like most of our other
sexual words, it has been turned into a bad-tempered
obscenity. The early English joked broadly about sex but they
had not yet fouled their sexual vocabulary to make it unfit for
poetry or civilised talk.

Even so, as Kemp Malone pointed out, if we take this
interpretation of the phrase (and even if we make Woden
himself the 'hero' of the story) the episode sounds quite out of

keeping with the rest of *Deor*, including the reference to Beadohild. Mæðhild's trouble is that Geat is enjoying her with such enthusiasm and vigour that she cannot get a wink of sleep; he is wearing her out.

That would do very well in one of Chaucer's comic stories: Alison's night with Nicholas, the Cambridge students' night with the miller's wife and daughter, old January's wedding-night with young May – 'Thus laboureth he til that the day gan daw'. Ribald humour has no place in *Deor*.

Kemp Malone made the interesting suggestion that 'frige' should be taken as the possessive form of the noun 'freo' – a free-born, hence well-born woman, a lady – and that the phrase 'Geates frige' is a variation of Mæðhilde': 'the lamentations of Mæðhild, of Geat's lady.'

In *An Anglo-Saxon Dictionary* (Bosworth and Toller), 'freo' is listed as indeclinable – that is, its form would not change whatever function it was performing in a sentence. 'Frige' is found, as a possessive form, as a place-name element and in the word Frigedaeg – Friday. But here, 'frige' is not part of a common noun 'freo' meaning a woman of good birth; it is the name of the Queen of the gods herself. Kemp Malone maintains that the common noun and the proper name were originally the same word – a lady and The Lady.

'Freo' is cognate with the Old Saxon 'fri'. Working backwards from freo through the sound changes would lead to the forms *frio and the earlier *frijo; freo and 'Frige' in Frigedaeg have both developed from *frijo. (The Old English development of the general Germanic consonant system ch X, sect 275, in Joseph Wright's *Old English Grammar*.)

Modern writers on Old English religious beliefs usually spell the goddess's name Frig or Frigg, the Scandinavian form, which has unfortunate associations in English eyes. Certainly, the goddess of love and fertility rules over sexual play and mating but she is too beautiful to be named by a bad-tempered obscenity. In spite of D H Lawrence's arguments, when a word has been used over a long period of time to show anger and contempt, or as a form of verbal indecent assault, it cannot be re-used to express pleasure, affection or mutual enjoyment. Also, the spelling 'Frig' suggests pronunciation with a hard 'g' as in 'get', when it should be a softer sound like the 'y' in 'yes'. The modern English soft 'g' as in 'George' would give the pronunciation 'fridge', which is even less appropriate to the goddess of love.

Using 'Freo' for her name avoids all these unsuitable effects. Also, it gives an English feminine and masculine pair of divine names or titles: Freo and Frea – the Lady and the Lord – to match the Scandinavian Freya and Frey and comparable to other pairs such as the Phoenician Baalat and Baal or the Gaia and Gaius of the ancient Roman marriage ceremony.

Kemp Malone suggests that the common use of the word 'freo' for a lady died out because Christians would avoid calling women by the name of a heathen goddess. However, the word did survive into medieval English; the beautiful and beguiling lady in *Sir Gawain and the Green Knight* is referred to as 'my fre' (1.1545) and 'þat fre' (1.1549). The lady is acting under the orders of Morgan le Fay – 'Morgne þe goddes', Morgan the goddess – and embodies her powers of seduction; perhaps there was still a faint memory that 'fre' had meant The Lady as well as 'a lady'.

Taking 'Geates frige' as meaning 'of Geat's lady' and referring to Mæðhild, we still do not know who she was. And if we do not take Geat as Woden, we do not know who he was either. If we take him to be, like Scyld, just a personification made from the name of a group, he will not have a love-story.

In the manuscript, 'Mæðhilde' is written 'mæð hilde', so some editors and translators have taken the name to be Hild. This leaves the word 'mæð' to be accounted for. 'Mæþ in Old English means 'hay harvest' or 'mowing' – the word might be fitted into a bawdy riddle about putting blades or hooks into long grass, but it makes no sense here. It has been argued that the woman's name 'Mæðhild' does not occur in Old English – which only means that it does not occur in any surviving document. However, both its elements are found in Old English names. 'Hild' is one of the most common elements in women's names. 'Mæð' is very uncommon but it does occur as a first element in men's names. Mæðhelm and Mæthcor were priests whose names were entered in the Durham *Liber Vitae*.

In Old German, the name elements 'matha', as in Mathild, and 'mahti', as in Mahtild, fell together, with Mahtild as the surviving form. When a German story about a woman with that name reached Scandinavia, the foreign element 'maht' – might – was replaced by the Scandinavian 'magn' – main.

There are Norwegian and Icelandic ballads in which a man called Gaute or Gauti and his bride Magnild have a threatened but finally triumphant union (the Norwegian version) or a fated and tragic separation (the Icelandic version).

I chose the Norwegian version as the starting point for my story because it fits best with *Deor* both in mood and in plot: in fact, it makes sense of the allusion in the Old English poem. For one thing, it has a finally happy ending. The theme of *Deor* is that all the disasters it mentions were endured and, in some way or other, survived. The desire of the water sprite to possess Mæðhild is indeed a 'sorglufu', both for the human beloved and in the end for the otherworld lover. Mæðhild's lack of sleep is not only because of her terror and her grief at the thought of being snatched away from Geat, but because she dare not relax her guard for a moment. I took the detail of Mæðhild weeping in bed at Geat's side from the Icelandic ballad, because at that point it seems nearer to *Deor*.

Another reason for keeping the happy ending is that these ballads are giving versions of the Orpheus story, celebrating the power of music, specifically of harp music. The most famous treatment in English of the Orpheus story, the medieval *Sir Orfeo*, also lets the minstrel win; this seems to be the English preference.

Perhaps they picked up the Orpheus legend before they came to Britain, from army service and trade across the Rhine frontier. Perhaps they knew it long before the Romans reached the Rhine – maybe it came north from Thrace along the old Amber Road.

Evidence about a 10th century English text, from a Norwegian ballad collected in the 19th century, would probably not be accepted in a law court – or a university examination room – but it is perfectly satisfactory to a story-teller's imagination.

In this harp lay, the 2nd, 4th and 5th lines of every verse are a refrain; when ballads were danced, the dancers usually sang the refrains while the ballad-singer told the story. The refrain has only been included in the first and last verses.

Gaute and Magnild

Gaute rides south to the island
    (here shadows darken the heath)
he is marrying Magnild, the fair maid.
(How can the young man win the maiden who replies in anger?)

He marries Magnild, takes her home as his bride,
knights and pages ride with them.

Magnild rides both out and in,
and all the time tears run down her cheek.

'Are you weeping for gold or are you weeping for goods
or are you weeping because you have married me?

'Are you weeping for your house or are you weeping for your land
or are you weeping because you will sit at my table?'

'I'm not weeping for either gold or for goods,
nor because I have married you;

'I'm not weeping either for house or for land,
nor because I will sit at your table.

"I am weeping more for my white body
that will not be able to rot in hallowed ground.

'I am weeping rather for my gold hair,
that must rot in Vending's river.'

'O my dear Magnild, do not be afraid,
you don't yet know what kind of husband you have.

'O I will build the bridge so high
and support it with strong iron posts.'

'Even if you build the bridge so new,
even so, no one can escape from their fate.'

And when they came into the green glades,
there stood a hart with gentle mien.

Everyone wanted to kill the hart,
no one wanted to go with the bridal procession.

Everyone wanted to catch the hart,
no one wanted to take care of the bridal procession.

And when they came to Vending's bridge,
the horse stumbled in its shoes of red gold.

Four golden horseshoes and four gold horseshoe-nails –
Magnild fell into the swift stream.

Gaute looks back over his shoulder:
'Where is Magnild, the pride of my procession?'

To this reply the two bridesmaids:
'We haven't seen Magnild since by Vending's bridge.'

Gaute calls to his page:
'Bring to me my fine harp!

'Say this to my father,
that Magnild is lying in the water.

'Say this to my mother,
that Magnild is lying in the river.

'Say this to my sister,
that the harp is in the chest.

'Say this to my brother,
that the harp is in the compartment in the chest.'

Away then rode the little page,
he rode five horses into the ground before he reached home.
(He repeats the four messages word for word.)

Back came riding the little page,
Gaute received his fine harp.

Gaute plays forth over the hill,
the bird is forced off the twig.

Gaute plays forth over the hillside,
the white bear is forced out of its lair.

Gaute plays over hill and dale,
the child is forced out of its mother's womb.

Gaute plays forth to the ford,
Magnild floated on the water –

Magnild floated on the water,
the water sprite tugged at her silken head scarf.

Gaute cast spells as best he could,
Magnild floated with saddle and horse.

Gaute cast spells and the harp resounded,
the water sprite sat in the water and cried.

The first words that Magnild spoke:
    (here shadows darken the heath)
'Blessed is the mother who has such a son!'
(How can the young man win the maiden who replies in anger?)

A man would not be named 'Geat' if he were a Geat living in Geatland, or as a member of a Geatish war-band or troop of Geatish mercenaries. The name would first be given as a mark of separateness – a nick-name given to a foreigner or a name given to a child born in exile, perhaps the child of a mixed marriage, in an attempt to keep a memory of a broken tribe.

In verses 4 and 5 of the ballad, Gaute seems to suspect that his bride is regretting she has not make a better marriage. That might suggest the touchiness of an exile, or someone who is not quite sure of his status.

The similarity between the goods found in the ship-burial at Sutton Hoo and the description of Scyld's departure in *Beowulf* has often been remarked. It can probably never be proved, but some English people like to day-dream that Geatish exiles (perhaps led by Wiglaf) got to East Anglia, so I have set the story there. Ballad tales of magic are free of the limits of time and space. For those who know Suffolk, the events can be imagined as happening beside, near, on, and at one stage under, the River Deben. The royal hall was at Rendlesham, Lord Helm's estate was at Helmingham, Geat's father lived at Brandeston and Geat had his meeting with The Lady at Aspall, the 'hal' – secret place – overgrown with aspens.

There is no surviving the record of Old English songs or dance music. The post-Norman historians, such as William of Malmesbury and Henry of Huntingdon, mention ballads about the early English kings, that were still sung by the folk. They sometimes quote phrases from them, translated into Latin. The earliest lyrics with music that have come down to us are the hymns of St Godric, who died in 1170. He was a seaman turned hermit who lived at Finchale near Durham. He said he 'heard' his songs in moments of mystic trance, rather than composed them himself:

> 'Sainte Marye, Christes bur,
> Maidenes clenhad, moderes flur,
> Dilie min sinne, rix in min mod,
> Bring me to winne with the selfe God.'

The editor, R T Davies, comments: 'It may be that he (Godric) writes in a native popular tradition about which very little is known.' *Medieval English Lyrics.*

Among the post-Norman lyrics there are some, often mere snatches jotted down in the margins of books, that are in very 'true' English. That is, they either have no trace of French or Latin, or just an odd word or two. Their themes are timeless.

Knowing how long folksongs can live in an oral culture, it is perfectly possible that songs like these were sung before the Normans came.

'Maiden in the moor lay' is the famous example; it must have been a dance. John Speirs has written an illuminating commentary on this song in *Medieval English Poetry*. The whole chapter on carols and other songs makes fascinating reading.

There are other delightful scraps collected at the end of *The Oxford Book of Medieval Verse*:

> 'Up, sun and merry weather,
> Summer draweth near.'

and this:

> 'The nightingale sings
> That all the wood rings,
> She singeth in her song
> That the night is too long.'

and this:

> 'Door, go thou stille (move silently)
> Go thou stille, stille,
> That ich habbe in the bower
> Y-don al myn wille, wille.'

I do not believe that songs like these were suddenly invented a hundred and fifty years or so after the Normans came.

Deor: ed. Kemp Malone Exeter Medieval English Texts Univ. of Exeter 1977. Kemp Malone worked on the text of *Deor* for many years and set out his ideas in several papers which chart the development of his thought:

Journal of English Literary History iii 1936 pp 253-6.
English Studies xix 1937 pp 193-9.
Modern Philology xl 1942 pp 1-18.
Studies in Heroic Legend and Current Speech 1959 pp 142-67.

Medieval English Poetry: John Speirs, Faber pbk 1971.
The Oxford Book of Medieval Verse: ed. C & K Sisam Oxford, Clarendon Press.
The Lost Gods of England: Brian Branston, Thames and Hudson 1974.
Rites and Religions of the Anglo-Saxons: Gale R Owen, David & Charles 1981.

Anglo-Saxon Verse Charms, Maxims and Heroic Legends

Louis J Rodrigues

The Germanic tribes who settled in Britain during the fifth and early sixth centuries brought with them a store of heroic and folk traditions: folk-tales, legends, rune-lore, magic charms, herbal cures, and the homely wisdom of experience enshrined in maxims and gnomic verse. In the lays composed and sung by their minstrels at banquets, they recalled the glories of long-dead heroes belonging to their Continental past. They carved crude runic inscriptions on a variety of objects including memorial stones, utensils, and weapons. In rude, non-aristocratic, verse, they chanted their pagan charms to protect their fields against infertility, and their bodies against the rigours of rheumatic winters. And, in times of danger, they relied on the gnomic wisdom of their ancestors for help and guidance.

Louis Rodrigues looks at those heroic and folk traditions that were recorded in verse, and which have managed to survive the depredations of time.

UK £7·95 net   ISBN 1–898281–01–7   176pp

A Handbook of Anglo-Saxon Food:
Processing and Consumption

Ann Hagen

For the first time information from various sources has been brought together in order to build up a picture of how food was grown, conserved, prepared and eaten during the period from the beginning of the 5th century to the 11th century. No specialist knowledge of the Anglo-Saxon period or language is needed, and many people will find it fascinating for the views it gives of an important aspect of Anglo-Saxon life and culture. In addition to Anglo-Saxon England the Celtic west of Britain is also covered.

UK £7·95 net   ISBN 0-9516209-8-3   192pp

The Battle of Maldon: Text and Translation
Translated and edited by Bill Griffiths

The Battle of Maldon was fought between the men of Essex and the Vikings in AD 991. The action was captured in an Anglo-Saxon poem whose vividness and heroic spirit has fascinated readers and scholars for generations. *The Battle of Maldon* includes the source text; edited text; parallel literal translation; verse translation; review of 103 books and articles.

UK £6·95 net   ISBN 0-9516209-0-8   96pp

Beowulf: Text and Translation
Translated by John Porter

The verse in which the story unfolds is, by common consent, the finest writing surviving in Old English, a text that all students of the language and many general readers will want to tackle in the original form. To aid understanding of the Old English, a literal word-by-word translation by John Porter is printed opposite an edited text and provides a practical key to this Anglo-Saxon masterpiece.

UK £7·95 net ISBN 0–9516209–2–4 192pp

Alfred's Metres of Boethius
Edited by Bill Griffiths

In this new edition of the Old English *Metres of Boethius*, clarity of text, informative notes and a helpful glossary have been a priority, for this is one of the most approachable of Old English verse texts, lucid and delightful; its relative neglect by specialists will mean this text will come as a new experience to many practised students of the language; while its clear, expositional verse style makes it an ideal starting point for all amateurs of the period.

UK £14·95 net ISBN 0–9516209–5–9 212pp

Wordcraft
Concise English/Old English Dictionary and Thesaurus
Stephen Pollington

This book provides Old English equivalents to the commoner modern words in both dictionary and thesaurus formats.

Previously the lack of an accessible guide to vocabulary deterred many would-be students of Old English. Now this book combines the core of indispensable words relating to everyday life with a selection of terms connected with society, culture, technology, religion, perception, emotion and expression to encompass all aspects of Anglo-Saxon experience.

The Thesaurus presents vocabulary relevant to a wide range of individual topics in alphabetical lists, thus making it easily accessible to those with specific areas of interest. Each thematic listing is encoded for cross-reference from the Dictionary. The two sections will be of invaluable assistance to students of the language, as well as to those with either a general or a specific interest in the Anglo-Saxon period.

UK £9·95 net ISBN 1–898281–02–5 240pp

Anglo-Saxon Runes
John. M. Kemble

Kemble's essay *On Anglo-Saxon Runes* first appeared in the journal *Archaeologia* for 1840; it draws on the work of Wilhelm Grimm, but breaks new ground for Anglo-Saxon studies in his survey of the Ruthwell Cross and the Cynewulf poems. It is an expression both of his own indomitable spirit and of the fascination and mystery of the Runes themselves, making one of the most attractive introductions to the topic.

For this edition, new notes have been supplied, which include translations of Latin and Old English material quoted in the text, to make this key work in the study of runes more accessible to the general reader.

UK £6·95 net ISBN 0–9516209–1–6 80pp

Monasteriales Indicia
The Anglo-Saxon Monastic Sign Language
Edited with notes and translation by
Debby Banham

The *Monasteriales Indicia* is one of very few texts which let us see how life was really lived in monasteries in the early Middle Ages. Written in Old English and preserved in a manuscript of the mid-eleventh century, it consists of 127 signs used by Anglo-Saxon monks during the times when the Benedictine Rule forbade them to speak. These indicate the foods the monks ate, the clothes they wore, and the books they used in church and chapter, as well as the tools they used in their daily life, and persons they might meet both in the monastery and outside. The text is printed here with a parallel translation. The introduction gives a summary of the background, both historical and textual, as well as a brief look at the later evidence for monastic sign language in England. Extensive notes provide the reader with details of textual relationships, explore problems of interpretation, and set out the historical implications of the text.

UK £6·95 net ISBN 0–9516209–4–0 96pp

The Service of Prime from the
Old English Benedictine Office

Text and Translation - Prepared by Bill Griffiths

The Old English Benedictine Office was a series of monastic daily services compiled in the late tenth or early eleventh centuries from the material that had largely already been translated from Latin into Old English.

UK £2·50 net ISBN0-9516209-3-2 40pp

Anglo-Saxon Runes
Tony Linsell

Books about runes tend towards the academic or the occult. This book bridges that gap and aims to help the reader understand how runes were used, and what meaning they had, for the people who used them. It also provides an insight into their values and how they perceived the world and their place in it.

Here the rune card illustrations are shown, one to a page, facing the appropriate verse from the Anglo-Saxon Rune Poem......this beautifully produced hardback book is well worth buying for this section alone which occupies just under half its 136 pages.....The remainder of the book makes fascinating reading and is full of – to me – unknown and interesting facts.....is a thoroughly enjoyable read as well as a delightful collection of evocative illustrations by Brian Partridge. Highly recommended.
Prediction Magazine

....Having read much about the Celtic influences on British life, I found it really interesting to learn something about the English history of these isles, and I actually found the general social and religious/magical background even more interesting than the runes and their meanings.....
Pagan Voice

UK £14·95 net   ISBN 0–9516209–6–7   Hardback 21cm x 27cm 144pp

---

Rune Cards
Tony Linsell and Brian Partridge

This package provides all that is needed for anyone to learn how to read runes.

This boxed set of 30 cards contains some of the most beautiful and descriptive black and white line drawings that I have ever seen on this subject.
..Pagan News

These are fantastic....Real magic, fabulous and brooding imagery, and an easy doorway to runic realms....
Occult Observer

There is a thick little book which includes clear and concise instructions on how to cast the runes. It is detailed without being overbearing and Mr Linsell obviously knows his stuff....
Clamavi

The illustrations on the cards include prompts that will quickly enable the user to read the runes without referring to the book.

UK £12·95 net   ISBN 0–9516209–7–5   30 cards + booklet

For a full list of publications send a s.a.e. to:

Anglo-Saxon Books
25 Malpas Drive, Pinner, Middlesex. HA5 1DQ England
Tel: 081-868 1564

Most titles are available in North America from:
Paul & Company Publishers Consortium Inc.
c/o PCS Data Processing Inc., 360 West 31 St., New York, NY 10001
Tel: (212) 564-3730 ext. 264

Þa Engliscan Gesiðas

Þa Engliscan Gesiðas (The English Companions) is a historical and cultural society exclusively devoted to Anglo-Saxon history. Its aims are to bridge the gap between scholars and non-experts, and to bring together all those with an interest in the Anglo-Saxon period, its language, culture and traditions, so as to promote a wider interest in, and knowledge of all things Anglo-Saxon. The Fellowship publishes a journal, *Wiðowinde*, which helps members to keep in touch with current thinking on topics from art and archaeology to heathenism and Early English Christianity. The Fellowship enables like-minded people to keep in contact by publicising conferences, courses and meetings that might be of interest to its members. A correspondence course in Old English is also available.

For further details write to:
Janet Goldsbrough-Jones, 38 Cranworth Road,
Worthing, West Sussex, BN11 2JF, England.

Regia Anglorum

Regia Anglorum is a society that was founded to accurately re-create the life of the British people as it was around the time of the Norman Conquest. Our work has a strong educational slant and we consider authenticity to be of prime importance. We prefer, where possible, to work from archaeological materials and are extremely cautious regarding such things as the interpretation of styles depicted in manuscripts. Approximately twenty-five per cent of our membership, of over 500 people, are archaeologists or historians.

The Society has a large working Living History Exhibit, teaching and exhibiting more than twenty crafts in an authentic environment. We own a forty foot wooden ship replica of a type that would have been a common sight in Northern European waters around the turn of the first millennium AD. Battle re-enactment is another aspect of our activities, often involving 200 or more warriors.

For further information contact:
K. J. Siddorn, 9 Durleigh Close, Headley Park,
Bristol BS13 7NQ, England.

Old English Newsletter

The *OEN* is a journal produced by, and for, scholars of Old English. It is a refereed periodical. Solicited and unsolicited manuscripts (except for independent reports and news items) are reviewed by specialists in anonymous reports. Four issues are published each (American) academic year for the Old English Division of the Modern Language Association by the Centre for Medieval and Early Renaissance Studies at the State University of New York at Binghamton.

General correspondence should be addressed to the Editor:
Paul E. Szarmach, CEMERS; SUNY-Binghamton,
PO Box 6000, Binghamton, New York 13902-6000, USA.